PRAISE FOR
DUBRAVKA UGRESIC

"Ugresic never commits a sloppy thought or a turgid sentence. Under her gaze, the tiredest topics of the 'tired' continent (migration, multiculturalism, 'new Europe') spring to life."—*The Independent* (London)

"Dubravka Ugresic is the philosopher of evil and exile, and the storyteller of many shattered lives the wars in the former Yugoslavia produced."
—Charles Simic

"Ugresic must be numbered among what Jacques Maritain called the dreamers of the true; she draws us into the dream."—Richard Eder, *New York Times*

"Like Nabokov, Ugresic affirms our ability to remember as a source for saving our moral and compassionate identity."—John Balaban, *Washington Post*

"As long as some, like Ugresic, who can write well, do, there will be hope for the future."—*New Criterion*

"Ugresic's wit is bound by no preconceived purposes, and once the story takes off, a wild freedom of association and adventurous discernment is set in motion. . . . Ugresic dissects the social world."—*World Literature Today*

ALSO BY
DUBRAVKA UGRESIC
IN ENGLISH TRANSLATION

KARAOKE
CULTURE

ESSAYS

DUBRAVKA
UGRESIC

TRANSLATED FROM THE CROATIAN
AND WITH AN AFTERWORD
BY DAVID WILLIAMS

(WITH CONTRIBUTIONS FROM
ELLEN ELIAS-BURSAĆ AND
CELIA HAWKESWORTH)

OPEN LETTER
LITERARY TRANSLATIONS FROM THE UNIVERSITY OF ROCHESTER

All changes and revisions to the original edition of this book (published in Belgrade and Zagreb as *Napad na minibar*, 2010), including the title, essay selection, inclusion of new essays, chapter headings, and amendments to individual essays originate with the author.

Library of Congress Cataloging-in-Publication Data:

Ugrešić, Dubravka.
    [Napad na minibar. English]
    Karaoke culture / Dubravka Ugrešić ; translated from the Croatian
and with an afterword by David Williams ; translation contributions from
Ellen Elias-Bursać and Celia Hawkesworth. — 1st ed.
        p. cm.
    ISBN-13: 978-1-934824-57-3 (pbk. : acid-free paper)
    ISBN-10: 1-934824-57-7 (pbk. : acid-free paper)
    I. Williams, David, 1976- II. Elias-Bursac, Ellen. III.
    Hawkesworth, Celia, 1942- IV. Title.
    PG1619.31.G7N3713 2011
    891.8'3454—dc23
                                2011020021

Printed on acid-free paper in the United States of America.

Text set in Caslon, a family of serif typefaces based on the designs of
William Caslon (1692–1766).

Design by N. J. Furl

Open Letter is the University of Rochester's nonprofit, literary translation press:
Lattimore Hall 411, Box 270082, Rochester, NY 14627

www.openletterbooks.org

CONTENTS

1.

KARAOKE CULTURE

1.

And by the mid-afternoon he was again overcome with the desire to be somewhere else, someone else, someone else somewhere else.
—Jonathan Safran Foer, Everything Is Illuminated

2.

"Help me. I had a dream last night. I was skipping through a meadow holding a picnic basket and the basket was marked 'Options'. And then I saw there was a hole in the basket."

"Mr. Kugelmass, the worst thing you could do is act out. You must simply express your feelings here, and together we'll analyze them. You have been in treatment long enough to know there is no overnight cure. After all, I'm an analyst, not a magician."

"Then perhaps what I need is a magician," Kugelmass said, rising from his chair.
—Woody Allen, "The Kugelmass Episode"

3.

. . . But one day
The sun will stand where the heart once stood
And there will be no words in human speech
That a poem would renounce
Everyone will write poetry . . .
                    —*Branko Miljković,* "*Everyone Will Write Poetry*"

4.

We human beings hog the limelight on this new stage of democ-
ratized media. We are simultaneously its amateur writers, its
amateur producers, its amateur technicians, and, yes, its amateur
audience. Amateur hour has arrived, and the audience is now
running the show.

                    —*Andrew Keen,* The Cult of the Amateur:
                    How Today's Internet Is Killing our Culture

1.
WHY KARAOKE,
AND WHAT'S CULTURE
GOT TO DO WITH IT?

It needs to be said upfront: I'm not a karaoke fan. This essay was not only conceived, but also half-finished, when it occurred to me to go and catch a bit of real karaoke. They say *Casablanca* is the most popular karaoke bar in Amsterdam. My companion and I, both neophytes, arrived at eight on the dot, as if we were going to the theatre and not a bar. *Casablanca* was empty. We took a walk down Zeedijk, a narrow street packed with bars whose barmen look like they spend all day at the gym and all night in the bar. Muscles and baggy eyelids—that pretty well describes our barman at *Casablanca*, to which we soon returned. On a little stage, two tall, slender young women were squawking a Dutch pop song into a couple of upright microphones. A concert featuring Dutch pop stars played on the bar's TV screens but was drowned out by the evening's young karaoke stars. The girls sang with more heart than the guys, and for a second I thought there must be an invisible policeman standing over them. The whole thing was a deaf collective caterwaul: deaf insofar as nobody actually listened to anyone. Amsterdam is definitely not the place for a karaoke initiation. I'm not sure why I even thought of going to see karaoke in Amsterdam—maybe because of the paradox that sometimes turns out to be true, that worlds open up where we least expect.

I was watching the film *Lost in Translation* for the third time and had stopped at the part where Bill Murray, with fatalistic forbearance, does his karaoke number. I sat down at the computer and opened YouTube. Trailing a few words behind and holding out little hope that I'd ever catch up, I gave singing "I Will Survive" a go. It was an invigorating experience. I had a go at opera too. I managed to warble along with a popular aria from *The Phantom of the Opera*, but on Andrea Bocelli's "Con Te Partirò" I could only get my tongue around the first line of the chorus. That song definitely has too many unpronounceable words.

I thought about buying the karaoke version of "Ti Voglio Tanto Bene" for $2.99, but gave it a pass. I didn't buy *Cantolopera* either, which would have let me sing operatic arias accompanied by a whole orchestra. I didn't even buy a teach-yourself pack, a *virtual coach for classical singers*. But when I saw an Internet ad for a karaoke program that promised to *recreate the joys, sorrows, ecstasy and anguish of opera*—while I was having my morning shower—I very nearly caved. It's not that I like warbling in the shower; it's just that I'm a sucker for emotionally charged ads with rich vocabularies. And I almost forgot, I also listened to a few karaoke singers on a site called *Singer's Showcase*. My favorite was the sad Mr. Sandy and his bear-like growl through "Georgia On My Mind."

What is karaoke in actual fact? Karaoke (Japanese for "**empty** orchestra") is entertainment for people who would like to be Madonna or Sinatra. The karaoke machine was invented in the early seventies by the Japanese musician Daisuke Inoue—who forgot to patent his invention, and so others cashed in. A few years ago Inoue apparently won the alternative Nobel Peace Prize (the Ig Nobel), awarded by *The Annals of Improbable Research*. They praised him for "providing an entirely new way for people to learn to tolerate each other."

Cultural critics are people who are prepared to see more in the craze for tattoos than just a passing fashion fad. I'm a member of this dubious guild. In karaoke I'm ready to see more than just desperate squawking to the backing track of "I Will Survive." Karaoke supports less the democratic idea that everyone can have a shot if they want one and more the democratic practice that everyone wants a shot if there's one on offer. The inventor of karaoke, Daisuke Inoue, is a humble man, most proud of having helped the Japanese, emotionally reticent as they are said to be, change for the better. As Pico Iyer wrote: "As much as Mao Zedong or Mohandas Gandhi changed Asian days, Inoue transformed its nights."[1]

What is the attraction of karaoke, which having first taken off in Japan (apparently it's still going strong) then made its way around the world? I suspect it is firstly its simplicity and stupidity, and secondly, the ambivalent position of the participant. Singing a song that someone else made famous, the amateur publicly declares his or her love for his or her idol (Sinatra or Madonna), while the inevitably flaky performance simultaneously devalues this same idol. This theft of the star's aura, or inadvertent subversion of a hierarchy of values, remains in the sphere of the innocent, empowering, and transformative. It's just a bit of fun. The performer is anonymous, and most often remains so.

---

1   www.time.com/time/asia/asia/magazine/1999/990823/inoue1.html

Letting one's imagination run wild, it's not difficult to imagine various other forms of karaoke-like fun. Someone with a bit of cash, for example, might hit upon the idea of hiring the ballet ensemble of the Bolshoi Theatre, commission a performance of Swan Lake, and insert his wife, mother-in-law, or even himself in the main dance section. The variants are endless. But the bottom line, it seems, is anonymity. Why? If we signed our first and last names, our gesture would have a completely different message. Our squawking along to "Mamma Mia" wouldn't be interpreted as a submissive imitation of the original, but as subversion, homage, parody, and so forth. An authorial gesture, as opposed to an anonymous one, sends a rather different message out into the world—Marcel Duchamp painting a mustache and beard on the *Mona Lisa* or Andy Warhol and his giant celebrity portraits come to mind. Were it not for an authorial signature, and general agreement that this signature be respected, much contemporary art—the product of an inseparable symbiosis between someone else's original model and an interventionist authorial gesture—could easily be filed under less flattering labels such as symbiotic art, appropriation art, or karaoke art. Because karaoke is an activity that belongs to those who don't sign their names—or don't do so for now. For the time being, karaoke-people stick within their communities, their fandoms.

There are of course inverse examples, where famous people do karaoke. The film *Romance & Cigarettes* (2005), a kind of karaoke-musical, stars superb actors (James Gandolfini, Susan Sarandon, Kate Winslet, and Steve Buscemi) who ham it up to the sound of others' booming voices, not least that of a certain Tom Jones. *Mamma Mia!* (2008), the hit film based on the West End musical, features equally superb actors (Julie Waters, Meryl Streep, Colin Firth) singing the evergreens of the Swedish pop-group ABBA. Like a karaoke session, both films are propelled by the spectator's recognition of the original hits; by the energy of the evergreen, and not, incidentally, by their poor imitations.

When did a harmless bit of anonymous fun grow into a culture? Should these two celluloid examples be considered karaoke culture, or are they simply examples of celebrity culture, a culture in which stars can do whatever they like—from clowning around in an onscreen musical to writing crappy books? Let's not forget: Karaoke is entertainment for ordinary people, who, within given codes (shaped by technology and genre), and protected by the mask of anonymity, fulfill their suppressed desires within their own communities, or fandoms. Karaoke-people are everything but revolutionaries, innovators, or people who will change the world. They're ordinary people, readers of *Pride and Prejudice and Zombies*, consumers and conformists. All the same, the world changes and ordinary people have their part to play.

The very foundation of karaoke culture lies in the parading of the anonymous ego with the help of simulation games. Today people are more interested in flight from themselves than discovering their authentic *self*. The self has become boring, and belongs to a different culture. The possibilities of transformation, teleportation, and metamorphosis hold far more promise than digging in the dirt of the self. The culture of narcissism has mutated into karaoke culture—or the latter is simply a consequence of the former.

The market on which the ego can be paraded is open to all comers, everyone and every variant is welcome. The ego, which for centuries lay buried in the subsoil, has seeped out onto the surface and, having changed its properties, become unusually strong. Metaphorically speaking, it's lucky that Andy Warhol, the inventor of karaoke in the visual arts, died when he did. Otherwise he'd have to look on in horror as a Campbell's Soup Can moved in to slurp him up. Today the humble Daisuke Inoue sells eco-friendly detergents and cockroach-killing insecticides, cockroaches being the very creatures that crawl down into the karaoke machine and chew on its electric wires. When we think about it a little more, everything runs on wires now. Without healthy wires, there wouldn't be karaoke culture.

Every text is sustained by the changing relationships between Author, Work, and Recipient. Modern technology has radically altered the structure of the text, whether this be literary, visual, or cinematic. The balance of power, formerly dominated by Author and Work, has been flipped in favor of the Recipient. This tectonic shift has changed the cultural landscape and wiped out many cultural species (while, truth be told, giving birth to new ones), transforming perception, comprehension, and taste—in fact, the entire cultural system. And we're not even conscious of it all, and neither are we in a position to articulate what has actually happened.[2]

That's why we're making a start with the awkward metaphor of karaoke. In the text that follows we're interested in the human *activities* in which an anonymous participant, assisted by new technology, uses an existing cultural model to derive pleasure. (And it has

---

2 Here's a quick anecdote. A teenager and I watched the "ancient" film *The Silence of the Lambs* together. There's that terrible scene in which Buffalo Bill's victim is trapped in an unused well. "The chick is dumb, she doesn't have a mobile" was the teenager's comment. "What do to you mean?" I asked. "If she had a mobile on her she could call the police." The teenager, a child who grew up with the mobile phone, watched the film in his own way—as a story about a "dumb chick" who got into trouble because she didn't have a mobile phone.

nothing to do with sex, if that was what you were thinking!) The models are most often drawn from popular culture (television, film, pop music, comics, computer games), but some belong to what was once considered "high culture" (film, literature, painting). Most often the anonymous participant derives *pleasure* and gets his kicks by simply getting to be "someone else, somewhere else." Amateur and anonymous, participants don't go in for artistic pretension, nor are they overly concerned with the authorship of their *creation* or their *activity*, but the desire to *leave their mark* is beyond doubt. Their *creation* can't be called *plagiarism*, nor can their *activity* be called *imitation*, because both terms belong to a different time and a different cultural system. Easily applicable to non-musical activities such as film, literature, and painting, karaoke is the most simple paradigm, hence the hasty and perhaps not completely apposite title of this essay, "Karaoke Culture." This *soft* term is less restrictive than those which are currently in use, such as post-postmodernism, anti-modernism, pseudo-modernism, and digi-modernism. All of these terms, including mine, are inferior to the content they try to describe. The content is new, and it's changing from one second to the next, so what we try and articulate today can disappear tomorrow, leaving no trace of its existence. We live in a liquid epoch.

Apart from "culture" this essay makes frequent reference to "wires." I admit that I don't know anything about "wires." The fact that I don't know anything about them doesn't prevent me from writing about them. Until yesterday these two sentences were in contradiction. Today they're not. Freedom from knowledge, from the past, from continuity, from cultural memory and cultural hierarchy, and an inconceivable speed—these are the determinants of karaoke culture and the leitmotifs of the text that tries to describe them.

2.
IT ALL BEGAN
SO INNOCENTLY

On my first visit to America in 1982 I found myself in Los Angeles, and of course I didn't pass up the chance to visit Universal Studios. The photograph of Clark Gable dates from this time; Clark in an open white shirt, a black curl falling on his sweaty forehead, a blazing orange fire in the background, and in his arms, my lithe body. Actually the body belongs to Vivien Leigh, but the head is definitely mine.

The pleasure was one I repeated on a visit to St. Petersburg, where in front of the Winter Palace, poking my head through a painted mural, I appeared in a photograph as Napoleon. Since then the idea has made its way into computer programs and on to the Internet. For Valentine's Day 2009, ScanCafe.com offered a bit of free fun: people could send in a photo of themselves with their partner and would be sent one back with a minor intervention. Instead of their partner, Barrack Obama was now in the photo.

Who knows, maybe this innocent fairground attraction, having one's picture taken with a painted mural, was the embryo of karaoke culture. The invention of the camera satisfied our desire to immortalize ourselves the way we actually are, but a painted mural, this hokey technological innovation, offered a better option: Why wouldn't we be someone else for a moment? We could have our photos taken with our idols (me and Clark Gable!), take someone's place (hey, I gave Vivien Leigh the shove!), fabricate the personal history we leave to our grandchildren (that's me kids, with Clark Gable!), enter a fictional world (hey, there I am in *Gone With the Wind*!), reshape oneself (ahh, look at my slender waist!), travel through time, or change one's class, race, or sex (hey, there I'm a man, Napoleon!). All in all, it gave us the chance to **intervene** in reality, in which we are held back by our first names and last names, not to mention our genes, class, race, sex, religion, and ideology. The experience of having one's photo taken with a painted mural was not only a bit of **fun** (which we knew), it was also **transformative** (which back then we didn't know).

But a lot of other things had to happen for the Pandora's box of our repressed desires to open. God had to die, so that our interventions in his work would go unpunished. The Time of the Great Inventions had to come to pass. Communism had to be born, and humanity, or least a part of it, had to be reset and convinced that the happiness of the collective would bring happiness to the individual. Freud had to appear, and humanity, or at least a part of it, had to be reset and convinced that the happiness of the individual would bring happiness to the collective. Modernism, radio, television, consumerism, the computer, mass media culture, postmodernism, feminism, postcolonialism, the mobile phone, the Internet, all had to step out into the light.

The **Internet** is the final, most explosive powder keg strewn on the eternal flame of our fantasies. The Internet is the cornerstone of both the new democratic revolution and the computer user's evolution into a free man, a man forever transformed (*Never again a slave!*), eyes fixed ahead on the screen (a "window to the world"), whose hands self-confidently control an emancipatory mouse: a proletarian-man, an amateur-man, a man finally worthy of the name.

The Internet has not only democratized but also internationalized the consciousness of its users. As if in one of Mao Zedong's nightmarish dreams, the Internet is a field on which a thousand flowers really bloom. What has happened to society in the intervening time is, however, difficult to say. It's entirely possible that in the democratic deluge of realizing individual desires **society** has dissolved and fragmented into millions of little pieces, into millions of virtual communities, or fandoms, held together by various obsessions—from Gobelin embroidery to the protection of earth worms. Having absolutely nothing in common, Gobelin enthusiasts and those worried about earth worms are two virtual communities that will never communicate. In this respect, sticking to our primitive karaoke metaphor, the Internet can be understood as mega-karaoke, a place with millions of microphones, and millions of people rushing to grab the mic and sing **their** version of someone else's song. Whose song? That's not important: **amnesia** is, it seems, a by-product of the information revolution. What is important is that we all **sing**.

There is little dispute that the Internet is a revolution, and as they say, every revolution occurs in the name of an enlightened idea. In his book *The Cult of the Amateur: How Today's Internet Culture Is Killing our Culture*, Andrew Keen claims that "the noble abstraction behind the digital revolution is that of the noble amateur." As Keen maintains, in this case the amateur has raised a revolution against "the dictatorship of expertise." Keen uses T. H. Huxley's infinite

monkey theorem as an example; it holds that if an infinite number
of monkeys sat down at an infinite number of typewriters, sooner or
later one of the monkeys would come up with a masterpiece to rival
Shakespeare. On the Internet "amateur monkeys" create "an endless digital forest of mediocracy." The forest is growing rampantly,
and Keen predicts that by 2010 there will be five hundred million
blogs "collectively corrupting and confusing popular opinion about
everything from politics, to commerce, to arts and culture." Keen
assails the notorious fact that Wikipedia is the work of amateurs,
of anonymous contributors, the end result being that "it's the blind
leading the blind—infinite monkeys provide infinite information
for infinite readers, perpetuating the cycle of misinformation and
ignorance." Things being as such, no one can be called to account,
and what's more, attempts by experts to intervene and assist amateurs usually end in failure. The Internet is a battleground for power,
and the "children" (often literally children) are in the control room,
"hackers" of one kind or another, their identities fluid and slippery.
There is a famous *New Yorker* cartoon in which a dog, sitting up at
a computer, explains to another dog that, "on the Internet, nobody
knows you're a dog." This thesis, suggesting the existence of a global
conspiracy of nameless amateurs, is one Keen supports.

Amateurs, Keen claims, devastate systems that are based on expertise and destroy the institutions of author and authorship, information (newspapers are slowly disappearing, blogs are taking
over), education (Wikipedia, the work of anonymous amateurs, has
replaced encyclopedias, the work of experts), and art and culture
(amateurs create their own culture based on borrowing, expropria-
tion, appropriation, intervention, recycling, and remaking; they are
simultaneously the creators and consumers of this culture).

Alan Kirby, an Oxford professor of literature, maintains that this new culture is in need of its own "ism," and as a provisional term suggests "pseudo-modernism." "This pseudo-modern world, so frightening and seemingly uncontrollable, inevitably feeds a desire to return to the infantile playing with toys which also characterizes the pseudo-modern cultural world. Here, the typical emotional state, radically superseding the hyper-consciousness of irony, is the *trance*—the state of being swallowed up by your activity. In place of the neurosis of modernism and the narcissism of postmodernism, pseudo-modernism *takes the world away*, by creating a new weightless nowhere of silent autism. You click, you punch the keys, you are 'involved,' engulfed, deciding. You are the text, there is no-one else, no 'author'; there is nowhere else, no other time or place. You are free; you are the text: the text is superseded."[1]

The exact nature of the revolution that has occurred is difficult to put one's finger on, because the revolution happened yesterday. Our lives are too fast and we don't have time to look back at what happened yesterday. Our biographies are little more than a history of stuff we bought and threw out, most of it stuff that helps "power" us through a little faster: typewriters, answering machines, fax machines, scanners, desktop computers, printers, laptops, mobile phones, video players, CDs, DVDs, cameras, iPods, iPhones, microwave ovens, televisions, CD players . . . We're barely able to catch our breath and get a handle on all this stuff, when just around the corner there's something new, the Kindle for example. One thing is certain. From the very outset the Internet has been accompanied by

---

1   Alan Kirby, "The Death of Postmodernism And Beyond" (*Philosophy Now*, November/December 2006). Available at: http://www.philosophynow.org/issue58/The_Death_of_Postmodernism_And_Beyond

revolutionary rhetoric, from McKenzie Wark's *A Hacker's Manifesto* (which follows the form and language of *The Communist Manifesto*) to the widely accepted term "the digital revolution."

In 2006, *Business* magazine compiled a list of the fifty most important people in the financial world. YOU topped the list: "You—or rather, the collaborative intelligence of tens of millions of people, the networked you—continually create and filter new forms of content, anointing the useful, the relevant, and the amusing and rejecting the rest . . . In every case, you've become an integral part of the action as a member of the aggregated, interactive, self-organizing, auto-entertaining audience."[2] Interestingly, the same year YOU also won *TIME* magazine's person of the year: "Yes, you. You control the Information Age. Welcome to your world."

This aggressive **YOU** reminded me of Soviet posters, the most well-known of which shows a soldier pointing at passersby, accusingly demanding: *Ty zapisalsja dobrovolcem?* (Have you registered as a volunteer?) The **YOU** from the poster belongs to a completely different time, and a completely different political, ideological, and cultural context, and at first glance it would seem that my association is inappropriate. But maybe it isn't?!

---

2   Ibid., Keen.

3.
KARAOKE IS A
COMMUNIST INVENTION!

It Certainly Is!

In the Soviet Union there were postcards that were about the size of a 7" single, and they had recordings impressed on them that one could actually play. One of these postcards turned up in my mail. I put the postcard on the record player and heard a friend's voice quietly singing away, wishing me all the best from the city he was visiting, Odessa I think. This quirky technological possibility actually existed; the voice of whoever bought the postcard could be recorded on it. This was the first time I ever heard karaoke, and it was in a time when karaoke, officially a Japanese invention, didn't even exist.

In the seventies and eighties many Yugoslavs would go abroad to buy whatever they couldn't get in Yugoslavia, or whatever was cheaper abroad. In Trieste, they bought fashionable clothes, jeans, and coffee; in Graz, or in Austrian shopping centers just over the border, they bought food; in Istanbul, fur coats and leather jackets. Eastern European countries weren't popular shopping destinations. Most of the Yugoslavs who went to the Soviet Union worked for Yugoslav construction firms. They brought home beautiful wooden chess sets, cameras, movie cameras, musical instruments (violins, accordions, trumpets, saxophones), sheet music, classical music records, and easels, canvas, and paint. Particularly sought after were these little wooden chests with oil paints and brushes that you could wear on your shoulders like a pack. Everything was dirt-cheap.

The first time I went to Moscow in the mid-eighties I also bought a little paint set. The amateur painter sitting on a stool at an easel was part and parcel of the Russian Soviet landscape, apparent confirmation of Marx's utopian vision that under communism people would throw off the chains of exploitation, enjoy their work, and dedicate their free time to the things they loved. A creek and patches of greenery, a chapel in the snow, a snow-laden hill, a frozen lake or lilac in bloom—these scenes were unthinkable without one compulsory detail: the amateur painter capturing them all at his easel.

In the Moscow of the mid-eighties, they thought of me as a "Westerner." An elegant coat and soft leather boots rising up above the knee from Trieste, Shetland wool sweaters and a cashmere one from London, a good quality Yugoslav overcoat (in Russian a *dublyonka*), a passport and hard currency (which got me into "Beryozka," where I bought a fox-skin cap for myself, and *Stolichnaya* vodka and copies of *The Master and Margarita* for friends); all of these passed as irrefutable evidence of my "Westernness." My Russian friends and acquaintances were what we might call fashion "incompatible," but unlike me, they all had hobbies. Most of them played an instrument, most often the guitar. At evening gatherings they'd take turns playing Okudzhava and Vysotsky chansons, or their own chansons in the style of Okudzhava and Vysotsky. Most wrote poetry or dabbled in painting, and I didn't know anyone who couldn't take a decent photo. To me, a "Westerner," this whole world of artistic amateurism was on the one hand quite delightful, but rather old-fashioned on the other. The truth is, there were all sorts in the underground Russian arts scene of the mid-eighties: amateurs without ambition, amateurs with ambition, swindlers, art lovers, informants, alcoholics, foreigners, political junkies, dissidents, losers, and not least, those who were sniffing around and hoping to be offered membership in the official state artistic organizations, which granted one "freelance" status.[1] There were also those such as Ilya Kabakov, who but a few years later would become darlings of the international art world.

The world of Soviet artistic amateurism seemed old-fashioned to me because by the mid-eighties the Yugoslav culture of amateurism (ham radio operators, choirs, community theatre, film clubs, amateur painters) was on the wane. Yugoslavs had passports and travelled. American films were in the cinemas, everyone had a TV, and these TVs showed popular American shows. Local cultural centers were slowly abandoned, "workers' universities" offering adult education began to close, and slogans such as "Knowledge Is Power" and "Workplace Education" had simply lost their credibility. Many ham-radio operators had become professional technicians, and many of those involved in amateur film and photography circles, formerly weekend dabblers, had established themselves as artists, most of them as "conceptualists." Amateurism kept its longest foothold in

---

1   Membership in the official Soviet literary, fine arts, film, and translation organisations gave one the prized status of freelance artist. In the absence of this status anyone who was unemployed could be prosecuted for parasitism (*tunejadstvo*), the law under which Joseph Brodsky was sentenced to five years of forced labor in 1963.

half-forgotten Esperanto clubs and the lively Haiku poetry scene, whose poets would send their work off to a mysterious Japanese commission, competing for an international Haiku poetry prize. Emerging out of the culture of amateurism, in the 1970s works by Yugoslav primitive artists were elevated to the status of "art," attracted international attention and the accompanying big bucks, and then together with buyer interest vanished just a few years later.

I remember bits and pieces from the time of Yugoslav cultural amateurism. The small town in which I grew up had a "House of Culture" with a library, a movie theatre, a music school, and an amateur theatre with an impressive number of productions under its belt. My friend Alma's father, a printer by trade, always played the leading man, and Ivanka, a typist and local beauty, the leading lady. In one production my father, who really didn't have a clue about acting, had a bit part as an American—because he was tall. The general consensus in our small town was that only Americans were tall. The audience was particularly enamored with the Hawaiian shirt he wore. We called it a *havajka* (a "Hawaiian") because it was brightly colored, the general consensus being that only Americans wore colorful shirts. The local audience enjoyed the performances, mainly because everyone had a personal connection to the actors. People often laughed in the wrong places, or commented loudly on this or that scene, but, having forgotten that the actors were their next-door neighbors and friends, they cried in equal measure.

All in all, alongside the cult of "technological progress," culture itself was a "cult" ideological tenet under socialism. Education and self-education were the obligations of every progressive socialist individual, and love of the *fine arts* went hand in hand with *humanism* and the *development of the well-rounded socialist personality*, all of which found expression in "artistic" amateurism.[2]

With the disintegration of socialist Yugoslavia in the early nineties and the emergence of new states and the ideology of nationalism, the practice of amateurism has seen its re-articulation. Today, as before, institutional, financial, and media investment is geared towards nurturing local folk traditions (songs, dance, customs), there being both ideological and commercial imperatives at work. On the one hand, local folk traditions are useful in cultivating regional identities, and on the other, they're handy in developing regional tourism. Under communism, folklore festivals offered symbolic support for the *brotherhood and unity of the nations and nationalities*[3] of Yugoslavia, and today these very same festivals offer symbolic support for the *particularities of national and ethnic identities*. The thing is, communism or post-communism, Eastern European amateurs dance their ring dances and pluck their *tamburice*[4] in exactly the same way

---

2   The Croatian writer Ivo Brešan's play *Performing Hamlet in the Village of Mrduša Donja* (Predstava Hamleta u selu Mrduša Donja) is a brilliant comedy about an amateur company in an isolated Croatian village. The company performs *Hamlet* in its local rural dialect, changing the meaning of Shakespeare's text to suit local ideas and the ideological principles of the (communist) time.

3   Translator's Note: In the former Yugoslavia the terms "nations" (*narodi*) and "nationalities" (*narodnosti*) had particular meanings. The constitutive nations of the former Yugoslavia were those named as such in the constitution: Serbs, Croats, Slovenes, Macedonians, (Bosnian) Muslims (from 1971), and Montenegrins. The "nationalities" designated what in other languages would be referred to as "national minorities," in this case, Hungarians, Italians, Slovaks, Czechs, Albanians, and others.

4   Translator's Note: A stringed instrument similar to a mandolin used to accompany folk songs, particularly popular in former Yugoslav regions along the Danube River basin and on the Great Pannonian Plain.

they have danced and plucked down through the ages. It's just that every now and then the ideological pretext changes.

Although the beliefs that culture was a matter for the people (and not just the elite), and that one day everyone would get to try his or her artistic hand, were firmly rooted in the practice of the communist culture of amateurism, the practice was never intended to undermine the canon. Amateur and "professional" art (literature, painting, ballet, opera, theatre) existed alongside each other. Amateur art tried to imitate professional art, but never set out to take its place. Amateurs knew they were amateurs and left the power games, turns, shifts, and battles over the canon to professional artists. Technology, market principles, globalization, and the death of communism have radically altered the order of things. The utopian cliché that one day everyone will get to try his or her artistic hand has actually become the dominant and completely chaotic cultural practice that we know today. Communism came to power with the Great October Revolution and ended as fiasco. But communist ideas (*Technology for the people! Culture for the people! Art for the People!*) have risen from the ashes, successfully realized in the Great Digital Revolution.

Karaoke for Comrade Tito

Let's imagine that in the future archaeologists will be able to put geographical regions through scanners, like the ones airport customs officers use to check our suitcases. Imagine the relief—no more futile digging in the wrong places! Now let's imagine putting Yugoslavia, a country that no longer exists, through this kind of scanner. Millions of mysterious phallic objects would show up on the imaginary scanner's giant screen. "What the hell is this?" the shocked archaeologists would ask. "What kind of relic could this be? What kind of civilization? A civilization that worshipped the phallus?"

It was a country that worshipped one man, not necessarily his phallus, although from a (psycho)analytical perspective we probably shouldn't exclude the hypothesis. The mysterious phallic object was neither a phallus nor a police baton. It was precious cargo. The object was known as the relay baton, was made mostly of wood, and in the middle had a hollow, and in this hollow, just like in a bottle, there would be a letter—containing birthday greetings for Tito. Yes, the man's name was Tito. And yes, the catchy brevity of his name contributed much more to his popularity than commonly thought. On this score, there isn't a president, not even Obama, who has ever come close. If this kind of thing weren't important, Bono would have called himself Engelbert Humperdinck.

The relay baton—both a letter and letter box in one—was shaped like a torch, easy to hold, and easily passed from hand to hand.[5] In May of each year every village, town, and city in the former Yugoslavia would organize a youth relay (Tito's birthday was also Youth Day), and the baton was passed from one pair of hands to the next. The baton was meant to symbolically link all Yugoslavs, all the

---

5 "As opposed to the sceptre in the hands of kings and religious leaders, which could not be touched by anyone else, the relay baton gained its symbolic political power from the very fact that it passed through many hands. While the sceptre, one end pointing down towards the earth, and the other upwards towards the sky, is a symbol of its bearer's connection to a heavenly power and his authority to represent this power on earth, the relay baton was a symbol of the connection between leader and people, of his legitimate power exercised in the name of the people." (Ivan Čolović, "O maketama i štafetama" [On Maquettes and Relay Batons] in *VlasTito iskustvo past present* (Belgrade: 2005)

country's nations and nationalities, and on May 25ᵗʰ, Tito's birthday, the baton would finally arrive, to much fanfare, in Belgrade. The boy or girl of the year would run the final stretch and solemnly hand the baton to Tito himself. The relay batons were unique handicrafts, and competition was fierce to make one's baton more original, beautiful, and impressive than the rest.

The day after Tito died (May 4ᵗʰ, 1980), the photographer Goranka Matić began taking pictures of the displays in Belgrade shop windows. She called the series "Days of Pain and Pride," the cliché on which the Yugoslav media seemed to have agreed. Overnight, ordinary people—hairdressers, butchers, and bakers—became artists. Tito's portrait with a black mourning crepe was the connective element in the many fantastic, touching, and grotesque amateur art installations. In one window display Tito's photo is happily set among fresh fruit and vegetables. In another Tito's portrait is among funeral candles. Then there is Tito's portrait with typewriters. Tito with sporting apparel (a tennis racket levitating from the side of the frame). Tito in the window of a hairdresser's, wedged among photos of young beauties who are showing off the latest styles. Tito in a cake shop window, among the cakes. Tito in a butcher's window, surrounded by legs of lamb, the butcher wiping his tears. Tito in a barbershop window (an enormous comb suspended overhead). Tito's picture on the wall of a hardware store, the photo taken through the glass display, on the left a board reading *Signs for Public Display* (the kind hung in public spaces), on the right, the shop's advertising slogan—*A Man Doesn't Have Spare Parts*—and in the middle, Tito's portrait and a mourning crepe.

In April 2009, Belgrade's 25ᵗʰ of May Museum hosted an exhibition of gifts given by Yugoslavs to Tito, the majority dating from the early seventies. Only a fraction of the diverse collection was actually exhibited. In Tito's lifetime, staff at the Museum of the History of Yugoslavia had diligently archived, classified, and numbered the items, and in the automatism of their jobs probably never thought that this "rubbish" would ever see the light of day. Following Yugoslavia's disintegration the archive gathered dust, and only today, thanks to enthusiasts, is this enormous collection slowly having its time in the spotlight. The overwhelming visitor interest was propelled by a number of factors, including the twenty-year stigmatization of communism, Tito, and Titoism; the tacit prohibition of "everything Yugoslav" (particularly in Croatia); the aftershocks of the nationalist hysteria and war; and finally, by the fiasco of the nationalist-inspired state projects and the inability of today's leaders to create "respectable," and at least semi-reliable, states.

The "women's" gifts include embroidered pillows, hand towels, knitted sweaters, gloves, tapestries, cushions (in the shape of a red star!), stocking caps, dolls in folk costume, children's slippers and clothing, Tito's portrait imprinted on silk, and hand-woven rugs bearing Tito's image, among them a bizarre specimen with the motif "Josip Broz's Sons Žarko and Miša Visit Their Father after His Operation." The many embroidered messages bear congratulations, little verses (*The bee belongs to the flower, Tito belongs to the world!*), and political slogans (*Let's go the unaligned route!*). The "men's" gifts are more "sturdy," either cast in metal or carved from wood, often representing the sender's trade. The gifts include a stuffed trout (from a fisherman); a stuffed snake (!); die-cast figurines of workers, cranes, cars, trains, yachts, boats, planes, ovens, ink pots; ash trays (Tito was a smoker); car-shaped cigarette lighters; and even oddities such as a mini artificial leg (from an orthopedic factory), a mini dental surgery (from the Yugoslav Dentists' Association), and a false tooth mounted on a plinth (from the Yugoslav Dental Technicians' Association). Some gifts distill the essence of Yugoslav ideology at the time, as understood by the sender, the amateur artist. Carved from a tree trunk, Ivan Demša's "Trunk of Peace" is emblematic in this regard. Tito's head grows out from the top of the tree, or, in other words: Tito is a tree, and his branches wrap themselves around the globe. Birds sit on the branches of the "Trunk of Peace" and build their nests, symbolizing the strength, fertility, and global reach of his pacifist politics.

Visiting the exhibition it occurred to me that this heap of "artistic" objects which were anonymously gifted to Tito was a kind of symbolic mega-magnet that had held Yugoslavia and Yugoslavs together. The most popular Yugoslav slogan was *We are Tito's, Tito is Ours*, but with the death of Tito, Yugoslavia fell apart, and nobody belonged to Tito any more, because in the simple, physical sense Tito no longer belonged to us. "The art of Josip Broz was called Tito . . . Tito is a romantic pop star, above all he is the realization of the romantic ideal that our life is a work of art."[6] As far as his media image goes, Tito was a kind of star, a communist James Bond. He wore a white suit, was a man of learning, had a lot of women, was a snappy dresser, smoked expensive Cuban cigars, liked fine wine, adored his two white poodles, and had famous actresses (Sofia Loren, Elizabeth Taylor, Gina Lollobrigida) and famous actors (Kirk Douglas, Richard Burton, who played Tito in the film *Sutjeska*) as his house guests. Tito was a "playboy" who dared to say "no" to Stalin. Tito founded the Non-Aligned Movement, played golf and tennis, was a keen photographer, and, judging by the many photos, liked to dance;

---

6   Rastko Močnik, "Tito: majstorstvo popromantizma," [Tito: the Mastership of Pop-romanticism] in *VlasTito iskustvo past present* (Belgrade, 2005).

he even had a yacht. All in all, "he could sit down at the piano, but he could shoot a bear just as well."[7]

A quick glance at the hundreds of miniature exhibits, and the thought of the thousands and thousands of similar objects stored in the basement of the Museum of the History of Yugoslavia, makes one's head spin. I asked myself what drove people to embroider, crochet, sew, and braid, to craft replicas of everything and anything, and then send their amateur "installations" to a single recipient, to Tito. And then I thought of the rituals of contemporary pop culture and tried to visualize the millions of letters, gifts, and artifacts that are sent to today's megastars. At rock concerts girls throw their lingerie on stage, their bras and knickers, in the hope that in a given moment their idol will use their knickers to wipe the sweat from his forehead, and in doing so, symbolically become one with his fans. For the same symbolic reasons, at concert's end a star strips off a T-shirt soaked in sweat and throws it out into the crowd. Famous tennis players do the same with their sweatbands. Let's rewind the tape. The grandmothers and great-grandmothers of today's young girls sent their mothers' slippers and bodysuits (from when they were babies), the most intimate things they owned, to Tito. Absorbing the sweat of thousands of runners, the relay baton passed from hand to hand and ended up in Tito's. Symbolically the people became one with their idol, and the idol one with his people.

And so, in the end, why are gifts sent by the anonymous masses karaoke? They are karaoke because the whole point of the gift is symbolic rapprochement with one's idol. Like the legion of Elvis impersonators who both idolize and carnivalize their "King," the

---

7   Ibid.

anonymous singer sidles up to Elvis by doing a karaoke version of "Only You," but inadvertently soils his aura in the process. The amateur portraits and miniature wooden sculptures of Tito exemplify this symbolic idolatrous "cannibalism," the idol transformed into his own farce. The gifts sent to Tito are collective karaoke, a mute collective song.

4.
KARAOKE PEOPLE

Doubles

Pulsing in the very idea of karaoke is the old legend of the *doppelgänger*, of the double, the lookalike, the twin and the surrogate. Karaoke-people are **wannabes**.

Legends about doubles have always fired the human imagination. With the epochal birth of Dolly the sheep, the first live clone, not to mention the recent first full-face transplant, this intriguing subject has left the unfettered sphere of the romantic and slipped into the domains of ethics, medicine, and the entertainment industry. Worried about the real possibility of the production of doubles, contemporary medicine moralistically trumpets that in life we are all one-offs and that we have but one life. The entertainment industry blares back that the market has room for everyone, secretly hoping that an anonymous karaoke singer will efface Elvis's performance of "Only You" from the collective memory, while simultaneously doubling sales of his CDs. The entertainment industry lives on recycling, and hailing its significance, theoreticians of popular culture dignify the profits.

As a child I was riveted by Mark Twain's novel *The Prince and the Pauper*. To me it was a story about risk, and it fueled my child-like fantasy that a little girl, my double, might appear and take my place, prompting a feeling of freedom that was both terrifying and exciting. (What if my double were to usurp my place in my parents' hearts for good?! What if I could never come home again?!) Whispered among the adults, stories about Tito got my child's imagination going, especially the one about Tito not being the real Tito, but his double. These rumors were given legs by the fact (real or imagined) that apart from speaking several languages, Tito also played the piano. People could never get their heads around that piano. How, for Christ's sake, did a poor kid from Zagorje complete a locksmith's apprenticeship, set up the Partisan movement, defeat the Germans, establish the Yugoslav state, *and* learn to play the piano?

Rumors about doubles have often accompanied kings, dictators, presidents, and generals. Irakli Kvirikadze's film *Comrade Stalin Goes To Africa* (*Poezda tovarišča Stalina v Afriku*, 1991) is a bitter comedy about an ordinary Soviet worker, a Jew, who as a result of his strik-ing physical resemblance to Stalin is arrested by the NKVD and drilled for months in how to impersonate Stalin. When the luckless worker finally completes his secret training, news of Stalin's death arrives from Moscow and the NKVD puts a bullet in his temple. It might seem quite by the by, but today, successfully cloned embryos are destroyed in laboratories when the embryos are between twelve and fourteen days old. For the time being that is apparently the allowed lifespan of a human clone.

In his 2008 autobiography Feliks Dadajev confirmed the rumors about Stalin's doubles. Dadajev, an old man pushing ninety, a former dancer and juggler, was Stalin's lookalike (apart from the ears, "My ears were smaller" claims Dadajev), his official double. Doubles served as targets for potential assassins (apparently there were two attempts on Stalin's life), stood in as Stalin's surrogates at parades, and traveled to and from airports to confuse the assassins. Trailed by journalists, in 1945 Dadajev traveled to the famous Yalta conference. The real Stalin was already there.

Literature and film have frequently exploited the motif of the double, the twin, and the lookalike. Alexandre Dumas (the story of Louis XIV and his twin brother), Charles Dickens, Mark Twain, Anthony Hope, and Bolesław Prus are but a handful of the writers who have been fascinated by the theme. Anthony Hope's novel *The Prisoner of Zenda* has seen endless movie remakes. Charlie Chaplin's masterpiece *The Great Dictator* is a story about a double. Karaoke-people, wannabes, fans, they buzz around famous people like flies. Give me a celebrity and I'll give you a double; it doesn't matter if it's Paul McCartney, Elvis, Princess Diana, Paris Hilton, or even Bill Gates.

Želimir Žilnik's film *Tito A Second Time Among the Serbs* (*Tito po drugi put među Srbima*, 1994) is an intelligent work of cinematic provocation. An actor who physically resembles Tito appears on the streets of Belgrade, and passersby, ordinary people, spontaneously get in on the joke and have a chat. During the course of the conversation, the game takes an unexpected turn. For a second people forget he's an impostor and, as if in a kind of regressive psychotherapeutic séance, some accuse Tito of being "guilty for everything" (for the war, for the disintegration of Yugoslavia), while others urge him to return, because "everything was much better" when he was alive.

There is an anecdote about Charlie Chaplin, apparently true, that underscores my childhood nightmare about doubles, the one inflamed by Twain's *The Prince and the Pauper*. The story goes that sometime in the thirties Charlie Chaplin entered a Charlie Chaplin lookalike competition. They say he didn't even make the final.

Fans

Ray Bradbury's novel *Fahrenheit 451* (and let's not forget François Truffaut's screen adaption) depicts a bleak future of a world without books. A forest-dwelling group of "outlaws," book-lovers, are humanity's only hope for salvation from total cultural amnesia. They are *book-people*, a living library, each having memorized a book by heart.

Visiting Moscow for the first time in the mid-eighties, I was invited by friends for a walk in a nearby forest. Given what I saw, my literary-orientated imagination promptly made associations with the community of book-lovers in Bradbury's novel. It was mid-winter and people sat on makeshift stools playing chess, their breath hanging in the air, others were just out for a stroll, and many (and not just in the forest!) recited Russian poetry by heart. My political imagination was inculcated with Tito's historic "NO" to Stalin, anti-totalitarianism, Zamyatin's novel *We*, Orwell's *1984*, dissident underground culture, and the Soviet everyday (many books really were banned), and so like everyone else I had read Bradbury's novel as a fierce critique of a totalitarian (of course Soviet) regime. Much later, Bradbury rejected this interpretation, and he claimed that his criticism was targeted at the totalitarianizing influence of television. In the early sixties Bradbury had believed that television would wipe out books and literature.

If we were to try to translate a few things from Bradbury's novel into today's language, Guy Montag (played in Truffaut's film by the unforgettable Oscar Werner) would be a newly-initiated **fan**, and the people huddled in the forest would be **fans**. Their community would be a **fandom**, bound together by their common fascination with books. For those outside the community—particularly those who write, produce, or sell books, the forest-dwellers would be a much-valued **fanbase**. Within their fandom, fans often communicate in slang, **fanspeak**. The forest in which Guy Montag meets the book-lovers would be called a **convention** (or **con**). If some of the book-people were dressed as literary heros, this would be called **cosplay.**[1] Given that people from the forest learn by heart and recite fragments out loud, this would be called **fanac** (fan activity). If the book-lovers were to offer Montag a publication that details their activities, it would be a **fanzine**.

---

1   The cosplay craze appears livelier in Japan than anywhere else. The following is an invitation to humanities scholars to present papers at a conference entitled *Cosplay: Media, Identity and Performance in Japan and Beyond* at the Institute of Comparative Culture at Tokyo's Sophia University: "A vibrant fan culture has developed around manga, anime and videogames, and perhaps the most visible indicator of its presence is 'cosplay.' A portmanteau combining 'costume' and '(role)play,' cosplay is for some people almost synonymous with Japanese fandom, but its roots are in sci-fi conventions in the United States. Connected with the rich media scene in Japan, the practice of costuming as favorite characters took on a life of its own. Conventions can draw 14,000 cosplayers, and websites over 200,000 users. The annual 'cosplay market' is estimated at $350 million. For a short time there was even a 'professional cosplay course' offered by a trade school. And this enthusiasm is fast spreading around the world, as evidenced by the annual World Cosplay Summit. The quality of costumes and passion of their wearers continues to draw media attention around the world. Unfortunately, cosplay has yet to draw much academic attention, despite the potential wealth of insights to be gained. This conference brings together scholars from a variety of backgrounds to consider not only cosplay, but also intersections with fashion, subculture, performance, identity and gender."

Bradbury's novel was published in 1953, in a time when television (in black and white) had just begun its historic invasion of American homes. The idea of television as opium for the people (Bradbury uses the word *opium*) would appear just a few years later. The commercialization of the Internet, a phenomenon of the past decade, has given the culture of fandoms and fans an unprecedented boost. Today almost every pop culture "product" has its own fandom, irrespective of whether this product is a TV show, film, cartoon, comic strip, video game, or book from any of the popular genres (horror, fantasy, romance, science fiction, vampire, gothic, etc.). If we take science fiction as an example, there are numerous forms (film, cartoons, comics, TV series, literature), genres within these forms, and within these genres, sub-genres. Further divisions run along the lines of age (children, teenagers, adults), gender, ethnicity, and sexual orientation. Fandoms themselves are broken down into groups, subgroups, and sub-subgroups, structured in complex communities.

Being a fan and member of a fandom means being an expert. A fan of the film *Planet of the Apes*, for example, particularly one with designs on becoming a **Big Name Fan** (a supreme authority, an initiator, a fandom leader) has to know that Pierre Boulle is the father of the fandom and that his novel *La planète des singes* was published in 1963. As a consequence, this ambitious fan will learn French and travel to France, finding out all he can about the author. The fan will watch Franklin J. Schaffner's four-part film adaption ad nauseum. The fan will know the name of the screenwriters who adapted the book, the names of the actors (both lead and supporting), and will memorize the smallest of details, from the music and costume design to dialogue lists. He'll know all the key lines by heart; he'll know everything about the television series and the "monkey" films

that followed; he'll have boned up on the graphic novels and be able
compare them with the book and the films; he'll be an expert on
monkey TV series, cartoons, comics, and video games; he'll know
his way around monkey websites; he'll chat on forums, Facebook,
and by e-mail with other fans; he'll go to conventions, buy signed
souvenirs, posters, and photos, adding them to his monkey collection; he'll buy a monkey suit and, all dressed up, haunt the convention corridors; he'll meet the actors, authors, graphic artists, and
costume designers of the "monkey planet"; he'll meet other fans,
swap addresses and experiences, and exchange all kinds of trivia on
monkey products.

Science Fiction has the oldest and largest fandoms, and apparently
their conventions draw the biggest crowds. Anime and manga fandoms are pretty popular too. Among many others, there are fandoms
for karaoke, Tolkien, Star Trek (fans are *Trekkies*), Harry Potter, and
something known as a "furry," whose fans are into comics, cartoons,
literature, painting, and other forms of cultural production that feature anthropomorphic heroes and motifs. A "furry" possesses both
animal and human characteristics, whether mental, physical, or a
combination of both. A "furry" can also simply refer to a "furry"
fan.

Fandoms use all available forms of media—websites, podcasts, song
videos, fan art. At conventions they work out schedules of activities, which include everything from promotional events to specially
organized tourist trips and foreign language classes. Manga and
anime fans go to Japan, the popularity of both having made learning Japanese cool again. Although informal communities, fandoms
become more and more complex, developing their own language
(incomprehensible to a non-fan), codes, rituals, and etiquette. A Big

Name Fan, for example, has the right to give his autograph to other fans, meaning that he can create his own personal fandom within the larger community. Fandoms are also gender conscious: there are *fanboys* and *fangirls*.

As far as Bradbury's anxieties about literature go, not all is completely lost. Although coined a century ago, today the word *Janeite* denotes a person who displays a voluntary idolatrous enthusiasm for Jane Austen. First adopted as a badge of honor by Austen lovers within the academic and cultural elite, the coinage has undergone a recalibration. When Austen was canonized in the 1930s, and her place within the upper echelons of English literature put beyond doubt, the coinage simply came to mean—a fan. In more recent times film and television adaptions of her work have made Austen a cult writer, and as such, today's *Janeites* engage in ever more elaborate fandom activities: reading clubs, outings, dress-up parties, tea parties, discussions, trips to where Austen or her heroes and heroines lived. *Janeites* practice their "mad enthusiasm" in every which way, studying everything from her characters' genealogy to the fabrics of the era.

Fandoms allow for a random, unstructured, and chaotic self-education. Fascinated by the films of Aki Kaurismäki, a young woman I know started learning Finnish. A friend of mine who is an actress has starred in two popular American TV series. The head of her fandom is a shy Canadian office worker, who, knowing that her idol is originally from Croatia, has spent the past several years diligently learning Croatian.

While unschooled and disadvantaged by his low caste, the boy hero of the film *Slumdog Millionaire* unexpectedly wins a television quiz show, the Indian version of "Who Wants to Be a Millionaire?" Everything he knows he picked up through random life experiences. Today, millions of adolescents acquire knowledge in a similarly wild, unstructured, and random way, owing everything they know to "playful enthusiasm" and technology. The wave they *surf* is popular culture. Injected with popular culture, few will become astrophysicists. The majority will just become fans.

Avatars

We live in a time in which fantasies of the surrogate are no longer reserved only for the famous. Today the Internet disseminates, enriches, and popularizes fantasies of the surrogate. The surrogate is no longer our replica, but a second, third, fourth, and fifth *self*, one we design and redesign, model and remodel, one we control or make disappear with the touch of a fingertip.

The *Guardian* article "Second Life Affair Leads to Real life Divorce" (November 13, 2008) reports the case of an English couple, Amy Taylor and David Pollard, who met in an Internet chat-room, fell in love, and got married. In *Second Life*, an Internet computer game, both had an avatar, and these avatars, "Laura Skye" and "Dave Barmy," were lovers. Then Taylor caught her then lover *in flagrante*: Pollard was watching his avatar make love to a prostitute. In virtual life, the embittered Taylor broke off the relationship between her and Pollard's avatars, but in real life she and Pollard remained a couple. Some time later Taylor decided to test Pollard's fidelity and went back into *Second Life* as a virtual private eye, setting a honeytrap, which "Dave Barmy" (i.e. Pollard) successfully avoided, claiming that he was in love with "Laura Skye." "Laura Skye" and "Dave Barmy" then got married, a marriage soon followed by the real life nuptials of Amy Taylor and David Pollard. The final twist was when Taylor again caught Pollard cheating in virtual life and so in real life applied for a divorce. Pollard admitted to the virtual ex-marital affair but said it hadn't even gotten as far as cyber sex, and that he hadn't done anything wrong.

Created by Linden Lab and launched in 2003, *Second Life* is but one of the numerous online virtual worlds, which users, or *residents*, enter through their avatars. Avatars can take whatever shape or form a user chooses, and although most often human, they can actually be animal, mineral, or vegetable. But few choose to be a plant in their second life. Avatars can be completely different or strikingly similar to their real life users. In the virtual world, avatars do more or less the same things as their real world users. They buy virtual goods (land, houses, cars, clothing, jewelry, works of art), they hang out, go to Sexy Beach, visit virtual sex shops, play computer games, spend special Linden dollars, and apparently, some also earn real American dollars. *Second Life* is home to companies, educational institutions, libraries, universities, and religious groups. Avatars can sign up for different classes and pray in the virtual temples of every faith. Embassies are located on Diplomacy Island. The Maldives was the first country to open a virtual embassy, followed by Sweden. The Swedish Minister of Foreign Affairs, Carl Bildt, announced that he hoped to get an invitation to his embassy's virtual opening. Serbia bought and created its own diplomatic island as a part of another virtual project known as "Serbia Under Construction." Visitors can visit the Nikola Tesla Museum, the famous trumpet festival in Guča, and the Exit music festival in Novi Sad. Estonia opened an embassy in 2007 and was followed by Columbia, Macedonia, the Phillipines, and Albania. Avatars can play sports, visit museums and galleries, and go to concerts and the theatre. In 2008 the *Second Life* Shakespeare Company gave a live performance of the first act of *Hamlet*. Many companies flocked to advertise on *Second Life* and many got burned. Coca Cola allegedly pumped big money into opening Coke's Virtual Thirst Pavilion, which attracted fewer than thirty avatars. All in all, it seems that *Second Life* is conceived as a paradise built to human dimensions. The only thing missing is funeral services.

Avatars fulfill our fantasies of being someone else, somewhere else. Adult users return to childhood, by definition a comfort zone. The virtual world is also a comfort zone. Adult users of *Second Life* experience life free of risk or consequence—they fly without falling, have unprotected sex, make risk-free acquaintances, and teleport themselves free from the risk of forever remaining in a virtual world. Users have the world under absolute control; they are Gods, able to connect and disconnect at will. Through this simulation game young users of *Second Life* learn about the world of adults. A young girl made her *Second Life* avatar a prostitute. It wasn't so bad, she said. And besides, she wasn't prostituting herself, her avatar was.

Can we live two lives? The American documentary *Second Skin* follows the lives of several players of the online game *World of Warcraft* (WoW). WoW is a "massively multiplayer online role playing game" (or MMORPG) situated in the fantasy *Warcraft* universe. Statistics suggest that some fifty million people, of whom sixty percent are between twenty and thirty years old, play the game. The documentary follows four addicts who live together; each spend about sixteen hours a day on the game. Asked why the "synthetic world" is better than the real one, the gamers reply that in the synthetic world the starting line is the same for everyone and that everyone has **equal opportunities**. They maintain that with their avatars they feel a greater **freedom** (the word they use most frequently) than

they do in the real world, that the game is an **extension of themselves**, and that in the world of the game **they are more than they
are** in the real world. Coming from someone who is confined to a
wheelchair, these reasons would be understandable, but they are terrifying when offered by healthy adults. Most of the gamers live with
the consequences of their obsessive connection to a fantasy world
and disconnection from the real world—unemployment, divorce,
suicide, alienation—the very things that accompany any kind of
severe addiction. Obsessive gaming changes one's perception, hearing, sensation, sense of color, and perspective—one addict confesses
that in his first days of abstinence it was the real world that seemed
fake. Other gamers say that in the virtual world they've struck up
partnerships and friendships that are more enduring than those they
have had in the real world. "We're alienated," says one gamer, "but
connected, because the game is a safe place to get more intimate."
The gamers band together, meet new people, set up associations
and virtual unions, and sometimes even meet in real "parallel" life.
Gamers share an intimate bond with their avatars, which they experience as the better part of themselves.

A *Wired Magazine* article entitled "How Madison Avenue is Wast-
ing Millions on a Deserted Second Life" and published in mid-2007
claims that eighty-six percent of *Second Life* users have abandoned
their avatars, and that corporate investment in the venture has
been a fiasco.[2] "It's really the software's fault," said the president of

---

2   *Second Life* might currently be a fiasco for investors, but it's fertile ground
for academic research. Zoe McMillan and Steorling Heron recently proposed a
collection of essays entitled *Challenging the Virtual: Women's Cultural Experience
in Second Life* and sent out a call to fellow female academics to contribute chap-
ters on the following topics: SL Economic and Business; SL Artistic and Creative Expressions via Building, Scripting, Animation; SL Subculture Identities

Linden Lab. Users returned to their First Life, impatiently waiting for better software solutions in their Second Life. In the now
deserted *Second Life* a user could only have a single avatar. But Sybil
had sixteen.[3]

Who's What to Whom?

Woody Allen's story "The Kugelmass Episode" revolves around a
middle-aged professor of humanities who teaches at The City College of New York. Bored with his life and marriage to Daphne,
Kugelmass wants a romantic escapade. At Kugelmass's request, and
assisted by a magic cabinet, the magician Persky teleports Kugelmass into the virtual world of Flaubert's *Madame Bovary*. Kugelmass
meets Emma Bovary, wanders the streets of Yonville with her, and
falls in love. Emma, however, wants to see New York, and with
the help of Persky and his magic cabinet is teleported there. After
a while she starts to tire Kugelmass, and so he asks Persky to send

---

(for example, Gorean, Furry, Neko, Sci-fi, Borg, Tinies, Roleplay, Child Avatars, etc); SL Relationships/Defending Personal Boundaries (Intimacy/Privacy
in Digital Environment). Concerned as it is with these two diligent academics
this footnote is not meant to be ironic. The fact is that from the beginning
of time humanity has used religion to passionately and devotedly live parallel
lives. The mere 2.2 billion Christians currently on planet earth believe in the
story of the Second Life. The fact that *Second Life* the computer game differs
slightly from the religious concept is quite irrelevant. The heart of the matter is
that the human mind has always been ready to teleport itself into other worlds.
And in this respect, the thesis that Google is actually the Heavenly Father is
also more plausible.

3   In the early seventies the psychiatric case of Shirley Ardell Mason, better known as Sybil Isabel Dorsett, aroused unusually widespread interest, her
rise to infamy helped by a bestseller written by her psychiatrist, Cornelia B.
Wilbur, and two movie adaptions of the book. Sybil's diagnosis was "multiple
personality disorder" (now known as "dissociative identity disorder"), and she
was reported to carry sixteen different female identities within her. Interestingly, Sybil's case inspired the computer security term "Sybil attack."

her back into the novel. Insatiable, Kugelmass soon requests Persky to get him into Philip Roth's *Portnoy's Complaint*. There is an explosion during transmission, the cabinet catches fire, Persky dies of a heart attack, the whole house goes up in flames, and Kugelmass is forever stuck—not in *Portnoy's Complaint*, but in a Spanish language textbook, chased by the irregular verb *tener* ("to have").

Allen's story was first published in *The New Yorker* in 1977. Today, thirty years later, its anticipatory charge is startling. Like Kugelmass's, our time is stuck, hounded by the irregular verb *tener*. In the story, as in interactive virtual worlds, no one is left unaffected. Every time Kugelmass is magically transmitted into Flaubert's novel, anyone reading the novel anywhere in the world has to read pages of bizarre dialogue between Emma Bovary and a character that wasn't even in the novel, a certain Professor Kugelmass. In his little comic caper Woody Allen has neither the time nor inclination to ask questions about the nature of the interaction, which in the intervening time has become known as "participatory culture." Allen's story was written in a different, pre-Internet context, when postmodern artistic practice (film, literature, visual art) toyed with the concepts of metatextuality, intertextuality, citationality, and the canon. Artistic and aesthetic canons still existed back then, their subversion a legitimate part of artistic practice. Today, thirty years later, the Internet, like a giant vacuum cleaner, sucks up absolutely everything, including the canons. The complex dynamics of turns and shifts take place in the interaction between the marketplace, the Internet, and the Internet user. In this process the market isn't a producer of goods, and neither are Internet users passive consumers. One feeds the other, and one feeds itself on the other. In spite of their incompatibility, Emma Bovary and Professor Kugelmass are still "old school" lovers. Today they both are Wikipedia entries.

Whether anyone will ever bring them together or separate them depends on the good will of AA, the anonymous author. Because AA is this beginning of a new cultural alphabet. Whether this alphabet will also be called "artistic" is hard to say.

Incidentally, as far as karaoke goes, there's a new gizmo on the market, the *Vocaloid*, a vocal synthesizer application that was developed by Yamaha. For the time being the anemic digitalized voice seems best suited to anime characters whose eyes are twice as big, round, and moist as Bambi's. But, any day now, imitating cutesy synthesized voices will no doubt be all the rage, all over the world. Maybe some plastic surgery clinics already offer clients eye-enlargements and socket sculpting so they can look like their anime heroes. Professor Kugelmass on the other hand—he's out of luck. He lived in postmodernism, in the pre-Internet age, at the very dawn of the digital revolution.

5

POST-COMMUNIST PRACTICE: VALENTINA AND EMIR

Valentina Hasan: *Ken Lee*

Who is Valentina Hasan? Valentina Hasan is a Bulgarian who auditioned for *Bulgarian Idol* in February 2008. She told the jury that she was going to sing the Mariah Carey song "Ken Lee" (the song's real name being "Without You"[1]). Valentina Hasan, a stumpy young woman in a cheap peach satin dress and glammy make-up, bravely sang the song in a completely unrecognizable language. To the jury's snippy question about the language in which she was singing (as if Henry Higgins himself had appointed them!), Valentina, taken aback that they didn't know, replied: "English."[2] A video clip

---

1 The song isn't actually a Mariah Carey song. It was written by Pete Ham and Tom Evans of the British band Badfinger, and first made famous by Harry Nilsson in 1972.

2 Listening to a recording of the song Valentina noted down what she thought were the words. Here's how her version of the chorus went:
Ken lee (I can't live);
Tulibu dibu douchoo (If living is without you)
Ken Lee (I can't live);
Ken Lee meju more (I can't give anymore).

with Valentina Hasan's appearance started doing the rounds on the Internet, and a regional war erupted on chat-forums soon thereafter. Bulgarian commentators distanced themselves from Valentina, claiming that she was Turkish, or maybe a Gypsy, but certainly not Bulgarian; the Macedonians and Turks jumped in and accused the Bulgarians of racism; the Greeks defended the Bulgarians and accused the Macedonians of themselves being "Gypsies" and having stolen the name Macedonia for their non-existent state. These anonymous outbursts, nationalist and racist, soon descended into a tedious Balkan soap opera that was comprehensible only to Bulgarians, Macedonians, Greeks, Turks, Serbs, and Roma. While all this was going on, a million-strong global audience watched "Ken Lee." Within a month the clip had four million hits and Mariah Carey had tipped her hat to her Bulgarian imitator on French television. Valentina Hasan's unexpected popularity forced the Bulgarian producers to invite her back for a repeat performance. Dolled up like a real star this time, Valentina sang the song in a slightly more comprehensible English, but to the audience's delight performed the chorus in her mangled English as she had the first time. On their feet and holding hands, the audience joined Valentina for the chorus of "Ken Lee." By the first half of May 2008 the video clip had thirteen million hits. Then a hit remix appeared. To this day Internet forums are full of people trying to imitate Valentina Hasan's unique brand of English.

Valentina Hasan became much more that an ordinary karaoke singer. For a brief moment this anonymous young woman was a "princess." A Bulgarian, whose appearance, figure, voice, and English had the jury rolling its eyes, won an unprecedented moral victory. Millions of YouTube viewers ruled in her favor.

Emir Kusturica: Drvengrad

Emir Kusturica is a Yugoslav film director with a deserved international reputation. On a hill called Mećavnik in southwestern Serbia, Kusturica has built his own town called Drvengrad or "Kustendorf."[3] Drvengrad really has tongues talking. Few people in the world get to build their own Graceland, Neverland, or Brioni, and very rare indeed are those who get to raise a pyramid to themselves in their own lifetimes.

On a trip to Serbia in April 2009 a friend talked me into visiting Drvengrad. Built on the crest of a hill and with its own gate, Drvengrad is just like a medieval village, but visitors need to buy an entry ticket. Everything is made of wood, the ground covered in wooden decking, the scattered wooden houses connected by flights of wooden stairs. The houses themselves are perfect examples of wooden architecture. In Drvengrad there is a movie theatre named after Stanley Kubrick, a swimming pool, a cake shop, two or three restaurants, a souvenir shop (in which the only DVDs and CDs on sale are Kusturica's films and their Goran Bregović-composed soundtracks), a library with a reading room, and an art gallery. The streets are named after Kusturica's idols, including Matija Bećković (a Serbian poet and member of the Milošević-era political elite), Ivo Andrić, Bruce Lee, Charlie Chaplin, Federico Fellini, Ingmar Bergman, Maradona, Nikita Mikhalkov, and Jim Jarmusch. The restaurants and cake shop are named after Ivo Andrić characters or works (for example, "Aska and the Wolf" and "At Ćorkan's"). I

---

3   Translator's Note: In Croatian and related languages "drven" is the adjective for "wood," and coupled with "grad," which means town or city in many Slavic languages, "Drvengrad" roughly translates as "wooden town." Kustendorf, on the other hand, pairs the (possesive) first syllable of Kusturica's name with the German "dorf," meaning "village."

don't think any of the street names are permanent; they change on Kusturica's whim. All the signs are written in Cyrillic, so the names are lost to many visitors.

Kusturica has successfully managed to become not only the owner of a "feudal estate" built on protected public land, but also the director of a national park. He is both a private landowner and a high-ranking public servant. Expensive "ranger" jeeps line the car park. The uniformed park rangers look like a cross between bodyguards, security guards, and the "rangers" one sees in American films. Kusturica's transport fleet also has a helicopter, which is often seen flying above the local peasants and Drvengrad's many visitors. At the foot of the hill lie the renovated Jatare railway station and an excellent restaurant. With Kusturica's helicopter nervously buzzing overhead, destroying the idyllic rural silence, my friend and I could barely exchange a word, let alone take a mouthful of our meals in peace. Kusturica has also put a short abandoned railway line into service. He doesn't own the tracks, but they work for him. The train is a typical tourist attraction, and over a one-hour journey travelers complete a "figure 8" and enjoy the untouched beauty of the surroundings.

The peasants who live as neighbors to this modern and modish feudal estate complain about Kusturica. As soon as he finished building an entire village out of wood, in his capacity as director of the national park Kusturica banned the peasants from felling trees for firewood or building wooden houses like his own. "With the forests I safeguard, I am part of the oxygen you breathe" is what he told them. At least that's what the Serbian papers reported. Others worship him, saying he's "brought tourism" to a God-forsaken region and employed many locals to help build and maintain his "dream."

A friend recently crossed the border between Republika Srpska (the Serbian part of Bosnia) and Serbia proper and apparently had to pay a special toll for passage through Drvengrad National Park. The customs officers weren't able to explain whether this little "tax" was enshrined in national law, a local council regulation, or a tithe payable to Kusturica himself.

There are a fair few things about Drvengrad that remain unclear, but Kusturica was obviously gifted his estate by the Serbian authorities. He publicly supported Milošević and passionately supported Vojislav Koštunica, effectively making him a supporter of the entire Serbian nationalist political and "entrepreneurial" elite. Kusturica has assets and revenue that directors of a similar international status can only dream of. At the same time he incessantly mouths off about liberalism being *the scourge of the earth*, and that art, honor, and spirituality matter, not money (*woe is us when the market becomes the measure of all values!*), railing against globalization, and publicly urging a return to nature. Judging by the earthworks and foundations being prepared for new houses, Drvengrad is set to expand down towards the foot of the hill.

As a true auteur Kusturica has played with concepts of the authentic and the fake. Not far from Drvengrad lies the museum village of Sirogojno, which was well-known in the former Yugoslavia and overseen by leading ethnologists. The village is home to many authentic wooden houses, an excellent souvenir shop (with carefully crafted replicas of village implements), and a restaurant with a modest selection of local dishes. Under the leadership of a number of fashion designers, the women of Sirogojno have for decades won international acclaim for their decorative sweaters, which are hand-knitted from local wool, and a special museum documents how the sweaters have made their way as far as Japan. Sirogojno has been deserted since Kusturica built Drvengrad. Today even school trips skip Sirogojno and head straight for Drvengrad. So the kids will get a sense of "authentic" village architecture.

Kusturica is a capricious ruler. Drvengrad has a prison, a little joke to amuse visitors I guess. The time I visited a painting of George W. Bush's head hung behind the metal bars on the prison's wooden doors. A glance at Bush's head prompted a fleeting smile, and then an immediate feeling of unease. It occurred to me that, depending on Kusturica's mood, anyone could (and can) end up there. The village has its own painter-in-residence, a full-time employee who works on the various wooden surfaces, changing details per Kusturica's instructions. I assume there isn't a special advisory board to decide on whom to symbolically imprison.

Kusturica is the absolute ruler of a village he himself *invented*, symbolically honoring people (with street names), symbolically imprisoning them, and symbolically burying them. The 2009 Kustendorf Film Festival opened with a spectacular funeral. The YouTube clip shows Kusturica demonstratively throwing a tape of the Bruce Willis film *Die Hard* into a wooden coffin, a burial of "cinematic rubbish," with Kusturica's No Smoking Orchestra bandmate Nele Karajlić in the role of priest, and a crowd of friends (some of them famous) and acquaintances standing in as mourners. During the later burial of Willis himself, an actor playing Willis bursts from the coffin, and in flames, flees into the distance, the burial candles having set his suit on fire. According to Kusturica this symbolic artistic gesture is meant to illustrate the apparent invincibility of the industry that produces "cinematic rubbish," and that, given the inevitably of a new

Die Hard sequel, again starring Bruce Willis, both will again need to be buried at next year's festival.

Kusturica chooses his guests in accordance with his own political and artistic preferences. Among others, Nikita Mikhalkov (a Russian director, cultural oligarch, and key Putin supporter), Vojislav Koštunica, Peter Handke, and the young Japanese director Kokhi Hasei have all put in appearances. Hasei was so taken by his experience at Drvengrad that he converted to the Serbian Orthodox Church and was baptized in the village's church of Saint Sava.

"I've created a place that looks like it was once inhabited. But it wasn't," said Kusturica in an interview. In another interview he says that he has created a mythical place in which the spirit of authorship will be reincarnated. Kusturica's website is called Kustopedia and is "the online encyclopedia on the universe of Emir Kusturica." He might not have dreamt up the name, but he surely approved it. Kusturica uses a hypermodern form (a fully-realized simulation game) and an antiquated authoritarian-utopian rhetoric (I **invented** a village; I built a **mythical place**; the reincarnation of the **spirit of authorship**, the **universe** of Emir Kusturica, **Kustopedia**).

Opposites

Valentina Hasan's is a textbook case in popular culture. Culture is a living, active process; it develops from the inside and can never be imposed from the outside or from on high. Valentina Hasan is both an active consumer of this culture and a potential participant. She is a representative of the millions of people all over the world who not only communicate via popular culture, but who also increasingly control it. Television is today dominated by "reality" TV (variants of

Big Brother), local and imported soap operas, and local and imported series (the majority being sit-coms). With transition cultures having adopted the *infotainment* model, real news and current affairs programming is very rare. Today untrained actresses not only act in soap operas, but also write and produce them, while memoirs and autobiographies are inevitably a by-product of the "celebrity business." In Croatia an anonymous young man became famous for being the first man (at least in Croatia) to have his lips pumped with silicon. Today he is a *celeb* and hosts his own popular TV program. Even local models and porn stars have their own programs. The examples are simply too numerous to go into—and they are no longer the exception, they are the rule. The media—newspapers, television, the publishing industry, the Internet—live off these "automatic-for-the-people-pop-stars," and these "people's pop stars" live off the media, together shaping and controlling popular culture. As exemplified by Valentina Hasan, this culture is no longer confined within local borders. Transitional post-communist cultures no longer ape American and Western European formats. They are early adopters; they imitate, embrace, communicate, and participate, never missing a beat. Like Valentina Hasan, popular culture is ideology-free, an empty screen on which consumers and participants together locate and inscribe meaning. But Valentina Hasan is no Cinderella. Like the many Bulgarians who headed west in search of work following Bulgaria's accession to the European Union, Valentina Hasan lives with her husband in Spain. Her unexpected popularity on *Bulgarian Idol* and the video clip that made its way around the world led to an appearance on Spanish television, where she impressed with her more than competent Spanish. As a consumer of popular culture, Valentina Hasan pushed all the right buttons: in the marketplace of popular culture everyone is welcome, everyone has the right to their five minutes of fame, and this five minutes of fame is a lottery—it all depends on the very second in which millions of people, themselves just like Valentina, choose their "star." The first time, silicon pumped lips might do it, a second, poorly pronounced English, the third time it might be exceptional talent. Valentina owes her five minutes of fame to inadvertently breaking the rules (her mangled English), to the jury who appointed themselves linguistic authorities (everyone in the jury began their careers like Valentina), and, most of all, to the audience who recognized this. The carnivalization of imposed values and of authority has always been a driving force behind popular culture. Valentina, "the people's princess," inadvertently carnivalized a body of authority (a Bulgarian television jury), inadvertently knocked a "queen" (Mariah Carey, the queen of pop) from her pedestal, and then made one final gaff: like a modern Eliza Doolittle, she knocked the English language off its pedestal.

As opposed to Valentina Hasan, Emir Kusturica is not only a representative but also a champion of "high culture." The Drvengrad project is very similar to computer simulation games such as *SimCity* (a "city building simulation game"); it's as if Kusturica followed *SimCity*'s promotional catchphrase—"Design, build and run the city of your dreams." With its toys for little boys—helicopters, rangers' jeeps, a railway park and old train—in its very realization Kusturica's Drvengrad resembles *SimCity*. Kusturica, however, is not a player of emancipatory-empowering computer games. He's a different kind of player, a transition mutant, a modern version of the communist state artist *par excellence*. In Serbia this position was long reserved for Dobrica Ćosić, who, known to his friends (including Kusturica) as the *godfather*, was in Milošević's time briefly president of "rump Yugoslavia" (consisting of the republics of Serbia and Montenegro). Kusturica is a new, neoliberal *godfather*, a landowner and entrepreneur, who has bundled his entrepreneurship into a personal ideological mishmash that includes anti-globalization, anti-liberal-ism, Serbian Orthodoxy as new spirituality, environmentalism, and the elitism of art. Kusturica could only realize his *utopia* with the help of the Serbian political and "entrepreneurial" mafia. He didn't have a choice; he built it in Serbia. The kindly hearted will intone that every state has a mafia, and this is true. But in Serbia—and the same goes for Croatia, Bosnia, and several other countries in transition—the mafia has a state. And that's how and why Kusturica has his Drvengrad.

Post-communist cultural practice blossoms between these two poles, between "Valentina" and "Emir"; between the ever more ex-uberant and dominant pop culture on the one hand and cultural representatives on the other, who, although they don't have their own Drvengrad, have heads buzzing with ideas that are similar to Kusturica's. There are the legions of "academics," covered in histori-cal dust, who every now and then let out an epileptic kick in the hope of reinstating the canon. There are writers who are retouching their self-images in the hope of winning back the audiences they lost in the historical change. And there are writers who have figured out that the media is king, who successfully combine roles (as writ-ers of newspaper columns and owners of newspapers, as publishers and owners of publishing houses, as TV personalities and TV show hosts, as bloggers and "twitterers"), having taken lessons from the media strategies of politicians and pop stars. For this reason we needn't bat an eyelid when we see the writer T. T. appear on Rus-sian television dressed up as Catherine the Great (cosplay!), her wig clumsily falling on her sweaty forehead. Nor should we be surprised to see the respected Russian writer L. P., in her twilight years (she's over 70), dressed up like a cabaret singer, performing her sad Edith Piaf karaoke. Nor should we worry when other prominent Russian writers use musical accompaniment (usually drums!) to liven up their showbiz-like appearances. And the last thing to startle us should be the Croatian writer V. R. practicing cosplay on television, appearing dressed up as a nun, a "woman in mourning," or a "beaten woman," visually underscoring whatever she has written or said.

Within the general karaoke culture, post-communist culture also wants the right to a voice. And that's why we really shouldn't be surprised that—just like Valentina—the aforementioned L. P. wanted to finally have her time under the bright lights, a right which, hand on heart, she truly deserves. The old dame woke from a dream, and having cottoned on that times have changed, she chose well: she went for a—hmm—"unique" karaoke gesture.

6.
THE FANTASTIC
FEELING OF OVERCOMING
EMPTINESS

Gobelins

I remember my distant relative Žana as a short delicate girl with a nacreous complexion and big grey-green eyes. I remember how she would lower her head to avoid direct eye contact with the person she was speaking to. Her body movements gave her away as a person who sought out the shadows in the hope of making herself invisible. If it hadn't been for her smile, one would have said she was a beauty. But when she smiled her mouth would contort into an awkward toothy grimace, more the imitation of a smile than an actual smile.

I met Žana again after about thirty years. She had graduated as an engineer and gotten married. She and her husband weren't able to have children, so they had adopted a boy. At the time I met him he must have been about thirteen. Žana had packed on the pounds since I last saw her. She looked like a monk seal. But the whiteness and glow of her complexion were unchanged. I noticed that she no longer lowered her gaze, but bored it right into you like a drawing pin. At first her husband seemed like a nice guy, but his voice made me uneasy, soft and arrogant when speaking to his wife and son, condescending when speaking to me.

Žana never worked in the profession for which she trained; the home was obviously her kingdom. The dining room table was heaving with food. The way she had set out the dishes, different cheeses, and ham decorated with vegetables, was sadly magnificent. *She is our artist*, said her husband. *Mom is a real artist*, the boy repeated after his father.

Before we sat down at the table, Žana gave me a tour of the house. Apart from the bathroom and kitchen, every room in the house was covered, almost wall-to-wall, in Wiehler Gobelin tapestries.[1] The entire catalogue was there: the *Mona Lisa*, *The Last Supper*, *Our Lady of Kazan*, Constable's landscapes, works by Francois Boucher, Thomas Gainsborough's *Blue Boy* and Thomas Lawrence's *Pinkie*, roses, autumnal landscapes, winter landscapes, motifs of German cities, birds, children with goats, children with cats . . .

"How many years did it take you to embroider all these?"

"It's not hard once you get going . . ." she replied noncommittally.

My visit was briefer than that demanded by courtesy. All of a sudden I had an attack of tachycardia and a dizzy spell. I don't know why, but it seemed that a terrifying emptiness gaped from every

---

1 Translator's Note: In 1893 Jakob Wiehler founded a company selling Gobelin embroidery patterns and yarns via catalog. Although no longer owned by the Wiehler family, the company that bears their name continues to flourish in Germany and many parts of Eastern Europe, not least Slovenia, Croatia, Serbia, and Bulgaria.

corner of the house. My host, Žana's husband, suggested that he drop me back to my hotel, an offer I accepted with relief.

Armed with needle and thread, Žana has fought her own battle down through the years: what kind of battle, I can't say. Whether those millions of stitches have meant victory or defeat . . . I don't know that either, but the bitterness that used to gather in her lips, the awkward toothy grimace where a smile should have been, has disappeared. The truth is, the bitterness has been replaced by a doll-like stare, and it's enough to make you shiver.

Later I checked out the whole Gobelin thing on a Croatian "recreational forum for creative people."[2] Half-heartedly I read the advice given to a woman who had decided to embroider a picture of her daughter based on a photograph, but hadn't been able to find a suitable fabric and was thinking about using mosquito netting. Forum users suggested the woman buy the fabric in Italy, or at the Unitas shop in Croatia. Some suggested she go to Slovenia, and someone else suggested Zweigart's Hardanger 100. Others warned that the Unitas cotton wouldn't capture the natural nuances of the face, and that Anchor or DMC would be better. Someone else suggested Cross Stitch Professional 2003 as the best computer program for printing her daughter's photo on the fabric, because it was used by the Austrian artist Ellen Maurer-Stroh, a noted reproducer of Berlin School works. The "thread" was joined by a Montenegrin who had been doing cross-stitch all his life, because he loved *the fantastic feeling of seeing a picture coming to life before my eyes, the feeling of creating something*. The Montenegrin explained a heavy stitch known as the "Gobelin stitch": *You do two diagonal stitches across two counts until you*

---

2   www.stvaram.com

get a life-size image, just like the old master painted it, but the motifs look
a bit rough, like when RTCG[3] has problems broadcasting and those big
squares show up on the screen, that's what a Gobelin stitch picture looks
like when you get a bit closer.

Cross-stitch is a mute song, a kind of "empty orchestra" or karaoke.
(In the Balkans there is also a mute *kolo* or ring dance, which is
danced in silence, unaccompanied by music.) The anonymous cross-
stitcher who completes a pattern with needle and thread is filled
with the "fantastic feeling of seeing a picture born before one's eyes,
of creating something," or simply, the fantastic feeling of having
overcome the emptiness.

Jelena Radić doesn't go in for classic works of art; she uses Gobelin
techniques to copy motifs from hardcore pornography. Embroidered
using traditional women's needlework and mounted in kitschy frames,
hardcore pornography is an unusual thing. Like some kind of anti-
Wiehler, Radić also designs and sells Gobelin patterns. Žana, were
she so inclined, could easily do a Gobelin picture with a fellatio
motif. Jelena Radić is a professional artist and member of the *Dez org*
collective. The collective promotes open source software and works
for the popularization and democratization of art, the goal being
that "all people, irrespective of financial status, religious, ethnic, or
other designations, have the opportunity to display their creativity."
As stated in one of the collective's manifesto type documents, "In
ever increasing numbers people from different walks of life, who
have nothing to do with the IT-world, are taking advantage of the

---

3 Translator's Note: RTCG refers to the Montenegrin state broadcaster,
Radio Televizija Crna Gora. Crna Gora literally means "Black Mountain"—or
Montenegro.

freedom that reigns in the computer world. More and more people are making their books, music, and images available in open license and free formats. Liberation from the repressive mechanisms of the corporate world is an inevitable phenomenon, which has its origins in the IT-world and has as its goal the creation of a free society in which the individual will take center stage."[4]

Edek

At the time when my own emigrant experience was still raw, and meeting my countrymen was like looking in a mirror, I had a chance encounter with a woman from Zagreb. The woman had married a Zagreb *somebody* (I should have known who he was, but I didn't), divorced, and, having followed the children abroad, had ended up stuck in Los Angeles, not really wanting to be there, but with little resolve to pack up and try her luck elsewhere. In the evenings she worked at a restaurant that was owned by one of our countrymen (who apparently I also should have known, but didn't) as an administrator or something to that effect. She shortened the daylight hours by painting. In a neat and tidy corner of her neat and tidy apartment sat an easel-mounted canvas and a box of paints.

"It reminds me of someone . . ." I said uncertainly, pointing at the canvas.

"It's our Edek . . ." said the woman, opening a coffee table book featuring the work of another of our countrymen. She pointed to the painting she had just started copying. The woman was copying the work of the most significant Croatian abstractionist, Edek, two of whose signed prints hung on the wall.

My first thought was that this woman's life must be *catastrophically*

---

4   www.draganrajsic.org/10.html

empty. And then a sadness crept up on me, not because of the woman, but because of the *catastrophically* dull automatism of my own reaction. What gave me the right to judge the richness or emptiness of someone else's life?! Was my own life that much richer just because I didn't copy other people's pictures?

"I adore our Edek . . ." said the woman somewhat melodramatically, putting the accent on the wrong syllable, a Zagreb girl born and bred. And it was only then that I understood the real reason for my irritation. It was Edek. Had she been copying someone else, I'd have had greater sympathy for her depressing hobby. But Edek, whether he liked or not, had become a poster boy for Zagreb's chattering classes. Just as every Croatian redneck proudly packs his little ethnic bundle with a Croatian flag, a Dinamo or Hajduk t-shirt, a picture of the Virgin Mary, and a prosciutto ham or paprika-flavoured salami, this woman had packed hers with the requisites of Zagreb bourgeois life. These requisites (and I'm guessing now) included the repertoire of the Croatian National Theatre, a concert at the Vatroslav Lisinski Theatre, buying a hat at Kobali's, haircuts at Kincl's, shopping in Graz or Vienna, skiing on Mt. Pohorje. And Edek.

I remembered the woman many years later. At Zagreb's Mirogoj cemetery I passed the gigantic headstone Edek had built in his own honor. Bordered with white ceramic tiles with colorful abstract motifs, the monument looked like a wall that been lifted out of a trendy wellness center and placed on the grave. It was an exemplar of artistic karaoke. The artist had copied himself.

Darger
The American and international cultural public only discovered Henry Darger posthumously. In his lifetime no one suspected that

the "oddball" (he is thought to have been autistic), the collector of "trash," the recluse who talked to himself, was actually an artist and autodidact, the meticulous creator of an autonomous world. Darger became a sensation in the art world when the American Folk Art Museum in New York opened the Henry Darger Study Center in 2001. In 2008 the Chicago room he rented from Nathan and Kiyoko Lerner, where he spent his solitary years, was re-created as a permanent exhibition at The Center for Intuitive and Outsider Art in Chicago. Over the past ten years Darger has inspired a radio drama, a play, a multimedia production, a number of songs, and a poem. In 2004 Jessica Yu released the Darger documentary *In the Realms of the Unreal*. I saw Darger's New York exhibition in 2002. My attendance isn't worth noting. In an episode entitled "Lisa the Drama Queen," Lisa Simpson also visited the exhibition.

The results of Darger's decades of oddball "activity" have been neatly tucked in the niche marked "Outsider Art." Darger didn't know how to draw, he was, as Michael Thevoz put it, "a thief of images,"[5] stealing from children's coloring and picture books, newspapers, advertisements, comics, caricatures, photographs, stamps, whatever he could lay his hands on. From this "trash" he selected his "little pictures," tracing them in pencil and coloring them in watercolors. Certain images (stamps, for example) he would have photographically enlarged.

Darger's personal world is shaped by a number of factors, including the trauma of growing up in an orphanage (which he later fled), a childlike interest in the American Civil War (which they say he

---

5   Michel Thevoz, "The Strange Hell of Beauty," in *Darger, The Henry Darger Collection at the American Folk Art Museum* 2001.

inherited from his father), Catholicism, mental illness, solitude, poverty, repressed sexuality, monomania, and a childlike fear of adults.

He would often glue his drawing paper into a long roll, painting it on both sides. Most of Darger's pictures feature little girls, nymphettes, the prototypes for which he copied from newspaper advertisements and children's fashion magazines. The soldiers in his pictures (largely inspired by American Civil War comics) represent the world of evil grown-ups. His nymphettes are located in rich phantasmagorical landscapes, in spaces that are part paradise and part war-zone.

Darger's sprawling composition *In the Realms of the Unreal* tells the story of the seven Vivian girls and their struggle against the evil Glandelinians who keep children as slaves. The Vivian girls free the children and defeat the evil Glandelinians. The child-slaves are naked and, were it not for their penises, would also appear as young girls. Nakedness points to innocence and sacrifice, with crucified children frequent motifs. The Blengins are giant mythical beings— naked young girls again, with penises. Their heads bear heavy rams' horns, their backs enormous wings and dragons' tails.

Darger's compositions provoke a conflicted feeling, somewhere between attraction and rejection, wonderment and unease. His visual world overflows with details, bodies, faces, and colors. His images of young girls are identical, one little clone next to another. It seems that Darger crammed his pictures with everything he saw, and everything he saw he "stole" from the surrounding "cardboard" everyday. His world is one in which giant frogs and horsemen, flying childlike beings, giant ducks, flowers of different colors and types, distorted Mickey Mouse heads, and sunflowers that dwarf clouds all simultaneously co-exist. A child's utopia and a kingdom of evil.

Identifying the original sources for the details copied in Darger's pictures is a treat for those familiar with the American everyday. The fantastic anthropomorphic beings with butterfly wings, for example, are stolen from advertisements for "Karo" syrup. "Darger steals his images, lifts them from conventional narratives, common everyday journals, and sentimental stories. He takes them out of context, disorients them, and re-enchants them. Indeed, he uses these images to reconstruct another narrative ensemble, but in the process, the images do not reject their origin but persist like foreign bodies, bodies with disquieting strangeness . . . Thus, Darger does not control anything: he is not the master of painting, nor is he even the master's assistant . . . he is a sorcerer's apprentice."[6]

Darger was proclaimed a great artist when his world, finally in tune with the Zeitgeist, could be understood as art. There is an inadvertent correspondence between Darger's world and contemporary cultural practice. His way of thinking can be compared to that of a child who spends day and night on the Internet. Cut and paste is Darger's primary artistic technique, and today, with *Photoshop* and programs such as *Illustrator* and *Brushes*, he would get the job done much quicker. Teenagers use different computer programs in this same way, the practice of *vidding*, making video clips and posting them on YouTube, is a good example. Teenagers trawl the alluring chaos of popular culture, selecting, combining, parodying, ridiculing, retouching, and beautifying, turning hierarchical relationships on their heads, making the incompatible compatible.

---

6   Ibid.

The second respect in which Darger's art corresponds with contemporary cultural practice is that his imagination, fired by popular culture, is perfectly in tune with the contemporary hunger for parallel fantasy worlds. In the world of *Harry Potter* children also create their own communities, fly, inhabit magical worlds, struggle against the forces of evil (most frequently embodied by adults), perform miracles, befriend mythical beings, and take control. In all of this the borders between worlds are *soft*. Darger's visual poetics likewise overlap with the aesthetics of popular mass media products, from comics to computer games. In this respect his poetics can be understood as a harbinger of manga and anime aesthetics.

Although canonized, Darger remains within the niche of outsider art. At least statistically, however, contemporary art practice *is* in the hands of amateurs, outsiders, autodidacts, the intuitive and anonymous, individual and collective authors.[7] Although "canonized outsider art" sounds paradoxical, it is a part of the cultural practice of our time.[8] At least for a moment, one can also put things the other way around. Using the iPhone *Brushes* program, David Hockney recently began sending his friends little sketches instead of SMS

7   Responding to a critic who had dared suggest that contemporary visual art was illiterate, Tracy Emin—an established and canonized contemporary artist—replied, "So what if I'm illiterate! I still have the right to a voice!" Although she herself belongs to the art world's elite, Tracy Emin spat out a sentence that sounds like the revolutionary slogan of a new artistic epoch.

8   The canonization of outsider art today occurs within traditional institutions such as museums (the *Museum of Everything* recently opened in London, providing a roof for outsider artists), but also in non-traditional spaces such as fandoms, blogs, virtual communities, and associations. Groups brought together out of a shared interest in popular culture are, however, often anything but "popular." A member of the virtual union of *World of Warcraft* gamers claims that joining the union is "as tough as getting into Harvard."

messages. On a symbolic level, the artist's self-amusement can be interpreted as a voluntary self-dethroning, an abdication of authorship and descent into the vast ocean of anonymous digital gestures. The artist no longer exists—there are only gestures that others can, but by no means must, declare as art. Symbolically becoming one with his predecessor, the anonymous author of prehistoric cave drawings, Hockney himself declared: "Him scratching away on his cave wall, me dragging my thumb over this iPhone's screen. All part of the same passion."[9]

9   Lawrence Weschler, "David Hockney's iPhone Passion," *The New York Review of Books*, October 22–November 4, 2009.

7

KARAOKE WRITING

Masters and Amateurs

Every time I come across a story on contemporary artists whose work uses anonymous human bodies I think of communist "bodygrams," the stadium crowds whose collected bodies would form and "write" messages of love and devotion to their leaders. Interestingly, for western observers these "bodygrams," communist *body art*, were, more than anything else, both crown proof of totalitarianism and first-class material for mockery. It's also interesting that for the democratically orientated citizens of these communist countries, "bodygrams" were, more than anything else, the triggers of frustration, rage, and shame at living in such absurd regimes.

In August of 2009 Nic Green brought her "theatrical exploration of modern feminism" to the Edinburgh stage, inviting ordinary, anonymous women, all volunteers, to appear naked. "Such a life-affirming thing to do" is how one of the women described the experience. At this time, Anthony Gormley was staging his "living sculptures" project *One and Other*, in which 2,400 volunteers each spent an hour alone on a plinth in London's Trafalgar Square. Having gotten it into his head that a sculpture had to be naked, Simon, a fifty-year-old, had to be removed by organizers. Later he explained that the event had been a turning point in his life. ("This event will serve to symbolize the beginning of a new age for me—I always wanted to be a sculpture"). Simon is a wannabe, a karaoke-man, and Gormley's project gave him the chance to "sing his song," experience a moment of internal emancipation, and make a dream come true.

Parallel to the Yugoslav communist culture of "bodygrams," Yugoslav actress and poet Katalin Ladik offered sophisticated examinations of the visual, phonetic, and gestural possibilities of poetry, appearing either naked or semi-naked. She never encountered censorship. Unfortunately, like many other conceptualist artists (among them body artists), she is today half-forgotten. Today, "translation" is required in order for the post-Yugoslav generations (young Croats, Serbs, and others whose parents were Yugoslavs) to understand that in the "communist darkness" a whole set of alternative practices also existed. Marina Abramović, then a Yugoslav, carved a star into her naked stomach with a razor. In the western art market, and in the context of body art at the time, the star was seen as a communist star, which it probably was. Abramović's sadomasochistic performance had a context, a reason and political charge for which no "translation" was necessary. Everyone understood what was going on.

Cultural dynamics unfold and develop in the paradoxes between the expected and unexpected, the translatable and untranslatable, the "read" and "unread," in the misunderstandings between sender and addressee, and in the errors of "translation" into a new language and new context. This was also true of Yugoslav cultural dynamics in the time of "Titoism." With the affirmation of "workers, peasants and the honest intelligentsia," a place within these dynamics was also found for amateur literature. The world of "outsiders"—amateur poets, bearers of oral traditions, *gusle* players, "living newspapers" (reciters of political events in traditional decasyllables), cranks, literati, epitaphists, the lot—was given wings. It was, however, largely thanks to established writers and filmmakers such as Želimir Žilnik, Dušan Makavejev, and Slobodan Šijan that this "underground" amateur literary activity was given its due. Exemplary in this regard is Moma Dimić's documentary novel *The Backwoods Citizen* (*Šumski građanin*) about Radoš Terzić, an eccentric, a Marxist, an amateur poet, and the author of the poem "How I Am Systematically Destroyed by Idiots" ("Kako sam sistematski uništen od idiota"). Terzić later sued his "portrayer," the court proceedings providing light relief for many. Together with Dimić, in 1983 Slobodan Šijan made a film about Terzić, taking his amateur poem as the movie's title.

Wanting in on the joke, the media would from time to time deliberately hype an amateur writer. As an exemplar of catastrophically poor literature, Miloš Jovančević's slim volume *The Male Virgin* (*Nevini muškarac*) briefly enjoyed cult-status among the culturati. Today it seems an early forerunner of "bizarro fiction." A number of amateur efforts such as the lathe operator Stanoje Ćebić's *Why I Became An Ox* (*Zašto sam postao Vo*) achieved well-deserved recognition, their rough and ready vernaculars rattling the terminally moribund sinecures of "established" literature.

The writer Milovan Danojlić conscientiously read his way through an enormous pile of amateur literary production, the end result of which was the novel *How Dobrislav Ran across Yugoslavia* (*Kako je Dobrislav protrčao kroz Jugoslaviju*, 1977), a highlight of its time and paean to the glory of amateur literature. Danojlić considers the efforts of his hero, an amateur poet, with respect, empathy, and tenderness, relativizing the borders and hierarchies established between amateurs, outsiders, and losers on the one hand, and the established artist on the other. At the same time, Danojlić's book was also a "textbook," showing us that there is no difference in the mechanism that moves the hand to pick up a pen—the differences lie in the execution, in the work itself.

Theoreticians of the day took an interest in this colorful anonymous "literary" production, the ethnologist Ivan Čolović's monumental study, *Wild Literature* (*Divlja književnost*, 1985), examined everything from newspaper obituaries and headstone epigraphs to retromodern folk songs and urban football legends.

It is unfortunate that today, thirty years later, Danojlić is a half-forgotten author, and that his novel, together with the time and context in which it was written, is completely forgotten. Criticism has changed. Today no one dares set out the differences between master and amateur, between good and bad literature. Publishers don't want to get involved; they are almost guaranteed to lose money on a good writer, and make money on a bad one. Critics hold their fire, scared of being accused of elitism. Critics have had the rug pulled out from under them in any case. No longer bound by ethics or competence, they don't even know what they're supposed to talk about anymore. University literature departments don't set out the differences—literature has turned into cultural studies in any case. Literary theorists have little to say on the subject—literary theory is on its deathbed, and the offshoot that tried to establish "aesthetic" values long in the grave. Critics writing for daily newspapers don't set out the differences—they're poorly paid, and literature doesn't get much column space in newspapers full-stop. Literary magazines are so few as to be of no use, and when and where they do exist, they are so expensive that bookshops don't want to stock them. Tracy Emin's bratty retort—*What if I am illiterate? I still have the right to a voice!*—is the revolutionary slogan of a new literary age. The only thing that reminds us that literature was once a complex system with in-built institutions—of appraisal, classification, and hierarchy, a system that incorporated literary history, literary theory, literary criticism, schools of literary thought, literary genres, genders, and epochs—are the blurbs that try and place works of contemporary literature along-side the greats of the canon. Vladimir Nabokov is the most blurbable of names. But if so many contemporary books and their authors are *Nabokov-like*, it just means that literature has become *karaoke-like*.

Fan fiction

I remember a childhood ditty from the region where I grew up. I think it's a folk song, and quite by chance I recently discovered that a Croatian pop group had done a successful remake. The verses of the song go like this:

> *On a hill sat a little house*
> *A house with two windows*
> *Where sat a pretty maiden*
> *Pretty as a spring rose*

> *Fair maiden, what are you doing*
> *On this a glorious night?*
> *Oh star so bright, my sweetheart*
> *He said he'd come tonight*

Three nights have passed
Alone I've been waiting here
And many more will come to pass
And many more a tear

My sweetheart is kissing another
Far behind he has left me
But curse him I shan't
Because who I loved was he

We sang the song with a wee addition, inserting the words "in her undies" and "with no undies" in the original verses. Here's how it went:

On a hill sat a little house (in her undies)
A house with two windows (with no undies)
Where sat a pretty maiden (with no undies)
Pretty as a spring rose (in her undies)

My young friends and I were delighted with our innocent intervention. Our delight was in vulgarizing the original text (we'd done something rude), in destroying the idyllic setting in which a "fair maiden" spoke with a star and waited for her sweetheart. It was in the liberty of changing the meaning of the song, in "taking its undies off." We were children and had no idea that our little gesture was fairly common in oral literary practice. Folk literature, myths, legends, fairytales, stories, fables, songs, puzzles, and nursery rhymes were all created in the telling and retelling, in the interaction between an original text, its narrator, and his or her listeners. In the retelling narrators either deliberately or accidentally modified the original narrative, something every parent telling his or her child the story of *Little Red Riding Hood* for the thousandth time well knows.

Fan fiction (fanfiction, fanfic, FF, or fic) is a term used for a new writing practice that has developed together with the Internet. Anonymous fans, their real identities hidden behind pseudonyms, intervene in an original source text, which is simply referred to as **canon**. These source texts are mainly gleaned from "trivial literature" (vampire and fantasy novels, gothic fiction, etc.), comics, graphic novels, and popular TV series such as *Buffy the Vampire Slayer*, *Xena Warrior Princess*, and *The X-Files*. **Ficers**, writers of fan fiction, remain within the closed virtual communities of their fandoms, their "interventions" intended exclusively for other fans. The key assumption is that everyone in the fandom is familiar with the **canon**. When J. K. Rowling finished her seven-novel Harry Potter cycle, Harry took on a new life in fan fiction. Ficers continue to dream up new adventures for her hero and intervene in his old ones. This sort of thing is hardly new. Throughout the centuries anonymous authors have served up all kinds of reworked stories to hungry readerships, from unauthorized installments of *Don Quixote*, tales about King Arthur and his knights, and new stories from *A Thousand and One Nights*, to re-workings and parodies of Lewis Carroll's *Alice in Wonderland* and the Sherlock Holmes stories. As a modern phenomenon, fan fiction is attributed to *Star Trek* fanzines, one of which—*Spockanalia*—is thought to contain the first examples of fan fiction.

Slash fiction is a genre of fan fiction in which fans write about the sexual preferences of fictional heroes from the world of popular culture. Fans get off on projecting, intimating, suggesting, and constructing lesbian and homosexual relationships between various characters. Most slash fiction writers (*slashers*) are said to be hetero-sexual women. *Slashy* is fandom jargon for homoerotic, and *slashy moments* are those in the canonical source text that a slasher implies are homoerotic. "Femslash," also known as *saffic* (from sapphic) centers on female characters. Of course computer programs such as *Photoshop* have seen amateur artists let loose, doctoring downloaded photos to create sexual images of their idols. For the moment these idols tend to be the actors and actresses who play their favorite TV and film heros/heroines, but it appears almost any celebrity will do.

Slash fiction even has its own sub-genre known as *real person slash* (*RPS* for short), in which fans invent biographical details and fab-ricate stories about real people (musicians, actors, pop stars, TV personalities, famous sportsmen and women). RPS has a number of sub-genres, among them, *popslash*, *musicfic*, and *actorfic*. Although there are almost no limits on what can be invented, there is an unwritten rule that suicide, murder, and rape are all off limits.

RPS is an Internet variant of a folkloric form mankind has prac-ticed since the beginning of time—gossiping or spreading rumors. The real people on whom RPS is based don't protest too much. It's never been clever to cut off the branch on which you're sitting, and gossip, of whatever nature, is the most effective form of publicity. Also interesting to note is that slash fiction has attracted a lot of attention from academics who are interested in feminist, gay, and queer studies.

The most entertaining part of the fanfic phenomenon is the new coinages, which supports the theory that fans are more interested in communication and interaction with other fans than the actual subject matter. *Fanon* is a story or situation that deviates from the canon. *Fluff* is prose to warm the heart, while *Kleenex warning* is an early signal that things are soon going to get sad. *Gen* (*general fiction*) denotes the absence of sexual content, although this doesn't exclude the protagonists getting together or *pairing*. A *hot bunny* is a story idea, and a *round robin* a story with which the author seeks help from other fans. *WAFF* stands for *warm and fluffing feelings* (a feel-good story), *Het* denotes a heterosexual relationship, and *AU* (*alternative universe*) stories modify a particular aspect of the canon. *Denial fic* is a good example of *AU*. Ficers intervene in the canon to either prevent a tragedy, or simply "put things right" afterwards.

A *crossover* work appeals to two or more fandoms, usually those that belong to the same literary "class." *PWP* stands for *porn without plot*. In *bodyswap* and *genderswap* protagonists temporarily enter someone else's body or change gender. *Darkfic* deals with death, torture, and molestation. A *Mary Sue* is a female character that's eager to please in every respect, the male equivalent a *Gary Stu*. For ficers, James Bond is a Gary Stu.

Fans have developed their "activity" with the help of the powerful and multi-faceted mass media industry. Fan fiction sites house archives with millions of "interventions." Whether short stories or novels, the texts are hard to follow for fandom outsiders. I had a go at a hundred or so pages of WhiteMidnightKitsune's "adaption" of Carroll's *Alice in Wonderland*, and although it's a book I adore, I couldn't make head or tail of the adaption. The publishing industry has swung into action in attempts to satisfy the enormous interventionist appetites of the potential reading masses, and the latest fashion—the production of "quirk books"—is in full bloom. The publisher Quirk Classics features novels such as *Sense and Sensibility and Sea Monsters, Pride and Prejudice and Zombies, Little Vampire Women, Jane Slayre,* and *Android Karenina,* the authors of which use "mash-up" techniques, inserting elements of popular culture (zombies, vampires, parallel worlds, science fiction, etc.) into classic canonical works. The spawn of such "mash-ups" also include *Vampire Darcy's Desire, Mansfield Park and Mummies, Emma and the Werewolves, Alice in Zombieland,* and *Romeo and Juliet and Zombies.* Their authors call them "adaptions," although the term is rather meaningless, as Internet forums confirm that readers haven't read the original—in the best-case scenario they've seen the film. Such a bizarre literary "mash-up" ensures it's own autonomy, and its readers treat it as an autonomous work: they haven't read Tolstoy's *Anna Karenina,* they haven't seen the film adaption, and the world of androids—which they know inside out—is, to their delight, given a new lease of life by the inclusion of "bizarre" details such as the names Karenina and Vronsky, not to mention "exotic" geographical and historical settings.[1]

---

1   This is the contemporary literary context in which Jonathan Safran Foer's latest book, *Tree of Codes,* finds itself. The title is "cut" from Bruno Schulz's *The Street of Crocodiles,* Bruno Schulz being Jonathan Safran Foer's favorite writer. By cutting pieces (literally) from Schulz's book, Foer has created a "new" book, a visual and aesthetic object, from what remained. It remains to be seen how readers and critics will appraise Foer's "intervention" or "adaption" at a time in which—Foer's literary reputation to one side—there is no cultural context in which his gesture might be placed and read (postmodernism, for example, provided such a context), and therefore, how the undoubted differences between the two kinds of adaptions—between the "androidization" of Anna Karenina and the "dislocated" authorial reading of Bruno Schulz—will be articulated. Born of love, both acts of "vandalism" are homage to classics. The unknown Ben H. Winters put Leo Tolstoy down as his co-author. Jonathan Safran Foer neglected to do the same with Bruno Schulz.

Fearing its own disappearance, "high literature" has today hooked its oxygen mask to the face of "trivial literature" and its derivatives (fan fiction being one of them), in the hope it might provide the breath of life. However much people have tried to explain the poetics of today's "rock star" writers and declare them "innovative," "experimental," or "Nabokov-like," the critical unanimity points to the very opposite: that the "literary novel" is returning to its roots, back to the place from where "popular literature" never budged. Aimed at a wide audience, the novel was originally considered a lower literary species. Any novelty in the contemporary novel lies in its regression, in the primitivization of narrative structure, characterization, and description—all in all, in its de-modernization (if we agree that the novel had its peak in the epoch of modernism). On the international market, geography is the only thing that gives the contemporary novel the illusion of dynamism, vitality, and richness. First a novel from Turkey turns up, then one from Pakistan, then France has a turn, after that Japan . . .

The borders between "high" and "low" literary production are either non-existent or extremely porous. Author, Work, and Reader are the three elements that create a literary work. Author and Work have had their time, and now it's the Reader's turn. Thanks to the Internet today's reader is passive no more. He reads and writes blogs, joins fandoms, contributes to Internet forums, recommends books, exchanges tips, issues challenges, has the chance to follow the author, intervene in his work, correct him, plagiarize him, ridicule him, "delete" him, or praise him to the high heavens. Novelists no longer write for their readers, they write for their *fans*.[2]

---

2 Sometimes the opposite happens: fans write for their authors, although they might not know who their author is. *Lolita* has found her place in the rich world

In this respect the institution of the author has been permanently displaced from its traditional position and is today located at two diametrically opposite poles. Writers are either totally marginalized, or (if one belongs to the privileged few) institutionalized like rock stars. The Internet and the new communicative ecstasy have given birth to the collective author, his work "collaborative fiction." With audacious ambition, and trying to piggyback on the success of Wikipedia, in 2007 Penguin Books initiated the wiki-novel project *A Million Penguins*. The project quickly tanked because the collective authorship couldn't agree on a thing. In spite of this failure, the specter of the collective novel, a communist idea, still haunts the Internet. The site *The Autobiography of Pain* invites the people of the world to help write "a community driven novel." The project initiators assure the artistically disenfranchised masses that *The Autobiography of Pain* project "belongs to everyone!" Although anyone can change whatever he or she wants, it hasn't yet occurred to someone to change the novel's title.

---

of Japanese subculture—actually, she's a Gothic Lolita known as "GothLoli." As a symbol of young female sexuality GothLoli has little to do with Nabokov's novel and much more to do with Japanese teenagers' love of Victorian-era children's fashion. As such, GothLoli look like Alices in Wonderland who like playing vampire dress-up. The GothLoli fashion hysteria emerged from manga and anime television series, computer games, and other phenomena of Japanese subculture. The fashion has been embraced by teen magazines (*Gothic & Lolita Bible)*, goth clubs, pop music, and the film industry (*Kamikaze Girls*). The fashion industry has developed a number of sub styles, including Sweet Lolita (*ama-loli*), Classic Lolita, Punk Lolita, Wa Lolita (Lolita style combined with the traditional Japanese kimono), Boystyle Lolita (Lolita style combined with Victorian boys clothing), Hime Lolita (a combination of Marie Antoinette and Brigitte Bardot), and Guro Lolita (or "broken doll style," which features wound-looking make-up and bandages etc.). A boutique selling clothes for Dutch Gothic Lolitas recently opened in Amsterdam. The end result of the hysteric fusion of cultural codes is best portrayed in Shion Sono's film *Love Exposure* (*Ai no mukisdashi*, 2008).

Keitai Shosetsu and Other Stuff

In recent years the cell-phone-novel (*keitai shosetsu* in Japanese) has rocked the powerful Japanese multimedia industry.[3] The cell-phone-novel is a new genre that has grown out of the mass usage of mobile phones, the Japanese site Maho-i-land (Magic Island), the largest of its kind, contains more than a million titles. Access to the site is free, and visitor hits run into the billions; anyone who owns a mobile phone is both potential reader and potential writer. Cell-phone-novels are amateur and unfiltered, the language simplified, the plot primitive, the forms traditional. The heroine is usually a girl from the provinces who endures an ordeal of one kind or another (she is raped, gets pregnant, her boyfriend leaves her, and so forth). The novels are written by barely educated high school dropouts, most of them girls, who hide behind fabricated identities and sign their work with short pseudonyms such as Mone (who apparently took her name "from some French painter"), Mei, Mika, and Kika. Their novels sell in print-runs of two or three million. In 2007 four of the top five books on the Japanese bestseller list were *ketai shosetsu*.

The father of the cell-phone-novel is Yoshi, who in the year 2000 began posting installments of his novel *Deep Love* on the web. *Deep Love* is about high school girls prostituting themselves to older men in exchange for designer clothes. It was soon picked up by the publishing industry, turned into manga, and adapted for film and television. The novel has sold almost three million copies.

Experts maintain that in Japan, where young people are obsessed

---

3   Many details about *keitai shosetsu* are taken from Dana Goodyear's unusually entertaining and instructive article "I ♥ Novels" published in *The New Yorker* of December 22, 2008.

with Internet games, the sale of two-and-a-half million books represents a huge cultural shift in the right direction. They say it's important that young people do any kind of reading or writing. Mone, the young authoress, has no literary pretensions, but defends the cell-phone-novel phenomenon, claiming: "They say that we're immature and incapable of writing a literate sentence. But I would say, so what? The fact that we're producing at all is important."

Those who work in the multimedia industry declare that it's important for young Japanese to feel integrated in their community, to feel they belong to a culture and "to have their voice." Sociologists and education professionals agree. The multimedia industry is of course most interested in a positive assessment of the *keitai shosetsu* phenomenon, because it makes them billions. A collective author or authorship is a sales guarantee. Millions of readers participate in the novel's creation, cheering the young authoress on, and then they buy the book, feeling themselves to be, in some way, co-authors.

Attributed to Murasaki Shikibu, "The Tale of Genji" dates from the eleventh century and is considered a classic of Japanese literature. Some in the literature business claim that cell-phone-novels are simply modern variants of this traditional chronicle of court life, which, as they would have it, is little more than a gossip-soaked tome. Others, such as Nobel Laureate Kenzaburō Ōe, place great literary significance on the work. Whatever the case, "The Tale of Genji" is required reading in Japanese schools.

Kiki, a new cell-phone-novel writing star, completed high school, but flunked Japanese. She wrote her novel because she had just gone through "a difficult thing" and writing was a chance "to get it off my chest." The novel is about a young girl called Aki who falls in love with a guy called Tomo and gets pregnant. Aki loses the baby and Tomo leaves her, but the novel has a happy ending. Asked whether she had ever read "The Tale of Genji," Kiki replied that the novel's language was complicated and that it had too many characters, but that she remembered another old book she had read a few years ago, and that it was really great because it was "very easy to read, very contemporary, very close to my life." The book was called *Deep Love*.

The cell-phone-novel trend is in steady decline in Japan (some think it will disappear the same way it appeared), but it is slowly making inroads in America. As in Japan, authors tend to be young, uneducated, and from the lower social strata. Julian Knighten, a twenty-two-year-old from Texas, works three jobs and writes cell-phone-novels in the evenings when he goes to bed. Julian likes the contact with his readers, who give him advice and encourage him to write, because only writing, "gives me the chance to escape reality."

It is interesting to note that in the cell-phone-novel phenomenon, as in all other karaoke-activities, the same simple rhetoric is repeated over and over: the right to a voice (the right to "get things off one's chest"), the defence of amateurism (illiteracy, ignorance) in the name of having the right to a voice (to "get things off one's chest"), or in the name of escaping reality.

And let's not forget Twitter here, which in the space of a few months had seventeen million registered users. Twitter is used for social networking and a quick "getting things off one's chest." Two writers have already announced plans to write Twitter novels.

In the meantime Penguin has published *Twitterature*,[4] a collection of sham citations ostensibly excerpted from the most famous works of world literature and narrated using the abbreviated acronynm-laced language of Twitter users. "Twitterature provides everything you need to master the literature of the civilized world, while relieving you of the burdensome task of reading it." The collections's authors, a pair of nineteen-year-olds, employ revolutionary rhetoric, because "like any good revolution, this one started in a college dormitory."

There's nothing wrong with a reappraisal or rethinking of the canon, quite to the contrary. In our college days my generation poked fun at the classics of our national literature, the dull and decrepit texts of required reading lists. Instead of reading the poems of our literary lions, we'd sing them in the vulgar style of retro-modern folk-pop songs, thus probing just how much of an "aesthetic" beating the canon could take. The most alluring literary discovery of my time was the Russian writer Daniil Kharms and his literary vignettes (not to mention his longer pieces such as the novella *The Old Woman*), in which the Russian absurdist delighted in dethroning the classics of Russian literature.

Literary "vandalism" is, therefore, nothing new. The current cultural climate and the new technology of twitter, however, make for a crucial difference. The literary canonization of the pair of nineteen-year-old literary "vandals" occurred at lightning speed (Kharms needed a good seventy years for his entire body of work to emerge from anonymity), their work bound in a Penguin Classics edition. What's more, the pair's humorless and dull wee book was received with

---

4   Alexander Aciman and Emmet Rensin, *Twitterature: The World's Greatest Books Retold Through Twitter* (Penguin, 2009).

praise ranging from warm to delirious (while poor old Kharms died in a Soviet prison, not necessarily because of his literary vignettes of course). As far as technology goes, a millions-strong social network gave the novices and "twitterature" their breakthrough. Although the literary "subversion" of the two young authors is little more than a shrewd and fleeting financial scam, the cultural market has set to work on transforming a lucrative joke into a revolutionary trend, and as such, "twitterature" is already embedded within the broader neologism of "amplified literature." The poorly-defined term also luxuriates in ecstatic self-satisfying revolutionary rhetoric. Here's how a successful "transmedia" European festival announced the content of its program:

> The complexity of the real continues to amplify and litera-
> ture continues to be the only discourse that does not try to
> shape the world with ideological clichés, disciplinary limits
> or absolute norms. The beginning of the second decade of
> the 21st century reveals a fascinating scenario. The hege-
> mony of the *printed word* is starting to lose ground to make
> way for other older and brand new words. We are witness-
> ing the rebirth of a *plural orality* and, at the same time, the
> seismic eruption of the *electronic word* is altering the way
> we create, conceive, publish and distribute literature. [The
> festival] is a sensor of these new cartographies generated by
> the revision of the western cannon, the transformation of
> genres and formats, the assault on the categories of fiction,
> the emergence of transmedia narratives, the diversification
> of reading devices, the appearance of new species of readers
> and writers, group authorship that is opened up by means
> of social networks and the explosion of literary creativity
> that is taking place inside and outside Internet. Faced with

all the crises we are proposing a solar festival with a highly intense program. A claim for amplified literature in permanent interaction with the arts and the sciences, in an open, mixed and changing world. Let's celebrate the unstoppable journey: the adventure of knowledge, the excitement and the surprise of creating in an open, mixed and changing world.

Chris Tolworthy doesn't defend amateurism in the name of the right to one's voice, or in the name of flight from reality. Chris's campaign affirms something completely different. Chris Tolworthy is fighting for "better stories," for the "accessibility of the classics," for "authenticity," against "greed," for "deeper ideas," for "diversity," for "creativity," for "ending global poverty," and all this by way of computer games based on literary classics. Victor Hugo's *Les Misérables* is already on the market and Dante's *The Divine Comedy* is in the works. You can watch the trailer on YouTube. First impressions suggest that it's actually a fantasy game about transformers. *Les Misérables* seems more sophisticated and features a certain Peri Laris, a kind of Tinkerbell and Wellek-Warren adapted for a one-year-old baby. Chris Tolworthy has plans to expand production and adapt Shakespeare's complete works, *Crime and Punishment*, *War and Peace*, Einstein's theory of relativity, *The Count of Monte Cristo*, *The World of Miracles*, and many others. Worried that his current and future products might be declared trivial, in a section of his webpage entitled "Deeper Themes" Tolworthy offers the following:

> Every story covers a major theme. It might not be obvious—you can ignore it if you like. But if you want to dig deeper there are people in the story who love to talk about deep topics and answer questions. They show how the ideas behind the stories all fit together.

Les Misérables: the theme is **justice**.

The Divine Comedy: the theme is **faith**.

The Nature of the Universe: the theme is the nature of **reality**.

Julius Caesar: the theme is **government**.

And so on. Don't worry if this sounds boring, you can ignore those parts. But if you hunger for a story with a little more substance, a little more ambition, this game will deliver.

The last time I stumbled across this kind of language, and this kind of "thinking about literature," was about thirty years ago when I bought a slim volume entitled *How to Become a Writer* at a local bookstore. It was written by Petar Mitić, an amateur, a wannabe, a literary instructor whose little book was the Yugoslav precursor of all those "how to" manuals (how to write a novel, how to turn one's life into a story, how to succeed in the literary world) I would later indifferently peruse in American bookstores. I bought a copy of Petar Mitić's little book, and what's more, I even wrote a parody in which I inserted Mitić's pearls of literary wisdom. At the time I had just graduated as a major in Comparative Literature and had published a couple of books. In the ocean of hardcore literary theory, Mitić's amateur effort was like finding sunken treasure. I could play around, invent a Petar Mitić theoretical school, ridicule or praise him, reinvent, integrate—in short, I could do whatever I wanted. I belonged to the literary "elite," Mitić to the literary "proletariat." He went about his business with no literary or theoretical "undies"; he was just a beggar who had dared raise his commoner's voice.

What is the difference between Chris Tolworthy and Petar Mitić? In essence, there isn't any. The difference is in the wires: it's in the reach of the ideas, the speed of dissemination, the penetration, and the visibility. Thanks to the Internet, Chris Tolworthy is visible. In the absence of the Internet, Peter Mitić was invisible. The difference is in me. Yesterday's Mitić made me laugh, today's Tolworthy I don't find funny. Mitić was just a "vagrant" hanging around outside "my house." Today I'm hanging around outside my former house. In that house—in literature—other people live there now.

THE MEANING
OF LIFE

I never asked Mom about the meaning of life. In any case, I know what she would have replied: "Well, my children of course!" This reply would contain within it the desire that I not ask her silly questions. The meaning of life is the new day and that's all. In her final months, when basic movements were painful and she had become half-blind, we didn't have any other option but to put her in a rest home. Having taken care of the formalities and settled her in, my brother and I got ready to leave. At that very moment the nurse came in with lunch. We waited around a little longer. As obedient as a soldier, Mom picked up the spoon, and, her hand shaking, scooped some soup from the bowl. A tear slipped down from her eye and into the soup. That tear falling into the bowl of soup struck at my insides. The image often flashes before my eyes, enlarged, and in slow motion. Mum's tear ricochets around my soul like shrapnel.

Mum's hypothetical answer wouldn't have been far from that given by a philosopher, who, responding to the same question, replied, "The meaning of life is reproduction." I posed the question to an acquaintance of mine, an older gentleman, who was hit by a car at age eighty-three. "It's a stupid question! Life doesn't have any meaning!" he muttered, before adding, "Collecting . . . Maybe collecting is what gives our lives meaning."

Many people think Zagreb's Mirogoj cemetery is beautiful, particularly the arcades in which notable Croats are buried. On Sundays Zagreb residents often visit the graveyard to place flowers on the graves of their loved ones and go for a walk. The different rows clearly demarcate the social differences among the deceased, the nouveau riche jostling for the first rows. With its imposing headstone, the grave at the very entrance to the cemetery is that of Franjo Tuđman, the first Croatian president, its strategic position suggesting symbolic leadership. Social differences are reinforced by the amount of marble and the size of the headstone, but the cemetery's architecture is traditional, nothing much is over-the-top. Serbian cemetery culture is more inventive, although money rules the day there too. I have a striking photograph of a headstone from a cemetery in a Serbian village. A computer monitor, "house," and keyboard carved out of white marble, all to natural scale, sit atop the gravestone. Imprinted on the marble computer screen is a black and white photograph of a young married couple.

The façades of Amsterdam houses are adorned with all manner of symbols, reliefs, and mini-sculptures (people, flowers, and animals—cats are the sweethearts of Amsterdam!), commissioned by the original owners to designate their professions and highlight their social standing. Today, Amsterdamers put photographs of their children in their windows (particularly newborn babies), alongside souvenirs (replicas of Amsterdam houses, cheap collections of little wooden boats, plastic flowers, and figurines) and personal effects meant to reveal something about their occupations, preferences, interests, and hobbies. The anonymous passerby is left to his own devices in interpreting these vivid autobiographical fragments.

Visiting Amsterdam for the first time, I was initially taken aback by this exhibitionism. The story goes (at least the one in the tourist brochures) that the Dutch are reluctant to invite new friends over, but, as a kind of compensation, they don't think twice about exhibiting photos of their children for all to see. It occured to me that Amsterdam was a European city inhabited by an unknown tribe, European Indians or something. The colorful "arrangements" in the windows, dolls, flags, teddy bears, the posters and slogans draped over the façades—all of it is incongruous with the dominant Protestant culture, or the Catholic one for that matter. It seems that the residents of Amsterdam practice urban voodoo: the things they put in the window or hang out on their façades are supposed to protect them from evil spirits. All this colorful urban infantilism beats in perfect rhythm with the bodies of prostitutes in the red light district windows and the city's carnival spirit.

Zorgvliet is one of Amsterdam's cemeteries, and it looks more "Indian" than European. It's not so much the sandy soil, but the graves, which the Dutch love to decorate with shamanic desiderata. If the deceased had been a barber, the blade he used all his life might be placed on his grave. If he liked a good drop, there'd definitely be a glass and a bottle. On one grave I saw Chinese take-out, fresh drumsticks, and rice in a plastic container. Who knows, maybe someone has a regular gig bringing the deceased a fresh lunch every day.

On a bench beside the grave of a child sat a family of teddy bears, the thirty or so of them bathed in damp. Pressed into the sand on the graves are touching colorful "arrangements": sea shells, pebbles, plastic toys, painted Easter eggs, plastic Christmas trees decorated with candles and little gifts. In place of headstones, many graves have glass reliquaries the size of home aquariums that exhibit little items that belonged to the deceased: a comb, a toothbrush, a letter, a favorite book, a CD, miscellanea of all kinds.

The arrangements belong to the burial subculture of a new time. These assemblages are brief biographies of the dead written by the amateur hand of their nearest and dearest. At Zorgvliet, religious and cultural syncretism reigns. Relics co-exist in fraternal fellowship: a cross and an Indian dream catcher hang on a nearby bush, slippers embroidered with native silver brought home from a trip abroad, a little Buddhist oil lamp, plastic airline cutlery, a Chinese wooden rattle . . .

Death is an empty orchestra. Those who remain behind try and brighten and fill the emptiness. They do so as best they can, either honoring strict burial conventions, or, more often, by breaking them. Zorgvliet graves remind one of MySpace or Facebook, of the final image of ourselves we leave behind. The bouquets of flowers and candles left on All Souls' Day are testament to the number of friends we have.

Or maybe it's actually the other way around?! Contemporary technology has given the ordinary individual the opportunity to indulge all kinds of fantasies, to live several lives, but the one thing it hasn't yet dreamed up is self-interment. In this respect, it's entirely possible that Facebook and MySpace contain within them the anticipation of death, the idea of the cyber tombstone, a display on which friends and acquaintances can, in our lifetimes, see who we are, what we are, what we like, the music we listen to, the films we watch. Here my elderly friend's suggestion that collecting is the meaning of life becomes quite plausible. Collecting and consumerism are not only ways of overcoming the emptiness, but also presuppose a fear of empty space, of *horror vacui*. Death is an empty space. For as long as we are alive we try and fill the emptiness. Collecting is a secret negotiation with death.

A few months before my Mom died I opened her wardrobe and spent hours going through it arranging her clothes. I don't know why. Her old Sunday best, a georgette blouse and pleated skirt, caught my eye. Mom had a lot of silk things, but it was that outfit, that skirt, which my eye happened upon. I spent hours carefully unstitching the pleats, one by one, not wanting to damage the silk. I cut the fabric into usable pieces, and then, almost in fear that someone might see me, took the scraps to a seamstress and asked if she could make me something. The seamstress protested that there was little to be salvaged from the assorted scraps, but she kept the bag and told me to come back in a few days. Mom died a month later. The bag is still at the seamstress's. I don't know why I did it. Maybe in mutilating her clothes I wanted to end her life? Or maybe it was the opposite; maybe I was trying to postpone her death. Maybe I was trying to slip into her "skin," to make the pain more bearable for her. Maybe her clothes were supposed to be a kind of amulet, a magic shirt to protect me from evil spirits? Maybe, anticipating what was to come, I was taking a small piece of her body in my mouth, as was done by primitive tribes, where women had to ritually eat a piece of the deceased's flesh in order that his or her spirit remain within the tribe? Maybe I was heading off the emptiness that would appear with her departure? Maybe destruction (ripping her clothes apart) is simply the flip-side of collecting, of the fear of emptiness?

In all its manifestations karaoke culture unites narcissism, exhibitionism, and the neurotic need for the individual to inscribe him or herself on the indifferent surface of the world, irrespective of whether the discontented individual uses the bark of a tree, his or her body, the Internet, photography, an act of vandalism, murder, or art. In the roots of this culture, however, lies a more serious motive: fear of death. From the surface of karaoke culture shimmers the mask of death.

9.
THE BEGINNING WAS
WHEN I WAS BORN, AND
THERE IS NO END . . .

The sentence above is from a book called *The Heart Moves the Pen* (*Olovka piše srcem*), a funny and intelligent collection of preschoolers' responses to various questions. Thirty years ago the book was a bestseller in the former Yugoslavia. The answer to the question, "What is the beginning, and what is the end?" is that of a boy, who today, if he is still alive, would probably be approaching forty.

The child's sentence encapsulates the beginning of the new digital epoch, its sense perfectly attuned to the modern understanding of time. A child believes that all things in this world begin with his or her birth (and that there is no end), which is exactly how the "networked" man of today lives in the present. The beginning is *log on*, the end *log off.* The touch of a key gives the user the illusion of unimaginable power, the illusion of control over time. On the Internet everything exists in the now. Maybe that's why delirious computer users believe that Google is God.

It's a notorious fact that technology radically changes one's perception of everything, including time. Thirty years ago I could wile away the hours on the cinematic aesthetics of Andrei Tarkovsky and similar directors. Today I am ashamed to admit that my eyes have simply been weaned off them; the shots are too long, too slow, and the plot, if there is one, plodding and ambiguous. I used to love all that auteur stuff, but today I don't have the patience. In the intervening time I've become hooked on cinematic "fast food." Flowing in my veins, this fast food has changed the rhythm of my heart, my attention span, and the rhythms of my respiration. The truth is that I overdosed on television, and so I don't watch it anymore. I've been clean for a while now, and I don't miss it a bit. But I do watch lots of documentaries—it doesn't matter what they're about, the most important thing is that they're "slow food," that they offer me the illusion that what is happening on the screen really is happening. The way I read has changed too. At first I was surprised when friends told me that they were going to speed-reading courses. Now I'm thinking about enrolling in a course myself. My eyes are too slow, the computer screen just gets richer and faster, and my attention span is ever shorter. From the sheer quantity of information my memory is getting worse and worse. It's not just that I have no idea what I consumed on the Internet yesterday, it's that I don't remember what I sucked up five minutes ago.

Between you and me, karaoke doesn't seem as stupid as it did when I started writing this essay. I've even been thinking about putting a bit of effort in and giving WhiteMidnightKitsune's version of *Alice In Wonderland* another go. I mean, why the sudden skepticism about some "fanficer"? Didn't I, thirty years ago, write a short story called "Who Am I?" in which I messed around with Lewis Carroll's original? Swaddled in literature like a mouse in cheese, wasn't I the one who was into the literariness of literature, deconstructing texts to see how the mechanism worked, protected by trendy jargon like intertextuality and metatextuality? Didn't I spread my literary feathers like a peacock, parading the elegance of my handiwork?!

Back then it was called postmodernism. Why do I now look at WhiteMidnightKitsune, whoever he or she is, man, woman, or child, with such "elitist" contempt? Isn't he just spreading his feathers? Doesn't he also have the right to a voice? "What if I am illiterate? I still have the right to a voice!"—the line keeps ringing in my ears. I think it's because with every new sentence I write, every new book I publish, I'm tortured by the question of whether I have the right to a voice. What have I got against Tracy Emin anyway?! Didn't I piously wait in a never-ending line at the Stedelijk Museum just to take a peek through a hole in the door of a make-shift outdoor toilet, an installation, the voluntary victim of artistic manipulation? Aren't I suffering from the same syndrome as Natascha Kampusch, the poor Austrian who was kidnapped by a maniac when she was a little girl and held prisoner in his basement for eight years?! Sometime in the years after her escape, Natascha Kampusch bought her torturer's house, and they say she now makes daily visits to do the cleaning. But don't I open the doors of my Internet-house every day, constantly bewildered by the expanse of the "rubbish"?

Maybe the problem is one of ideological manipulation? Today AA (the Anonymous or Amateur Author) is as untouchable as the teenager comfortably lounging on the tram seat. At sixty-years of age you stand next to him with bags full of groceries, struggling to keep your balance. Your legs hurt, and your single obsessive thought is how to give the uppity little schmuck a well-deserved slap in the face. You know it's never going to happen, but the fantasy is good for your soul. If a little open hand communication isn't an option, maybe a gentle word might help. But that's not an option either, because, armed with his iPod and iPhone, the kid is both physically and mentally untouchable. And in any case, the kid is innocent, because he doesn't see you. You don't exist in his world. But he exists in yours.

Under communism, at least in the early days, fetishizing "the people" ("the little guy," "the comrade," "the citizen," "the workers, peasants, and the honest intelligentsia") was all the rage. The class enemy (the bourgeoisie) had to be overthrown. The people had to requisition his armchair, storm his mansion and summer house, smash his piano, trash the artwork on his walls, stigmatize him, hound him out, replace his values with one's own, and get all that old bourgeois crap the hell off "the steamship of contemporaneity."[1]

You stand there in the tram, secretly hoping the kid will get up off the seat and make room for you, and what's more, you're convinced that this would be "normal," that it's the "natural" order of things. You need the kid, the kid doesn't need you. He's visible, you're invisible. So you stand there next to him and grumble, trying to establish communication that's not there, because it can't be there. The kid just doesn't speak your language. You feel as if you've been personally tossed from "the steamship of contemporaneity."

Armed with his high-tech toys, our Anonymous Author, just like the kid in the tram, has today **occupied** a lot of territory. He has

---

1   The "steamship of contemporaneity" is a syntagm from the 1912 Futurist manifesto *A Slap in the Face of Public Taste* (Burliuk, Kruchenykh, Mayakovsky, Khlebnikov), which called for the destruction of old traditional values in the name of a new future.

occupied the television—and all power to him, television was always meant to be his medium, and today it finally is. The intended viewer is also "one of his people," and also passive no more. Today's viewer is (inter)active, his phone calls are broadcast live mid-program, he sends SMS messages and e-mails, he comments and makes requests, he's there on stage and in the studio—in actual fact, programs wouldn't exist without him. AA has occupied the newspapers; protected by the mask of anonymity (a kind of condom), he spends hours firing off comments. Because only authors—people with first names and last names—are responsible and vulnerable to attack. AA's power lies in his namelessness, irresponsibility, and invulnerability. All the same, AA forces you to communicate with him, and if you don't, he simply excludes you from his field of vision. Remember: he doesn't need you, you need him. He has his online newspapers, his blogs, his network of readers, he is himself both an author and a reader. AA has occupied YouTube and hundreds of similar sites, which were all invented for him in the first place. Don't even dream they were for you. He is an anonymous creator, editor, contributor, and end-user of his own encyclopedia, Wikipedia. And hey, amazing, he's now the most consulted global source of general information. Protected by the mask of anonymity, AA establishes his hierarchy of values. He decides whether his Mom is worth a Wikipedia entry, how much space Paris Hilton deserves, and how much Nikola Tesla. AA has his own literature, determines canons, and then does whatever he likes with them. And nobody can hold him to account, because he is nameless. He has his own culture in which others just like him, the nameless, actively participate. He has set up his virtual institutions, developed his forms of education, his information, and his leisure activities. AA doesn't need existing institutions—he will invoke, destroy, and reference them; AA has created his own parallel world in which everything belongs to him. AA is in the majority.

That's his strength. He controls the most powerful toy in the world, the Internet, that's where his strength lies. He is fluid, changeable, ephemeral. He is a morph, he is infantile, he is elusive, he is mobile, he "rides" and "surfs," he moves around, he appears and disappears. He doesn't have a declared program to contest or dispute. Actually, he doesn't have a program at all, but this doesn't stop him from making his fanatical and penetrating voice heard—that's where his strength lies. You are in his power. You have a first name and last name, you're an author, you stand behind your work; you are responsible for what you've written. He's not interested in responsibility (To whom? To what? I mean, do the superstars of the contemporary art world show any responsibility?!), nor is he interested in authorship. He takes whatever he likes, and justice is on his side. His constructions are virtual, he builds and destroys them with ease, and like a good thief, he leaves no trace. He is a representative of the new, you are a representative of the old, that's his strength and your weakness. He's young, you're old—that's his advantage. Fighting him is as senseless as punching the wind. Getting into an argument with him is stupid, ignoring him more stupid still. This is his time and his culture, you're on the margins. Learning his codes is tough, but if you don't know his languages, you're condemned to linger there on the margins. It is both a comforting and terrifying thought that he too is vulnerable: the source of his strength lies—in wires.

In wires?! Standing next to the kid in the tram, your hands loaded with bags of groceries, him having occupied the seat, headphones on and iPhone in hand, suddenly you reconcile yourself to the fact that yes, this is the normal order of things. Because AA lives in a world that "has narrowed, not broadened, in the last ten years," he lives in the "ideology of globalised market economics raised to the level of the sole and over-powering regulator of all social activity—monopolistic, all-engulfing, all-explaining, all-structuring."[2] AA is a child of the consumer and conformer age, an age dominated by fear of loss (of one's job, one's identity, one thing or another) and the ideology of catastrophe and global crisis. And it can't be ruled out that the delirium of communication—his everyday life practice—is in fact a form of autism, of apathy, a refusal to confront a world that has the measure of him and threatens to swallow him up.

"The steamship of contemporaneity," from which you for a moment felt thrown, is a metaphor for a revolutionary age, a time when steamships symbolized progress, speed, and modernity, when artistic gestures really were "a slap in the face of public taste." The revolution in society at the beginning of the twentieth century was marked by concomitant revolutions in literature, painting, film, architecture, poetics, and systems of thought. The entire cultural system was turned on its head. AA doesn't incite revolutions, and he's too much of a conformist to give anyone a slap in the face. In any case, a slap in the face is an authorial gesture. AA is a child of his time, his gestures—irrespective of his occasional self-adulatory revolutionary rhetoric—are neither great, nor powerful, nor subversive, nor mind-blowing. Deep down, AA is just a small-time hacker. He's not even driven by a powerful and passionate Salieri-like envy. He hardly knows who Mozart and Salieri are—questions of copies and originals are lost on him. He is a sophisticated barbarian, the sophisticated part his mobile phone, the barbaric his message, which he films live and sends to other users. AA shouldn't be underestimated. Don't get all worked up, just meekly bow your head: this is his moment, his era, and his culture. While he sits there comfortably sprawled out over the seat, you stand there with your shopping bags

---

2 *Ibid*, Kirby.

thinking about him. There's no need to worry about him throwing you overboard, if that's what you're worried about. His authentic "revolutionary" gesture is not invention, but intervention, not originality, but appropriation, not explosion, but implosion.

10.
AND THERE IS
NO END . . .

I just came across a newspaper story about the opening of a virtual "ABBAWORLD" in the Earl's Court Exhibition Center in London. Visitors have their photos taken at the entrance so they can later buy an ABBA record sleeve with their portrait, or a poster on which they have swaggered their way into a group photo with the famous four. But that's not all. Visitors will be able to get up on a stage with a spectacular three-dimensional holographic illusion, and sing with the virtual ABBA while watching themselves on video screens. Visitors will then be able to buy a DVD of their performance, so that back in their meaningless lives they can watch themselves and ABBA until their hearts are content. Forecasts suggest that this interactive mega-exhibition is going to attract millions of visitors. Abbasolutely fab, isn't it?

Cultural managers, curators, festival and event organizers, cultural theorists and commentators all assure us that the concept of the professional artist, he who "knows knowledge," belongs to the past; that the false cordon between the amateur and professional artist has

finally given way; that the professionalization of art killed spontane-
ity and the fun of the artistic gesture; that amateurism is the only
hope; and that today art finally belongs to the international creative
masses.

Apparently "I Will Survive" (written by Freddie Perren and Dino
Fekaris and made famous by Gloria Gaynor) has been top of the
pops with karaoke fans for years now. It's been parodied often
enough and performed and remixed any number of times. It's turned
up in films, served as a hymn for women's solidarity, as support for
AIDS sufferers, and has served many purposes and been used on
many occasions. It's entirely possible that CDs with the song lie
scattered underground, with the corpses of the deceased, irrespective
of whether they believed in reincarnation or not. It's easy to imagine
that "I Will Survive" has already been catapulted into outer space
as a contact message, the earthling hymn sent out to life on other
planets. It's also easy to imagine the video clip: billions of people
opening their mouths like fish and singing. Actually, the people *are*
the song. They've all got the right to a voice too.

I've always had an inkling that there was something in "making one's
voice heard"—whether this voice be collective or individual, amateur
or professional. In 2005 the artist-activists Tellervo Kalleinen and
Oliver Kochta-Kalleinen initiated the "Complaints Choir" project,
bringing people together irrespective of nationality, race, class, gender, religious, sexual, or other identifiers. Choir members start by
making a list of their complaints (their "complaints' book"), which
are then set to the tunes of well-known melodies. The project began
in Birmingham, and since then choirs have popped up in Helsinki,
St. Petersburg, Hamburg, Melbourne, Jerusalem, Juneau, Chicago,
Malmö, Budapest, Philadelphia, Vancouver, Florence, Singapore,

and even on Gabriola Island. Zagreb recently got a choir. They sang their lists of complaints at the main train station. The local authorities wouldn't let them sing in St. Mark's Square, in front of the Croatian Parliament.

I'm joining the ranks of this rhapsodic Complainers Internationale. I'm making my voice heard against lax public services; traffic lights that don't work; overcrowded trams; lines in the supermarket; long queues in doctor's waiting rooms; expensive dental services; the antiquated school system; the unbelievably thin bags in supermarkets that you can barely prise open and which send your blood pressure through the roof; the racket caused by mobile phones and their owners; price increases on public transport; corruption; low salaries and small pensions; rubbish in the city streets; narrow seats in aeroplanes; complicated telephone messages that click in when you're trying get hold of a public service; loud advertisements on television; television; 3D films for children that give children nightmares; against the mass (ab)use of deodorants; against preservatives . . .

And then I stop for a minute and add *karaoke* to my list. I raise my voice against karaoke: kindergartens are karaoke, newspapers are karaoke, television is karaoke, fashion is karaoke, books are karaoke, values are karaoke, the education system is karaoke, religious faith is karaoke, the free market is karaoke.

I raise my voice against cosmetic plastic surgery that produces karaoke people; against political plastic surgery that produces mentally identical individuals; against religion, because it produces sectarian lackeys; against karaoke politicians; against karaoke states and state systems; against karaoke ideologies and ideas; against the global karaoke spectacle and the millions of us who are birds of a feather and karaoke devotees. Totalitarianism is dead, long live totalitarianizing freedom! And that's why, earthlings, complainers of the world—unite! Let's clear our throats, raise our red fists, and sing without risk. Because even our protest is nothing other than karaoke.

Do we have any other choice? We wanted freedom, we got the freedom of a game, and we even thought the game was the freedom to just clown around. We wanted individual freedom and achieved the freedom of imitation. So let's tighten our vocal chords, there's no quick and dirty exit from this game. We voluntarily got ourselves lost in a house of crooked mirrors, and there's no way back to our authentic reflection. Our bodies move of their own accord, and our mouths do the same. A voice emerges from our throats, but nothing is under our control any more, although they constantly reassure us to the contrary. In the mirror we see our distorted image: what initially filled us with childlike glee has turned into our nightmare. We spin around like an old gramophone record, our hopes pinned on hearing a benevolent click signaling the end, but an invisible hand has already placed the needle back at the beginning. And we again open our mouths. It's too late, there's no going back. This is our glorious age, the age of karaoke; we embrace it, sink down into it like quicksand. There's no cause for alarm, we won't drown, but we won't swim our way out either. We will remain, we will survive. Survival is, in any case, our only purpose on this earth. Sure, we will survive.

2009–2010

2.

BUY THE JELLYFISH THAT STUNG YOU

MY DIGITAL LIFE

Someone said that God is disinformation, and someone else that God is Google. For a long time I believed the former, but recently I've been more inclined to believe the latter. They say only God is all-knowing, omnipresent, and invisible. Oh, hold the phone—that's Google!

Despite my atheism, lately I've been having these strange, inexplicable "spiritual" cravings. I go to bed late, get up early, and in the time between navigate the Internet like a demon in the hunt for divine vitamins, a metaphysical supplement to nourish my famished soul. I glide over the online newspapers, American, Macedonian, English, Serbian, German, Russian, French . . . their menus, news, and pictures all the same. I've got a habit, and local newspapers are no longer enough for my daily fix. I set a course horizontally and vertically, eastwards, and westwards, from the Arctic to the Antarctic, but the same vacuity and same abundance await me everywhere. Maybe the excess of information is actually the cause of my unrelenting hunger. I dive into Internet forums with a passion. Maybe divine revelations are buried in the screeds written by the studious folk who like fly-fishing, cooking, tarot cards, and who knows what else. I recently stumbled upon a site about underwater gymnastics. There are no metaphysics under water. I checked.

The computer screen is constantly flashing junk in my face, about Shakespeare, Tutankhamen, Seinfeld, Sarkozy, the economic crisis, Thai resorts, Italian pasta, child molestation, herbal remedies, and budget flights. Sometimes I get the feeling that the Internet is an enormous global gossip-driven soap opera. I look for the truth hidden between the lines, exhausting myself watching American films with Russian subtitles, Russian films with Korean subtitles, Korean films with Azerbaijani subtitles, you name it. I feel like a penitent, flagellating myself from morning to night, without ever knowing the point of it all. The only thing I do know is that a deep hunger drives me to it all; I'm constantly on the prowl for a metaphysical morsel.

Scientists tell us that our brain's ability to adapt to new experiences is called neuroplasticity. They claim that from an evolutionary perspective this elasticity can be useful, but that it also means that left unused, brain function simply atrophies. Tests show that the brain structures of London taxi drivers have changed since they became reliant on GPS navigation systems, their own sense of navigation having simply shriveled away. I sympathize with those London taxi drivers, and in future I'm going to leave them a slightly bigger tip than usual.

At this very moment my neuroplastic consciousness believes that God is an octopus and that his name is Paul. Because that's what happens when you've more-or-less become an Internet junkie. I

spend hours watching the YouTube video, over and over. I watch
Paul's supple tentacles open the box with the Spanish flag. Why the
one with the Spanish flag? I ask myself. Then I quickly remember
that it's not my place to ask questions—*God knows*. And then I fog-
gily remember the cry from the stands at village fairs—"*The white
mouse shows his nous!*" A small fee to the owner and the white mouse
would pull a scrap of paper from a hat, each scrap bearing a suitably
portentous message, just like the ones hidden in fortune cookies.

In English *God* and *Dog* are inextricably linked. In my search for
God my life has become that of a Dog. Google has drilled a dog's
loyalty into me, and with tongue dangling out, I obediently toddle
around after my master. My master's hand beckons me with a divine
bone, but it's one he never lets go.

So here I am, back at the beginning. God is a trickster. And God's
son, Jesus, is a trickster too (after all, isn't he the one who turned
water into wine and fed thousands with just a couple of sardines?!).
But the creator of the Internet is the biggest trickster of them all.
He took two things—*panem et circenses*—and joined them in an
unshakeable union: in a game as vital as our daily bread, a game
that really is our bread.

July 2010

CANS OF TUNA FISH
AND THE EUROPEAN
CLASSICS

I'd be hard-pressed to claim that Europe is coming apart at the seams. All I know is that a friend of mine, a Dutch writer, decided to put aside his career as a writer for a while and actively stand up to the imminent crisis. He opened a how-to-survive-the-recession advice center. Work is booming, and the newly minted "crisis coach" has no complaints. Except that his own transition, he says, sounds like a bad joke.

Another Dutch friend of mine, a journalist, lost her job. She turned the living room of her apartment into a kitchen. She makes pâtés and sells them to fine restaurants and specialty food stores. Her work is going well, and she has no complaints. The only thing is, as she remarks with a tinge of melancholy, *she is up to her elbows in meat.*

Seen from without, everything seems to be in its place. Venice hasn't sunk; the tower in Pisa stands firmly aslant. But every now and then a seam rips open somewhere: immigrant youths go wild in Paris suburbs and smash everything in sight, the young of Athens are in a frenzy, and then the northern dominoes topple: Vilnius, Riga, Tallinn. For the wild and embittered players in these *incidents*, the media word is *hooligan*. This word, by the way, was in lively usage during communist times. Back then they called boys who sported Elvis-Presley haircuts hooligans. European *hooligan* outbursts are treated in the media almost as if they are meteorological phenomena, like a sudden hurricane, for instance. Once the hurricane has passed, the media stitch up the seams as skillfully as if there had never been seams at all—until the next hurricane strikes.

Internet sites about the world recession have the drawing power of porno sites. I can't say the recession has much to do with pornography, but I do know that Charlotte Roche's book *Wetlands* has had a Botox-like effect on the European masses: The worry lines have been smoothed on German faces. Every country has its Charlotte Roche. This is how ordinary people forget for a moment that they have been, or will be, laid off; they forget their worries about their children and how to get them through school, about evaporating welfare funds and the future, which no one, besides the blessed who have drowned in *denial*, imagines in the form of tourist ads for travels in the southern seas.

Ordinary Europeans ooze solidarity. The circulation of human cargo—thanks to the fall of the Berlin wall (Europe is celebrating the 20th anniversary this year!) and the benefits of globalization—is greater now than ever. First Polish plumbers went off to fix plumbing from Dublin to Madrid, then Romanians flooded European train stations with their accordions. Young Moldovan teachers joined the western European prostitutes who were soliciting on every corner of Europe; Bulgarian women are fine maids in the homes of western Europe; Albanians are clever traffickers and pimps; Serbs and Croats are trusty drug smugglers; Croatian women are sought as caregivers for the Italian elderly, while Slovakian women tend to the elderly in Germany and the Netherlands. Ordinary people, the *Wessies* and *Ossies*, have struck up a dialogue.

If Europe is not coming apart at the seams, the idea of European multiculturalism is showing its cracks. Romanians pelt a Gypsy (because he is a Romanian just as they are); Hungarians flog a Romanian (thinking he's a Gypsy). Dutchmen trounce a Moroccan; Moroccans thrash a Dutchman. Italians clobber a Romanian, an Albanian, or whomever they can grab. The number of Europeans complaining that Jews are getting the cushy jobs in banking and politics is mushrooming. Apparently this is because of Gaza and the recession, they say (history clearly is not the teacher of life!). The young, self-appointed champions of national values, in some places called street gangs, elsewhere (as in Hungary) called the young guards, go after someone every other minute: The Russians go after people with non-Russian faces, Croats thrash a tourist (thinking he's a pedophile), Serbs clobber a Gypsy (claiming he's gay), Bulgarians beat up a Turk, Austrians a non-Austrian, the Italians a Moldovan, and Silvio Berlusconi, the Italian master of life and death, has forbidden people to die. People are edgy, but for now, as far as the analysts are concerned, these are merely *incidents*.

Ordinary people in the West and the East are sinking slowly into the underclass, according to the sociologists. They're losing their faith in banks, courts, institutions and politicians, though a majority of them gave their free votes, what a paradox, to those same politicians. Indeed, some western European politicians, (those transitional leaders of the people who thumped the nationalist drums, the semi-criminals and criminals, the profiteers, smugglers of cigarettes and guns, the liars, compromisers—don't offer much hope. Political apathy and a deficit of social imagination are on the rise.

Europe is holding on tight despite it all, and even if seams were ripping, all were magically re-sewn on the day of Obama's inauguration. Many Europeans roused from their political lethargy, put down their bottles of beer, and listened to Obama's address with rapt attention. Obama (briefly or not?) united millions of legal European citizens of non-European origin; he united the French, the Moroccans and Dutch, the Walloons and Flemish, the German Turks and Germans, the Serbs and Croats, the Catholics, Protestants, and Muslims. Even the Slovenes momentarily forgot their quibbles with Croats over the Adriatic on the day of Obama's inauguration. What was the trick? Obama succeeded in doing something not a single European politician has been able to do. People believed him. Obama gave the word *change* back its credibility; he gave solemnity to the word *hope*; he made the word *future* real. Obama brought back forgotten values. One of them is *decency*. With Obama, many not only feel better, they have, at least for a moment, become better.

Europe and America are bound by an umbilical cord. Like my friends, I prepared for the recession. I ordered many tins of tuna fish from a Yugoslav dealer in Amsterdam who supplies the diaspora with products from home. Adriatic tuna is the best; the tins are square, flat, and thin. You can pack an entire library with them: the European classics—Proust, Kafka, Joyce—in front, and behind, tins of tuna. Like in Russian homes during communism: in front, the classics of socialist realism, and behind, the dissidents.

February 2009

CAPTAIN, SIR, WE HAVE PLENTY OF COFFEE!

The lips pursed in the shape of the letter "O." "Pu"—a little door bulging with pressure from within. A mouth full of morsels. O-pulence. "Lence"—rings like a brass bell. The word swells, then pops like a fountain gushing with sprays of gold coins. Opulence: rivers flowing with milk and honey, plump pancakes dropping from the sky.

"What image does the word *opulence* evoke for you?" I ask a friend.
   "An American refrigerator!" he shoots back.

The American refrigerator is an accurate representation for many Eastern Europeans—especially those Yugoslavs who watched American movies from their earliest childhood—of the mythical "horn of plenty." The image of that vast American refrigerator, so full to overflowing that food tumbles out of it; the picture of the *fridge* (what a warm, soothing word!) out of which the half-awake American pulls a plastic half-gallon jug of milk or orange juice and chugalugs it down; or removes a whole tub of ice cream, brandishes a soup spoon, and sitting cross-legged on a comfortable sofa, clicks on the TV and slurps the ice cream from the tub as if it were soup. This has been etched on the imagination of Eastern Europeans for generations as the clearest and most appealing image of wealth and ease.

There are as many notions of opulence as there are people! To know what it means to be full, you have to be hungry; to know what wealth is, you have to be poor. In an episode of that old American mammoth soap opera *Dynasty*, Joan Collins's Alexis and her lover Dexter are soaking in a jacuzzi, sipping champagne. Dex scoops something up with a spoon from a bowl and downs it.

"Hey, go easy with the spoon," says Alexis, chronically vulgar, "that's caviar!"

The director probably thought it gauche to zoom in on the salty roe, yet the audience still needed to register the couple's indulgence, hence Alexis utters her improbable sentence. Out of place in the scene of luxury, of course. The champagne, the caviar, the jacuzzi: simple symbols of opulence the media have foisted on the imaginations of the poor in America and all over the world. Yet during the famines that followed the Red Revolution, many Russians had so much caviar that they were sick of it; there was absolutely nothing but caviar to eat. Those who were short of a spoon scooped it up with their bare hands.

Poverty knows affluence best. Maybe that is why one should go rummaging around the open markets, the flea markets, the big retail chains for the poor, and see the pile of "garbage" that the poor spend their money on. Because "garbage" is the most precise expression for a poor person's general impression of opulence. Perhaps it is only in this context that we can make sense of why the Vanderbilt family imported, brick by brick, lavish sixteenth century Italian rooms and built them into their "cottages" in Newport; and why today's rich Russians blast great holes in the Montenegrin cliffs to build villas that are reminiscent of the Guggenheim Museum, with swimming pools from which the swimmer gets an eagle's eye view of the azure of the Adriatic.

Peer into a poor apartment where the largest wall in the living room is wallpapered with a lavish sunset. Or into the little city gardens done in plastic grass with a flock of plastic flamingos and plastic frogs swimming in a plastic fountain. Peek into the stores selling gilded nylon brocade, synthetic lace, polyester silk and satin. Check out the Eastern European hot springs that date from the communist period, where weary Western retirees purchase accessible pleasures: a swim in the shabby pools, a massage with the hotel masseuse, a pedicure.

The idea of opulence is the *meeting point* between the poor and the rich. We all encounter each other at that place, as if it were an old abandoned railway station at which trains never arrive or depart. We came to the station, it seems, when God banished us from paradise. For opulence exists only in paradise. Everything else is a substitute, regardless of whether the silk is real or synthetic.

There was a popular ad for *Franck* coffee on Croatian television back in the early nineties. A space ship with its crew. Sudden turbulence. The horrified expressions on the astronauts' faces signal that the spaceship will never return to earth. A stewardess wearing a Gagarin costume steps into the captain's cabin and smiles brightly: "Captain, Sir, we have plenty of coffee!" An explanatory line of text runs along the bottom of the screen: "The first Croatian expedition into outer space." The ad was a nostalgic evocation of a time of turbulence on the former Yugoslav market when there were coffee shortages, while at the same time announcing that a new Croatian future was coming in which there would always be coffee. For three things signified opulence in Yugoslavia: coffee, detergent, and cooking oil. Yugoslav women went over the border by bus on day trips to Trieste or Graz to buy their supplies. For no apparent reason one of the *must-have* items on the list was raisins. My mother's cupboard at one point was nearly bursting with little packets of them, and I nearly burst with pity for my mother.

Opulence is kept shut away in the realm of the imagination. For death usually lurks just beyond it. (Moths will get into it! Mice will nibble it! Fire will reduce it to ashes! People will snatch it! The banks will go bust! The money will be gobbled by inflation!) There is nothing lurking beyond poverty but the necessity of survival.

When I was a child, we lived in a small town near Zagreb, a couple of miles from the Zagreb-Belgrade highway. In summer the traffic of Turkish and Greek guest workers on their way home from Western Europe inched along the road. One day the local police knocked at our door and asked my mother to help as an interpreter. That very day the Bulgarian ambassador to Mali had been on his way home for a hard-earned summer vacation, and just where the exit splits off the highway toward our town, the ambassador had collided with another car. His wife was killed instantly; he and his two little girls were unharmed. There were many formalities to attend to, far too many for the local police, but the poor man and his children also needed to be cared for. So the Bulgarian and his two little girls were our guests for several days. When the ambassador departed, he left behind two large sacks of peanuts he had been taking to Bulgaria in the trunk of his car. He probably felt it no longer appropriate to deliver them home along with the news of the death of his wife. Perhaps this was his expression of gratitude; he had nothing else to give us. None of us had ever seen or tasted a peanut before. Our whole neighborhood roasted peanuts with us in the oven, shelling the unsightly husks and nibbling at the unusual oval seeds for months. From the horn of plenty, peanuts showered down upon us.

I have disliked peanuts ever since. Opulence should be left where it can do the least harm—in the realm of the imagination. I make an effort, as much as I can, to steel myself to its siren call. That *Captain, Sir, we have plenty of coffee* will do for my daily dose of happiness.

June 2008

NO PLACE FOR SISSIES

When God created the world, and donkeys, dogs, monkeys, and man along with it, he gave each a lifespan of thirty years. The donkey knew life would be hard, so he asked God to shorten it: God sliced off an eighteen-year chunk. The dog and the monkey had similar complaints, so theirs were cut short too, the dog's by twelve years and the monkey's by ten. But as for Man, he felt thirty years too few and asked for more. So God went ahead and gave the greedy one the years he'd taken from the donkey, the dog, and the monkey. Now greedy humans would live for seventy years. The first thirty years are the human years, the ones we enjoy, happy and healthy; then come the difficult donkey years, when we have to carry others, and receive only kicks and blows for our trouble. The dog years follow, the twelve toothless years we spend growling in the corner, with no teeth with which to bite. Finally, there are monkey years, the ten years we spend as old fools, mocked by young children.

The Brothers Grimm heard that story from a peasant and recorded a version of it as *The Duration of Life*. I read it (or something similar) when I was a child. My socialist readers were bursting with didactic stories, proverbs, puzzles, and other forms of oral literature. Naturally I've now forgotten all of them, but ever since I've had an aversion towards folksy aphorisms. I can't stand those little pearls of wisdom you find in Chinese fortune-cookies either. I don't like people who parrot folksy sayings; they're usually old and half-senile.

Man is an insatiable being, and our haggling with God over the duration of our lives continues to this day. With all our might we try to usurp God's throne, to take the question of our lifespan into our own hands, a tendency that goes on apace. There's the pharmaceutical industry, the cosmetic industry, the self-help industry, not to mention the tons of products designed to both prolong our life and improve its quality. People spend enormous amounts of time going running, working out at the gym, dieting, frequenting health food stores, going to the dental hygienist, the sauna, meditating, cutting out stress and meat, consuming healthy fats, reducing unhealthy fats, cutting out sugar, working on their mental health, practicing work-out routines, relaxing, quitting smoking and drinking, gulping down water, having regular health checks, speed-walking, avoiding tomatoes, eating more tomatoes, carefully reading product labels, learning exercises to prevent wrinkles and firm the buttocks, starving themselves, steam-cooking, detoxing and botoxing. All told, were Hitler to today rise from the grave, it would warm his heart to see the millions-strong masses of potential *Übermenschen*, optimistic and disciplined, glowing with rude health and physical vitality.

Longevity is currently right up there on the ladder of our civilizational values. Flanked by the media, the Croatian President recently offered his personal congratulations to a woman who had just turned 104. Why? Because she is the oldest Croatian woman alive.

Premature death, particularly if it's due to terminal illness, is no longer seen as lucking out in the divine lottery, but as a personal failure, like a self-induced bankruptcy. The more benevolent treat untimely death due to sickness as a kind of genetic affliction, which is also seen as a kind of personal failure. We should have chosen forebears of better genetic material. Today life is like a marathon of uncertain duration, at the end of which—providing we aren't disqualified by a higher power—the head of state might be waiting for us, a bouquet of flowers in hand.

By and large, in the past fifty years life expectancy has dramatically increased. Today every Tom, Dick, and Harry is eighty years old. There are experts who maintain that this increase in life expectancy will result in a tectonic global disturbance more dangerous and alarming than global warming. Yes, people are living longer, but their pensions are increasingly precarious, and when they do have one, it's too meagre to live off. People are living longer, but a longer life means greater susceptibility to illness, and the health services in many countries often refuse to treat the elderly. People might be living longer, but their children are so overworked, struggling to support their own children, that they have neither the time nor money to look after their parents. In many countries, rest homes, just like prisons, are in seriously short supply, and the expensive private ones are raking it in as a result. The state is keen to see private rest homes prosper, but lacks the desire or means to monitor them. If we then factor in the global economic crisis, things look all the bleaker.

In many cultures euthanasia and geronticide were inescapable rituals. Such rituals were often innocuous (leaving the windows open so the draft would hasten death and allow the soul an easier departure, or sealing the house shut so the soul wouldn't have anywhere to hide), but could also be quite pragmatic and efficient (murder, incineration, starvation, drowning, abandonment, being throwing off a cliff, etc.).

A Serbian newspaper recently ran a story about two sisters from the village of Lučica near Požarevac. The old women had no means of income and survived on scavenged scraps. When one died, the other apparently lay down beside her, took a sharp object, and began slicing flesh from the soles of her sister's feet. Suspecting something amiss, the other village residents called the police. Asked why she didn't declare her sister's death, the old woman replied: "What would I have eaten then?" Other newspapers reported the story of a poor Italian family who hid their deceased grandmother in the fridge for months. They didn't declare the old woman's death, as doing so would have meant forfeiting her pension.

These kinds of stories probably fall into the category of sensationalist modern folklore, but they could also prove a bleakly comedic foreshadowing of the near future. Faced with the dilemma of feeding their children or their parents, that the poor will revive a form of geronticide can't be ruled out. In wealthier countries, as a result of both expensive gerontological services and the general economic crisis, a different practice is in evidence. The practice is still very hush-hush, because people would rather keep mum about it. The Swiss and Germans pack their parents onto one-way flights to low-cost Thailand, where the Thai medical staff nurse them until their deaths. Funeral services are included in the package. In one hit, cash-strapped children combine the recreational and the functional, returning from holiday with parental ashes in their luggage.

Croatian entrepreneurs are on the ball. One is currently building a rest home for Swiss clients, while another apparently already has a contract with the Japanese. It turns out that it's cheaper for the Japanese to send their parents to Croatia and visit them twice a year than to have them cared for in their exorbitantly-priced homeland. In the years to come, hundreds of elderly Japanese might make their way to Croatia. The Japanese will end their days looking out across the idyllic rolling hills of Croatia, slowly letting out their souls like little shriveling balloons. That is, until the day our overheated and overcrowded planet hastens things along.

April 2009

THE CONSOLATION
OF THE LAST RESOURCE

On a grey housing-estate wall somewhere in the former Yugoslavia there's a piece of graffiti that reads: *My boyfriend's so rich he doesn't need to lick the lid of the Eurokrem jar!* In the gastronomic conscious-ness of its citizens, *Eurokrem* is remembered as a) a cheap snack for children; b) morning-tea for soldiers of the former Yugoslav Peoples' Army; and c) a hotel breakfast for budget-conscious pensioners, both local and foreign, who spent their "summer" holidays in Adriatic hotels in mid-winter.

It seems that the idea of poverty has finally gotten through to the average citizen of the former Yugoslavia. Stupefied by the country's disintegration (*The Communists robbed us blind!*), patriotism, war (*the war impoverished us*), and hatred for Serbs, or Croats, or Slovenes (*they economically destroyed us!*), until now the average citizen has rejected any confrontation with his own social status. He has sur-vived thanks to the consolation provided by last resources (*We'll sell the village land dad left us; We've got a good garden, big enough to feed us; If it comes to the crunch, we'll sell the summer house; My uncle's a big-time Charlie, he'll always be able to sort me out; Grandma will leave us the house in her will; My brother's doing well in Germany, there's no way he'll leave us to starve; We'll rent the house on the coast to foreigners; If nothing else, we'll always be able to sell the family grave).* These resources, however, are now fully depleted, the options exhausted, aces up the sleeve thrown. Grandma's house is gone with the wind, the family land sold, society has stratified into a tiny minority of wealthy and a massive majority of poor—"fuckers" and "suckers." Much hastily-acquired wealth is slowly slipping away, businesses are shutting up shop, people are losing their jobs en masse, that big-timer uncle Charlie is in jail, the money from the family grave long spent. Many go to work, not having been paid in months. The lucky receive half their monthly salaries in cash and the other half in coupons. Naturally the coupons can only be redeemed at the workers' own companies. They trade them for sausages that are past their expiration date, and *Eurokrem*, which doesn't have an expiration date. Many work Saturdays, although no one sees the point, except, of course, the owner of the firm who's doing all he can to engineer voluntary resignations.

A married couple by the name of Pevec own what was until very recently a successful chain of stores in Croatia. Today the Pevecs are bankrupt. They left behind hundreds of ragged employees who, having been unpaid for months, were then made redundant. At a recent party at a local hotel, the Pevecs had a great time dancing into the wee hours. Employees at the hotel—also in receivership, and who themselves hadn't been paid in months—watched the obscene shimmy of the failed Croatian tycoons, barely able to draw breath.

Only these kinds of "entertaining" details find their way into the Croatian media. The bitter everyday is left to gurgle away in anonymity. Headlines—such as those informing us that the American actress Jennifer Love Hewitt not only has her, um, you-know-what, regularly shaved and trimmed, but that she recently had it "vajazzled" with a Swarovski crystal, so now her "vajayay" *shines like a disco ball*—stupefy the impoverished masses like a non-stop water sprinkler. They see their own lives of servitude shimmer like a disco ball.

Are they really lives of servitude? As a new slave trade snakes its way along subterranean European pathways, the united European idyll is slowly revealing its dark underbelly. An "innocent" asparagus farm in the Czech Republic, growing asparagus for an "innocent" importer in the Netherlands, employed a convenient group of Romanians as pickers. Why convenient? EU passports in hand, they could cross borders unhindered, and the question of their non-existent work permits was somehow swept under the rug. As it happens, a good part of Western Europe exploits itinerant Romanians, Bulgarians, and others, and the question of work permits always magically disappears. It turns out the Romanian asparagus pickers were recruited by a Ukrainian gang. They never saw the promised wages, the food and lodgings were subhuman, and their brutal Ukrainian masters threatened them with death if they tried to escape. Thanks to the few who managed to escape and bravely complained to the Romanian Embassy in Prague, the slave-running ring was (temporarily) broken. There are scores of similar farms scattered all over Europe, scores of slave drivers, innumerable desperate wretches, and more than enough corrupt police and members of the judiciary.

The media, particularly the transitional Eastern European media, have for years done their utmost to prove that education, expertise, and competence are no guarantee of a stable and prosperous life. *Big*

Brother, authentic entertainment for millions of viewers, proved that anyone could be a star for any reason under the sun. At the same time, it was also a harbinger of what was soon to come. The media, life experience, and often educators themselves took education down from its throne, and on the pedestal of values the body took its place. With its own market value, the body is both the first and last resource. The body can be sold, beautified, inflated with silicone, injected with Botox, shrunk, thinned, enlarged, bulked-up, tattooed, clothed, or stripped naked. Of course one can increase the body's market value—one just needs to know how. Prostitutes, both female and male, sell their bodies directly. Some parents sell their children, and some children sell themselves, without a middleman. Some parents maim their children, banking on compassion to increase begging revenue. Many Indians sell their organs. Some people sell their blood. Even a dead body has a market value. According to Amnesty International, the six thousand Chinese prisoners executed every year supply ninety percent of black-market kidneys. Wealthy foreigners pay between ten and forty thousand dollars a kidney. The organ harvesting doesn't, of course, end with kidneys. In Chinese prisons executions are carefully conducted: if the convict is in poor health, he's shot in the chest; if he's a suitable candidate for organ harvesting, he's shot in the head.

Wanting to build himself a house, King Erysichthon of Thessalonica cut down trees in a grove that was sacred to Ceres, who punished him with an insatiable hunger. Erysichthon ended up eating himself to death. If we ignore the ecological reading, the story of Erysichthon offers another example of how, when our survival is in question, our own bodies are, indeed, the last resource.

January 2010

MY EAR THE CHAUVINIST, MY EYE THE MISANTHROPE

He moves towards me like a soldier in full combat gear. He strides along an imaginary straight line, rucksack on his back, iPod in hand, earplugs inserted in his ears. His sunglasses exclude all possibility of negotiation by eye contact. He uses his body like an invisible plough clearing the snow ahead, and I stand obediently to the side. In the urban public space, more and more people use their bodies like ploughs. I'm always the one who steps aside.

While queuing at my local Lidl, a muezzin's call pierces my eardrums like a sudden pain. I turn around and see a young woman decked out in a *hijab* and long denim skirt, chintzy-decorated flip-flops on her feet. She takes a mobile phone from her handbag and has a fiddle. Perhaps a reminder to prayer, I think calmly. My ear goes back to sleep. But then it's rattled again, this time by the sound of a young Chinese woman screeching something into her mobile. Both voices are equally piercing, I think to myself. Embarrassed, I delete the thought. I swear, this isn't about me—it's my ear. Where it grew up high Cs were never popular. My ear is a chauvinist!

I've noticed that more and more cyclists are singing in the streets of Amsterdam, pedaling along and singing at the top of their lungs. This public reclamation of personal freedom, showing off just how relaxed you are, is a new thing. My ear is uneasy, unaccustomed, and un-accepting. My ear is a spiteful control freak.

I'm sitting in a café with a view of the lake, waiting for my coffee, when a young couple at the next table catches my eye. The young woman, long blond hair, casually puts her bare feet up on the table, right alongside her partner's bowl of soup. The young man gently massages her toes with one hand and finishes his soup with the other. The young woman titters with delight and tries to tip the soup over with her toes. The sight of her bare feet on the table makes me slightly nauseous. My eye is a misanthrope. I don't have an invisible remote to switch the scene from the opposite table off, which is what I secretly want, and so defeated, I get up and leave.

In many European cities the metro station elevators (used mostly by mothers with baby strollers, old folk, and cyclists carrying their bikes) are always plastered in piss and spit, used by men as urinals and spittoons. Taking the lift up to the platform, I cover my nose with my hand or scarf. The stench is unbearable. My nose is the guilty one. It's a damned elitist.

I've noticed that as soon as they find a seat on the tram, an ever-increasing number of young women take out their makeup bags and do their make-up for the day. They've got everything there: eyeliner, mascara, nail files and nail polish. But why, of all places, do they have to do their make-up on the tram? If they really have to do it in public, why not in a public toilet or on a park bench?! Metro stations are obviously more convenient—I recently saw a middle-aged woman plucking her chin hair with a pair of tweezers while she was waiting for a train.

I'm standing on the street when a passing cyclist tosses a drink carton towards a non-existent rubbish bin, missing my head by about ten centimeters. Hey!—I yell, but there's no chance of having it out with him as he quickly disappears from view.

There are several places of worship in my Amsterdam neighborhood. One of them is obviously a bit small, so when the weather's nice the faithful head outside, unfurl their little prayer mats or whatever they have, and kneel down. When the faithful pray, no one, neither believers nor non-believers, can use the sidewalk. A signpost stands watch next to God's temple; on it is a dog with a cross through it. A friend of mine has a dog. The self-appointed religious police have already warned him several times that dogs aren't allowed to be walked past God's temple. The space around the temple is, incidentally, filthy, because the children visiting the temple ditch their soft drink cans and snack wrappers there. But God obviously has his preferences: rubbish doesn't bother him, but dogs do.

On both the trams and the metro, adolescents, kids, occupy most of the seats. Older folk meekly stand. The urban public space has become a field on which to exercise repressed sadomasochism. The stronger have their way, the weaker suck it up.

For months now, a thirty-something jerk has stood banging on his guitar in front of my supermarket. The guy is tone-deaf, and obviously can't play, but he just stands there and doodles away, clearly hoping the racket will draw attention to his presence and that people will toss him a coin.

In apartment blocks some residents think it's funny to throw food out the windows onto the street. To feed the birds. These birds, seagulls and pigeons mostly, hover overhead and crap on the windows below. What the birds don't eat the rats finish up. At night rats freely roam the public space. This pushes animal rights activists' like buttons.

In New York I climb into a taxi. The taxi driver, white knitted cap on his head, is saying his prayers. Holding a little prayer book in one hand, he repeats his mantra. From time to time he needs to brake or pay attention at a traffic light, so he interrupts his prayer. The monotonous mantra jars my agnostic ear, but I politely put up with the situation I've happened into. Not having anything smaller, I give the driver a large bill when I get out of the taxi.

"How much is the tip?"—he asks gruffly.

I notice how his tone of voice has suddenly changed: that meek spiritual bleating from a minute ago was for God, the threatening tone is for me. He's already holding the bill in hand, so negotiation isn't really an option; he could floor it and make off with the lot. Hoping for at least something back, I give him a generous tip.

In an Amsterdam metro station I take the steps down towards the exit, holding the side rail. A kid climbs towards me, stops in front of me for a second, and just glares. Hypnotized, I forget to move aside. The kid swears, hits me, shoves me aside, and continues on his way. Frozen with fear, I slowly make my way down, terrified that he could have ended up pushing me down the stairs. It was my mistake; I was on the left side, the wrong side.

The urban public space, which is governed by both written and unwritten rules of behavior, today serves as a stage for the exhibition of personal freedom. The old rules of etiquette no longer apply. "No Spitting" signs are long gone, seen as absurd and a bit of joke. As a result, nowadays, many simply spit wherever they like. Spit, piss, the body, the voice—it's all about marking out one's space. Nobody wants to go unnoticed. Everyone fights for his or her personal rights, but few respect the rights of others. Incidents of this demonstration of freedom are becoming increasingly common and increasingly violent.

I notice that I go outside less and less. I've put three locks on the front door, and I keep the curtains pulled. My apartment is slowly turning into a guerrilla nest. I notice that I don't love my neighbor anymore either. Loving one's neighbor requires a superhuman effort. It's love without reciprocity, and I'm just a common, fallible human specimen. In any case, that's God's department, he created man in his own image, let him love him.

A blogger recently accused me of using exaggeration as a writing strategy. I allow that this is the case. It's true that not *everyone* spits on the floor, puts their feet up on restaurants tables, walks the streets naked, or pushes people over for walking on the wrong side. My exaggeration is a form of concern for the future. It's completely possible that in little more than a decade this document will seem like an unintelligible snapshot of the urban everyday. Future readers won't know what phrases like urban public space mean, nor will it be clear to them what the writer meant to say. I admit, at this very moment I don't know either. I'm not a prophet. Nor am I a saint, like Mike.

Mike is a well-respected sixty-something American university professor, who collects empty bottles and cans while walking each day from his home to the university. He stores them in his office for the day, and at day's end takes the morning stockpile and supplements it with whatever he collects on the walk home, as much as he's able to carry. He then sorts the empties into piles; glass, plastic, cans, stacking them neatly on his porch. At night, when everyone is asleep, human shadows converge on Mike's Los Angeles home. Young Puerto Ricans. They spirit away Mike's collection and recycle it for a little small change.

November 2008

FEAR OF PEOPLE

When Stanley Kubrick's *A Clockwork Orange* appeared in 1971 (based on Anthony Burgess's eponymous novel) it was seen as a dystopian film, a black comedy, a futuristic satire. The adolescent protagonist Alex and his three friends (called *droogs*—from the Russian *drug*) amuse themselves with *ultra-violence*. Alex undergoes the Ludovico treatment, which induces in him a powerful aversion to violence, but then he himself becomes a victim of both his *droogs* and his former victims. Today Kubrick's film is one of the key cultural references on juvenile violence. It seems, however, that today's youth violence has far surpassed that imagined by either author or director.

For a time Golding's allegorical novel *The Lord of the Flies* (1954) was regarded an iconic work of modern literature. But when Golding's vision became reality, the novel was stripped of its allegorical power, the fate of all such prescient works.

One of the most powerful episodes in Kundera's novel *The Book of Laughter and Forgetting* is the phantasmagorical portrayal of Tamina's death. The young angel Raphael takes Kundera's heroine by boat to an island, where, in a setting reminescent of a Boy Scout camp, children molest, abuse, humiliate, and rape her, acting out their basest instincts. In Kundera's dark phantasmagoria, children are executioners, the angels of death.

The Peter Jackson film *Heavenly Creatures* (1994) is based on a true story from the 1950s that took place in Christchurch, New Zealand. In spite of their class differences, two fifteen-year-old girls, Pauline Parker and Juliet Hulme (played by Kate Winslet), form an obsessive mutual bond. The girls brutally murder Pauline's mother, who they see as an obstacle to their future plans together. The media attention generated by the film led to the discovery of Juliet Hulme's subsequent identity. After five years in a youth prison, Hulme left New Zealand and is today known as Anne Perry, a well-known writer of Victorian-era detective fiction.

Austrian director Michael Haneke first filmed his feature *Funny Games* in 1997, and in 2008 shot a remake with American actors. In the film a pair of good-looking, well-mannered young men (who could be the post-Ludovico sons of Burgess's hero, Alex) brutally torment a family of three in a summer cottage, ultimately murdering them, just as they had previously murdered their neighbors, before calmly proceeding with a new wave of violence. Their brutality is driven solely by their delight in a sadistic game in which they have the upper hand. Watching Haneke's film, as voyeurs, we too become parties to the crime.

Early in 2008 a Dnepropetrovsk court sentenced Viktor Sayenko and Igor Suprunyuck to life imprisonment on twenty-one counts of murder. A third accused was sentenced to nine years. Armed with hammers and metal bars, these former local school pupils beat random people to death, gouging out the eyes and slicing off the ears of a number of their victims. They filmed the murders with a video camera, and there's at least one of these terrifying clips out there in cyberspace. You hear their voices (*Vitja, neater, you fuck!*), but their faces remain out of view. The camera painstakingly records a battered old man drowning in his own blood, as screwdrivers are stabbed into his stomach. The two adolescents apparently documented their murders on camera so that they would have *memories to look back on in their old age.* The father of one of the killers accused the police of fabricating the charges, because, he said, his son was a *normal boy.* The mother of the other claimed that her son *couldn't even kill a cat.* A defense lawyer for the young killers stated that the boys killed to *overcome their fear of people.*

Recently an eleven-year-old boy from the community of Wampum in Pennsylvania was accused of murdering a pregnant woman and her eight-month-old unborn baby.

In Yorkshire two brothers aged ten and twelve attacked and robbed two other boys, subjecting them to a physical and sexual assault that included poking them with sticks and stubbing out cigarettes on their skin. It was not the first criminal incident in which the brothers had been involved.

News stories like these have become part of our everyday lives. One can no longer separate juvenile violence from regular adult violence; violent children feature in newspapers' court pages as frequently as violent adults. We regularly read stories about gangs of boys who have beaten one of their classmates to death, young people bashing old women while trying to snatch their handbags, or physically assaulting their parents. Youth violence is on view everywhere, captured on mobile phones, in newspapers, on television screens, in documentaries, and on the Internet. Several girls were interviewed in a documentary on teenage Russian killers. One had killed her newborn baby, another her grandmother, a third, helped by a couple of boys, a friend. Typically these young offenders were coolly indifferent to their crimes. Asked by a journalist why she had killed, one replied more-or-less: *Why do you think? It's a jungle out there!* Responding to the same question in a documentary about young American killers, one young killer replied bluntly: *Because it's a thrill!*

Crimes committed by children occur everywhere. The stereotypical psychosocial model—an impoverished and traumatic childhood, a mother who was a prostitute or drug addict, a violent father—still predominates, but can no longer be assumed. Violence is a part of children's everyday lives, and children's violence is part of the everyday lives of adults. Parental violence in the home, the prevalence of pedophilia, child prostitution, adults purchasing the services of children, criminal exploitation of children, training child soldiers to become cold-blooded killers, forcing children into crime—these are all part of the contemporary everyday.

The young Ukrainians tortured and killed people and animals with the same cool indifference, filming their crimes as mementos to look back on in their old age. Their crimes can't be explained away; there are no answers to be had, no messages, no meaning. The evil is a dull, empty space. As the judge handed down his verdict, one of the two boys from Yorkshire yawned. The killers in Haneke's film dress in white, on their hands they wear white gloves, the golf ball is white, as is the egg they use to begin the game. The murders are bloody, but there isn't a drop of blood on the killers. The killers are free of remorse: there are no second thoughts, no compromises, no compassion, and no respite.

"There are no children anymore!" announces the nine-year-old Victor in Roger Vitrac's classic absurdist drama *Victor, or Power to the Children*. There are no children any more because, simply, there are no adults. During the brutal siege of Sarajevo, asked what she feared most, a young Sarajevan girl replied: "People!" The little girl had adults in mind. Today, *people* also implicitly includes *children*.

March 2009

FILIPINAS

I recently visited some friends who live in Hong Kong. My friends do well for themselves, and although their apartment was large by Hong Kong standards, it was still smaller than I expected. My friend and hostess showed me a narrow cubicle that exited onto the balcony, the purpose of which wasn't immediately clear. What do you do with a pokey recess that you can't use for anything and just makes the apartment smaller?

"Lots of people in Hong Kong keep their Filipinas there," she said.

Hit by the jetlag, I woke up early those few days, and in the morning stillness I watched the Filipinas from the balcony. In the early morning the Filipinas walk the dogs around a beautifully-maintained (not to mentioen gated and guarded) residential compound. A little later, I saw them carrying shopping bags from the nearby supermarket and shepherding the children to the school bus. Sometimes—in the lift, at the pool, in the massage studio, or in a restaurant—the fashionable owners of these Filipinas would appear: stylish young white women, two or three gorgeous children in tow.

My hosts say that Hong Kong is a magnet for young business people. The money's good, the accommodation luxurious, the Filipino maids cheap—ideal conditions for keeping the family wheels turning.

Aside from their work, in the evenings and weekends my friends live within their own, Anglo-American, enclave. In the evenings they have drinks in bar owned by a Filipina whose husband is a successful English businessman.

One evening, my friends were invited to the birthday of a Filipina who was happily engaged to a Dutch guy, so they brought me along. It was a Filipino bar, there was a Filipino band, the singer was a Filipina, and, apart from my hostess and myself, the female guests were all Filipinas. The male guests?—"Englishmen." The Dutchman was still somewhere in the air on board a Hong Kong bound plane.

Entering the bar felt like entering a cave full of bats. The twenty or so Filipinas were quick off the mark, their movements finely honed. They swarmed on us from all directions, omnipresent, amiably plying us with food and drink, patting and nudging us, intermittently letting out short sharp bursts of laughter. For a moment I thought they might all be sisters—they all gesticulated in the same way, their bursts of laughter on cue, all of which made me uneasy.

The shenanigans soon got underway. The Filipinas wiggled their butts, wrapped themselves around invisible poles, and flashed their breasts. Lining up one behind the other, each grabbed the hips of the woman in front, bumping and grinding their pelvises into her rear. Or one would stick her rear out and another would bend down and nestle her nose where the other's anus had to be. This vulgar pantomime was accompanied by peals of laughter. Each wave of laughter rang out like a command for others to laugh along. One Filipina popped her breasts out, asking those present to rate them.

"Don't pay any attention," said my hostess, catching my disapproving glance. "They always carry on like this."

Yes, Filipinas. Some are married to "Englishmen," and others are on their way to finding one, says my hostess. The husbands, "English" businessmen, come to Hong Kong to earn money and lay the foundations of family life. That's how it starts out: They bring their wives over, have children, earn money—and then a Filipina turns up on the scene. I spoke to an Englishman at the bar, a friend of my friends, who told me that he had an adult daughter and a wife in Australia, and here, in Hong Kong, a Filipina. As we spoke, she kept coming over, rubbing herself against him. It was as if she were running around on an invisible leash, like an impatient dog.

Another Englishman had the same story: an ex-wife and two children—and a Filipina. His Filipina was the star of the evening, her routine unforgettable. She took a largish bone from the table (dinner was delicious grilled pork) and performed a lengthy and well-rehearsed *fellatio* pantomime. The Englishman was wealthy; my friends told me that he'd built the Filipina a luxurious villa in the Philippines, that he supported her many relatives, her child from her first marriage, and her ex-husband, while she just goes wild, spending and spending. This Filipina has carved out a career sought by many; for while many are currently still the home help, which is how they feed their parents, unemployed ex-husbands, and their children to unemployed ex-husbands, they all dream of one day finding their "Englishman." Back in childhood someone drilled it into them that "Englishmen" don't fall from the sky and that only girls who are good at gyrating their hips and shaking their asses deserve them. Later, life just confirmed the truth of the story. Although many of them completed their schooling, gyrating their hips has proven to be a more secure and profitable path. That's why in the evenings many Hong Kong Filipina Cinderellas transform themselves into porno-comedians. The night belongs to them.

"Look at them," my new bar-friend says warmly, "like snakes . . ."

He was obviously looking for a way to tell me to relax, to not be so judgmental, because it's all a bit of innocent fun, for Pete's sake, "we're all the same under the skin," "a drop in the ocean," our common home is "a valley of tears." I didn't say anything. Allowances for life in all its color, for its peaks and troughs, are usually sought by those who stand to gain from such an "anything goes" position—an excuse for themselves at the very least.

I spoke with two Filipinas, who, like me, had gone outside for a smoke. One complained that everybody thinks Filipinas are prostitutes. The other nodded in agreement. They just came here to earn an honest living. They dream of buying a little homestead in the Philippines and growing vegetables. For a moment I'm carried away, I feel like Betty Friedan: "Yes, veggies," I say, "good idea." They shrug their shoulders and sadly exhale cigarette smoke into the steamy Hong Kong night. In their heads they tally up the dog walks, the bags of groceries, the mornings getting the kids on the school bus, and the nights spent wedged into the cupboard-like space where some keep Filipinas, others washing machines. Then they go back inside. From the street I watch them rejoin "their kind," wiggling their rears, curling up "like snakes," household knick-knacks, efficient little sex-machines.

"Englishman" and "Filipina." The only irony is that the players in this game don't know how to enjoy what they've achieved in life. In a Gucci dress and Prada shoes, the Filipina licks stubbornly at the pork bone, although there's no longer any need. The Englishman, I assume, has it in mind that although his Filipina still works—her expiration date not yet up—he could still trade her in for a new one.

Filipinas have left a dark stain on the glittering panoramas of Hong Kong, like sepia ink. Half-crazed bats lay siege to the tall and slender Hong Kong skyscrapers, flapping their wings and flushing gold coins out from somewhere. The coins fall to the ground like snow, like fireworks. The sound of the metal coins hitting the ground echoes like short sharp bursts of laughter that chill me to the bone.

July 2010

SERBIAN HOLLYWOOD

1.

I recently visited a small settlement near Groningen in the north of Holland. The place is called Eelde, and the chances are fairly remote that I'd ever go out of my way to visit. Eelde is home to one of the most beautiful small museums of figurative art I've ever seen. Everything is perfect: the unusual architecture is perfectly integrated into the natural surroundings, which were perfectly designed by Holland's most famous landscape architect. The museum catalogues are exquisitely designed and the café wonderfully situated in the museum's natural landscape. It was a Sunday, and the museum was full of locals. I'm not sure if it was because the museum shop was open or because there are only two things one can do in the tiny settlement: go sailing, or go to the museum. The museum in Eelde would represent a commendable example of the synergy between money (a Dutch bank is one of the sponsors), meticulous environmental awareness (the museum is in perfect harmony with its surroundings), and art, if only it fulfilled its primary function. Namely, the museum has everything except art! Yes, there were a few pictures hanging on the walls, but you couldn't even call them amateur (even amateurism can have its charms); what you got instead were exemplars of the worst kind of pretentiousness. A quick look at the prices in the catalogue, and the only thing a visitor could possibly conclude was that being an artist really does pay, particularly if you're a crappy one.

2.

A few years ago I attended the unveiling of an Ilya Kabakov installation at a wealthy Californian university in Santa Barbara. The installation was situated in one of the university's parks, and it consisted of a bottle made out of wire, or more to the point, wire shaped like a bottle. The bottleneck pointed down towards a barely visible stream of water trickling from a small opening in the grass. The installation was called *Mother and Son*, although it wasn't clear what was supposed to symbolize what. You could see the satisfaction on visitor's faces, Kabakov devotees the lot of them, myself included. Indeed, out of a deep inner feeling of having been cheated—or out of shame—many of them launched into passionate explanations of the somewhat less than transparent—and therefore all the more profound—meaning of Kabakov's installation. Kabakov is one of the stars of modern art. We never call a star's fiasco a fiasco, but rather, a new phase, a new high in the ouevre of a celebrated artist, actor, musician, or writer . . .

3.

If you type "Mutanj, Serbia" into your search engine, it will immediately respond with the question: "*Do you mean: Mutants, Serbia?*" I mean, yeah, whatever. The little test proves that geographers are the most passionate, precise, and pervasive professionals on the Internet. Mutanj is a hamlet on the mountain of Rudnik in central Serbia, and on the Internet you can find maps, satellite pictures, and all kinds of other information about it. Geographers don't differentiate between massive New York and minuscule Mutanj, which has all of eighty-four inhabitants. Why is the village of Mutanj important? It's not. Nevertheless, driving down the Ibar Highway in late-October 2007, someone caught a glimpse of a group of phantom white letters spelling "Holywood" up on Straževica hill and set off to investigate what appeared to be a bizarre teleportation of the famous sign. It turned out that the lone creator of this peculiar installation was twenty-year-old Ivan Jakovljević, a Mutanj villager and employee at the local lead and zinc mine. Above the big "Holywood" letters, there was a smaller sign in Cyrillic that said "Srpski" (Serbian). Jakovljević's "Holywood" was missing an "l," which he deliberately left out, wanting, as he put it, "to avoid copyright issues." Apparently, Jakovljević wants to attract the "Seventh Art" to his village, and in particular, creators of "films about ecology, history, and ethnology." He has stated that his campaign doesn't have a "political background," and that his "installation" is just a "symbol of the seventh art and nothing more." In order to realize his project, Jakovljević took out an 800 euro loan, and over the Christmas and New Year holidays he plans to have "Srpski Holywood" up in lights.

4.

In the countries of the former Yugoslavia a capricious culture of public sculptures is in full bloom. The situation might be best explained as a kind of wild "monumental" polemic: the destroying of monuments bearing one ideological message, and the erection of new ones bearing a different message. The countries of the former Yugoslavia also boast an authentic and spirited headstone culture, with fierce competition for originality. In America the celebrated Ilya Kabakov today reconstructs vanished Soviet toilets, schools, and other emblematic Soviet constructions (*Mother and Son* is one of his rare fiascos), while in a God-forsaken Serbian village a replica of the famous Hollywood sign surfaces. If this happy teleportation of symbols continues in our world without borders, the field is wide open for New York's Twin Towers to one day rise again in Shanghai, and the numerous decapitated heads of Stalin and Lenin to re-emerge from the Antarctic ice.

All of this is understandable, and a bit of a laugh. Only one thing remains a mystery: earthlings' obsession with art. It's almost beyond comprehension why someone in Eelde in the north of Holland would pay five thousand euros for a picture they could get at a flea market for three, or why anyone would pay ten, twenty, or thirty times more to have an ugly wire bottle in a university park, or why someone would take out a loan of several hundred euros to put up big metal letters in a forest next to his hamlet, especially when those letters already exist on another hill, on the other side of the world.

Although the motivations remain incomprehensible, the obsession with art, and art itself, are facts of life on earth. Thus I can but only encourage Ivo Jakovljević from the village of Mutanj. If he were a Serbian conceptual artist, somebody would have already lauded his installation, acclaiming it as an intelligent and incisive satire of Serbian megalomania. Were Ivo Jakovljević Andy Warhol, his installation would be exhibited in museums, acclaimed as a work that wittily unites the symbols of two cultures, Latin and Cyrillic. But Ivo Jakovljević works in a lead and zinc mine and his "Srpski Holywood" is just the lonesome enterprise of a lonesome village idiot. I don't know if it would be of any comfort to the currently out-of-pocket Ivo Jakovljević to understand that the difference between "high art" and amateurism is negligible, and that it's all just a question of context. People in the art world behave like the majority of people do in other spheres of life—like a majority. In other words, they behave just like those Serbian voters, who, when asked by a representative of a small anti-nationalist party whether he'd get their vote in the next elections, responded: "First of all get elected, and then we'll vote for you!"

December 2008

BITCHES

Even those who can barely say their name in English know what *bitch* means. *Bitch* is as promiscuous and freely-spouted as the word *fuck*, its circulation global. *Bitch* rings out everywhere, for the simple reason that American films and TV series are everywhere. In Slavic languages, *bitch* has displaced the imposingly inventive local repertoire of words with the same meaning.

Who knows where the word *bitch* was ripped from? Maybe from the phrase *son of a bitch*, where the word renounced its *mother*, abandoned its *son*, and shimmied off on its own carnivalesque conquest, elbowing all similar words aside. *Bitch* is not only an expression of familiarity among young women (*nigger* serves a similar function among young urban African-Americans), nor is *bitch* simply social, gender, and age-defiant American slang. *Bitch* is more than this.

The word's global conquest came with the seal of approval of "third wave" American feminism, which grew out of the punk and hip-hop scenes and the eras of consumerism and the Internet. *Bitch* is most often used in reference to young women. Having adopted the slogan *To Be Real*, women thought it better to endow the word with a positive connotation rather than censor it. While Gloria Steinem united American feminists under the auspices of *Ms.* magazine, "third wave" feminists are associated with the magazine *Bitch*. Having rejected the assumption of a universal female identity built on the life experiences of middle-class white women, the mixed bag of "third wave" feminism contains many divergent schools of thought. All of these tendencies—the "Riot grrrl" movement, ecofeminism, transgendered feminism, queer culture, anti-racism, postcolonial theory, and traditional activism—are linked by a female perspective on the contentious issues of race, class, and sex.

So who, then, is a *bitch*? People say a bitch is a woman with a mind of her own and who isn't afraid of speaking it loud and clear; a woman who knows what she wants and uses everything at her disposal to get it. A "bitch" would seem to have adopted the title of the popular American song "Whatever Lola Wants, Lola Gets" as her catchphrase.

Everybody knows that the media—television, film, the Internet—is the most powerful promoter of images, ideas, ideologies, and trends, and that it shapes our consciousness. As a passionate devotee of Hollywood film, my mother became a smoker, emancipated by Hollywood stars. Today, only bad guys smoke on-screen, and everybody knows that a smoker is capable of anything.

When my mother was a teenager, there was no such thing as teenage popular culture. She didn't have much option but to go to the cinema (most often on the sly), where she would dream away and identify with the great Hollywood stars of the 1930s and 1940s.

Thanks to my mother's cinephilia, and the same absence of teenage culture when I was growing up, my childhood pleasures came from books—and Hollywood films.

Today, the mass culture market is spectacularly diverse and caters to the needs of all consumer age groups; even impecunious children have become serious consumers. Children, teenagers, twenty-somethings, the middle-aged, each group has its own stars, although the boundaries have become uncannily porous and elastic. Take the notorious *Sex and the City* as an example: The show's anorexic thirty-something women look like teenagers, put on teenage affectations, speak in squeaky anemic voices, and the problems of these seemingly self-confident urban women—embodied by Sarah Jessica Parker and her fellow heroines—appear to be almost identical to those of the average twelve-year-old girl—the twelve-year-old of our time course. Because, when I was a little girl, in the absence of richer and more entertaining cultural offerings, my hero was Gregor Samsa from Kafka's *Metamorphosis*.

In the dynamic, diverse, and generationally-divided world of popular culture, capturing every typological representation of women is no walk in the park. Representations frequently carry mixed messages, and patriarchal content is often packaged in emancipatory images. In the broad typology of female characters, of those with feminist pretensions only the "woman-warrior" seems to be truly emancipatory—the tough girl, the wonder woman, the action chick, all of which have spin-offs in various forms of popular culture. "Women-warriors" are generally first seen in comics and video games, then "spun-off" into films, television series, and genre novels (fantasy, gothic, etc.), before finally becoming products for the toy and souvenir industries. "Buffy" from *Buffy the Vampire Slayer* is a good example of a teenage "woman-warrior." Buffy isn't an adventurous type keen on hunting vampires, they're right there for her at school. In contrast to the demure Buffy, Lara Croft is a real adventurer, a wealthy and athletic noblewoman, an archaeologist and expert in ancient civilizations and languages. A female Indiana Jones, Lara Croft was originally a video game character, before going on to appear in films (starring Angelina Jolie), comics, novels, and cartoons. *Xena, Warrior Princess* is a product of the tacky genre of historical fantasy. An Amazonian, Xena is a female version of Hercules, and although they never actually say that she's Bulgarian, her battle cries sound like something out of a Bulgarian folk song. Bulgarian yelps and New Zealand landscapes make for a pleasant emancipatory cocktail. Played by Uma Thurman, the woman-warrior character from Tarantino's *Kill Bill* is a mash-up born of Hong Kong cinema, spaghetti westerns, and Japanese Samurai films. More recently, the imaginary of popular culture has been colonised by mysterious and aggressive women warriors from visually striking Chinese films.

The emancipatory transformation of a woman is most explicit in the film *Batman Returns*, where Mousy Selina (Michelle Pfeiffer), a feminine, insecure, and demure secretary who lives in a world dominated by men, is transformed into the dangerous and seductive Catwoman (*Life's a bitch and so am I!*). Cultural products with pretensions to seriousness such as the iconic film *Thelma and Louise* use the same principle of transformation—a woman goes from mouse-woman to cat-woman, from a woman in danger to a dangerous woman.

When I imagine my mother and her granddaughter, compare their cultures, and consider their formative influences and icons, the differences are striking. My mother's formation was shaped by Hollywood films; her icons were Katherine Hepburn, Carol Lombard, Lauren Bacall, Barbara Stanwyck, Bette Davis, Joanna Crawford, Ava Gardner, Marilyn Monroe, and many others. When I watch those films today, I'm gobsmacked by the fact that the male and female characters appear as equals, above all because they converse as equal and intelligent human beings. Whenever I think about the eloquent and witty dialogues between Katherine Hepburn and Spencer Tracy, or between Cary Grant and his female partners, I'm dumbfounded by the humiliating fact that today's supposedly emancipated female characters inevitably hold their tongues. And they hold their tongues because they evidently have nothing to say. The old Hollywood film and television scripts were predominantly written by men, and while the male-female relationships in them were clearly idealized, they concomitantly established an ideal standard of behavior between men and women. The absence of dialogue in contemporary films is stark proof of the humiliating absence of the need for dialogue.

For all that, it seems, at least in part, that female popular culture revolves less and less around men. Lara Croft and the heroine from *Kill Bill* are both solitary, independent "players" and barely differ from their male counterparts. Female culture is slowly becoming monological, as is male culture—the monologue being not only a confessional form, but also a form of domination over the listener. Women are slowly establishing this domination of the monologue in many spheres: in literature, in the genre of the personal memoir, in newspaper columns, in television shows, in contemporary art. Women are now "loose tongues," "loudmouths," "chatterboxes," and "fishwives." They have won the right to their monologues, to their "loose tongues," although they'll respond to that with the claim that a loose tongue was always the weapon of frustrated court jesters, fools, and of Scheherazade. They might be right about that, but they might also be wrong.

How women will use the position they have won both now and in the future is up to them. My only hope is that one of today's female icons, Victoria Beckham, will have faded from the media horizon by the time my mother's granddaughter begins imitating her female icons. Why single out VB from the multitudes like her? Because VB is notorious for saying that she's never read a book in her life.

June 2008

KNOWLEDGE
IS POWER

In the closing scene of *The Kingdom of the Crystal Skull*, Harrison Ford, reprising his role as Indiana Jones, responds to his son's question about the meaning of the legend of the city of gold by explaining that the word *gold* translates as *treasure*. But the treasure wasn't gold—it was *knowledge*. *Knowledge is treasure*, declares Indiana Jones, his gaze fixed towards the gold-tinged past, but also towards the future represented by his son. The film takes us back to the America of the 1950s and the McCarthy era, and in this respect the evil Irina Spalko (Cate Blanchett) is a worthy opponent. Having imbibed the slogan *Knowledge Is Power* with her communist milk, Irina remains loyal to that idea to the bitter end, paying for it with her head. The antagonism between Indiana Jones and Irina Spalko is actually false, because the same passion for knowledge draws both into the dangerous adventure of the film. But Irina is a woman, a communist, and, unlike Indiana, has no family, all of which makes the outcome of their battle clear from the outset.

I drank the slogan *Knowledge Is Power* with my socialist Yugoslav milk. Hand in hand with Greek mythology, as a child I swallowed the myths about communist leaders who crammed for hours on end, who from humble beginnings as poor village children became PhD scholars, polyglots, and "Great Men." The story about Maxim Gorky, the orphan boy who read books by the light of the moon, was forever burned into my consciousness. Communist leaders posed for their portraits with glasses on their noses, the backdrop a symbolic row of books. The glasses were an incontestable sign of erudition. Tito also underwent a similar mythological transformation: from a poor village urchin, then a locksmith's apprentice, he, in his turn, became a man with glasses on his nose.

Such images of glasses-wearing, book-loving communist leaders had a propaganda function and highly visible results. In Yugoslavia the spread of literacy among the people began with Partisan courses during the Second World War (bolstered by the legends of wizened old peasant women who learned to read and write). The popularization of education began in earnest, studying became accessible to all, and a network of "workers' universities" and "evening schools" for adults was created. (*Education in the workplace!* was one of the more popular Yugoslav-era slogans). With the arrival of television sets to Yugoslav homes, and the production of educational programs for both adults and children, the education of the socialist masses went on apace. At the time, newspapers also had an educational character.

Abraham Lincoln, the self-educated American president, is one of the founding fathers of the educational-enlightenment myth in American culture. The propaganda-like and Enlightenment-inspired mythologizing of literacy and education and the right of citizens to education took hold in America long before they did in the short-lived Communist epoch. America created college culture and, along with it, campus films and television series, literature and fashion, rituals and customs, all of which are inseparable from this culture. In America the slogan *Knowledge Is Power* never lost its credibility and strength, Barack Obama being its new torchbearer.

In Yugoslavia the slogan *Knowledge Is Power* vanished before Yugoslavia itself did. "Workers' universities," evening schools, and educational programming on radio and television simply disappeared. Newspapers yellowed with scandal and pornography, and television became lowest-common-denominator entertainment. Writers became comedians and salespeople. Nationalism became an alibi for self-pronounced "avengers" hell-bent on knocking "Yugoslav" giants, literary and otherwise, from their pedestals—and I mean literally. In Croatia, the monuments to Nikola Tesla (because he was a Serb) and those of the sculptor Vojin Bakić (also a Serb) came crashing down, as did the monuments to Ivo Andrić (a Nobel Laureate in literature) in his homeland of Bosnia. In a moment of furious ethnic and ideological cleansing many books were tossed out of libraries, some ending up on bonfires.

On an October visit to New York in the run up to the 2008 US presidential election, I was invited to the Union Settlement Association in East Harlem, a visit organized by the Unterberg Poetry Center. Union Settlement is an American version of a "worker's university." I was the guest of an adult education program, which for many years has helped immigrants master both written and spoken English as efficiently as possible.

There were about two hundred people in the auditorium, and the program coordinator translated my English into Spanish. My audience

consisted of Mexicans, Puerto Ricans, and other immigrants whose
first language was Spanish, men and women working tough physical
jobs to put food on the family table. It wasn't important to them
where I was from; for them I had a symbolic value: I was a writer,
and a female writer at that. I represented all the values my audience believed went hand-in-hand with a writer's calling: erudition,
courage, moral values, honesty, and a commitment to justice. For
them I spoke a language that "recognizes no borders," a language
understood by all classes and all races. In short, I was a woman with
glasses on my nose, and that night signed many books and shook
many hands. I received a bouquet of flowers and, as a memento, a
plush teddy bear. My throat tightened. Accepting the role they had
bestowed upon me, I really did feel like a writer, though a bit like
Rosa Luxemburg too.

Later, walking the New York streets armed with a bouquet of flowers and a teddy bear, I wondered why I had been so moved, and
where all the soppy sentimentality had come from. Then I wondered
how my countrymen, those semi-literate do-nothings, those Yugo-
shitters and smart-asses, who get off on making jokes at the expense
of others' talent, knowledge, and work ethic, would have fared
among those earnest Mexicans and Puerto Ricans, who still believed
that literature can save the world. I wondered how those who used
to taunt Ivo Andrić with "Hey, four-eyes, done your scribbling for
the day?" would have fared, let alone those who still today get off
on regurgitating the anecdote, thinking it oh-so-funny. Actually,
it's for the best that I couldn't explain to the Mexicans where I was
from, I thought to myself. I mean, what could I have said? That I
come from a place where arrogance is a kind of unwritten etiquette,
and ignorance a treasured human value? That I come from a place
that cultivates disdain for every intellectual effort, a place where

they understood the slogan *Knowledge is Power* literally, and, this being the case, the Bosnian Serb leader Radovan Karadžić set his cannons on the Sarajevo Library? That I come from a place where local politicians, criminals, liars, thieves, thugs, and murderers are models of courage, morals, honesty, and progress?

I gave the teddy bear to my six-year-old niece. When she's a little older, I'll tell her the story of how the teddy bear found its way to her, the story of impoverished immigrants who arrived in America with the belief that knowledge is the only real treasure. I'll do everything I can to instill in her that same belief. She might say, "Thank you, Indiana Jones," or "Thank you, Irina Spalko," but that really doesn't matter.

November 2008

THE HAIRDRESSER
WITH THE POODLE

A homeland is a fact in a person's private life just as a person's place of birth and date of birth are facts. The encounter with the homeland begins at pre-school. One of the first things a child learns is the famous sentiment: *My country is* . . . Here, at a tender age, begins the homeland briefing that lasts *from the cradle to the grave.* This briefing continues at school, through classes in the history, language, and literature of the land. The poets tell us that the homeland is the *land of our grandfathers, our home and hearth, our native soil, amber waves of grain and eyes the color of the sea, the prairies, mountains and valleys, seas and plains,* and other such things. Today, particularly from a broadly neo-liberal vantage point, all these thousands of patriotic verses— particularly the ones which urge expropriating the native hills, rivers and plains, hearth and home, sky and sun (*my sky, my sun, my prairies and my mountains*) can be read as a list of real estate holdings which were acquired under suspicious circumstances. Poets, of course, as proof of their right to this imaginary property, unfurl their direct ancestral line, claiming that the homeland is their *mother,* which, from a gender perspective, is discriminatory, but easy to understand. Homelands are generally *mothers* for their sons. Poetically inclined daughters seldom refer to their homeland as *mother.*

Whatever the case, the homeland and the state meld in an alloy, two concepts merged into one, a traditional marriage: the homeland— the female emotional charge; the state—the male rational side. The alloy comes more readily into focus after the first call to military service and the first tax bill. A divorce between homeland and state is not permissible, and the notion that the homeland might be a Utopian project is out of the question. So it is, for instance, that the poem by the Croatian poet S. S. Kranjčević (*I have a homeland, I hold it in my heart, with all its hills and plains/Where will I spread out this Eden? In vain I ask the world, and choke back my pain*) is interpreted in schools as a Croatian document confirming the exclusive Croatian copyright to *hills*, *plains*, *pain*, and *Eden.*

A person needs to trudge down a long and hard road on the way to figuring out how to relate to things, among them the homeland/ state. Profound insights do not come dropping out of the sky like the roast chickens of fairy tales. When I left my homeland of Croatia, the one which had slipped out of my Yugoslav homeland, and turned up here in the Netherlands, my feelings were at first confused. I didn't know how to think about homeland. And then—though this took some ten years of cogitation—I discerned within myself an unusual urge. As soon as I turned up in a new country or city, the first thing I'd look for is—a hair salon! My hair grows slowly, and I haven't much to spare, so getting a haircut is not a high priority. When I go to the hairdresser's, I don't get all the bells and whistles, I just have it cut. So my neurotic urge to have my hair cut would be difficult to classify as simple female vanity.

I will not list all the cities and countries where I've had my hair cut, but as evidence of my competence I can say with a certainty that that the cheapest haircut currently available in New York City is at salons run by Uzbeks, no longer with the Russians the way it used to be a number of years ago. The able Uzbeks will cut your hair in Brooklyn for ten dollars. Not even the barbers in the Serbian town of Čačak will pick up a pair of shears for that kind of money.

I thought about what all this means, and I wondered whether my neurotic urge to get my hair cut in each new place I visit is a form of masochism or a ritual form of internal apology—apology for what I don't know. In the Netherlands I long felt that I had been missing something. Yes, I had friends, a tax accountant, my own dental hygienist; I had mastered the many facets of ordinary life that made life more ordinary. Then, as a result of the deficit I mentioned earlier, I embarked on painful introspection, until at last I stumbled upon a moment of epiphany: my biography suddenly emerged as a chronicle of all my haircuts. In Amsterdam I have changed many hairdressers, the fancy ones, the famous ones, and the cheapest ones at the barbershops run by Moroccans, but none of these felt like a comfortable shoe on a weary foot. And then Liesbeth took over the hair salon in my neighborhood.

Liesbeth is a tall, large, young woman with a very pale complexion, who must have grown up on Dutch cheese and milk. Liesbeth has blue eyes and a slightly melancholic look, perhaps from her porcelain complexion. All in all, she has a charming face, which looks diminutive next to her vast posterior. It is difficult not to notice Liesbeth's behind, especially because she prefers tight pants. Liesbeth has a different hairdo and hair color every time I see her. Sometimes she dyes her bangs platinum blue while the rest of her hair is black.

Liesbeth knows that the hairdo of the proprietress is the best ad for a salon. She has a boyfriend every bit as large as she is, and the two of them are like young walruses; they adore each other, and together they adore a poodle. Liesbeth has the tiniest poodle in the world, the size of a squirrel, except that unlike a squirrel her poodle has a short tail. The poodle, unusually docile and adorable, never barks, or at least I have never heard it. It spends most of its days in a little basket that Liesbeth sets by the window, so that the poodle won't be bored. It is a little odd that Liesbeth's salon is always empty. I call in advance to make an appointment for a haircut, and she invariably hesitates a moment, consults her calendar, no, ten o'clock wouldn't be so good, how about eleven. We go back and forth about the time, although I know that Liesbeth is free at ten and eleven, and whenever I want. Liesbeth's salon is done up in bright colors, the door is violet, the door frames light green, the walls pink. Whenever I cycle by Liesbeth's always empty street, I can see her out on the grassy patch in front of the salon walking her poodle on a slender leash. Liesbeth is large, the poodle is small. She looks as if she is walking a mouse. She and I speak of nothing but the haircut, whether I want it this way or that, shorter or longer. The conversations are pointless because she cuts my hair exactly the same way each time, and each haircut is every bit as bad as all the others.

I don't know why, but sometimes a fear gnaws at me that Liesbeth, with her shears and her poodle, might vanish like a soap bubble one day. The murky stab of terror drives me to dial her number.

"When would you like. 11:00?"

"What about 12:00?"

"Sorry, that won't work. 12:15?"

"OK."

With a sigh of relief I hang up.

As far as hair is concerned, this is what I recently learned: In ancient cultures, the act of cutting the hair was a symbolic sacrifice for the good of the people. Through history long hair was worn by martyrs, hermits, the holy, kings, warriors, aristocrats, dignitaries. The servants and the underclass had short hair. Cutting hair was a ritual of obedience, sacrifice, grief, disgrace, punishment, and self-punishment.

After the long, painful, and geographically diverse experience I have gained traipsing through hair salons, the very essence of the home-land/state finally became crystal clear to me. Yes, I am the perfect subject! I am what every homeland-mother desires.

February 2009

A POSTCARD
FROM BALI

The "postcard" is here a literary genre that presupposes three things: the presence of its author in a particular place, brevity, and randomness of content. The reality is that nowadays people send e-mails from Bali. The postcards I stumbled across in a small shop at a Bali resort reminded me of Eastern European ones, sixties-style. Back then, few had cameras, and digital cameras were in the distant, inconceivable future.

Postcards, frankly, just aren't around anymore. What Bali has is Vespas: everyone's got one. This makes traffic lights and gas stations few and far between, so they sell gas in plastic bottles, like home-made plonk. All in all, settlements on Bali have little in common with the European conception of urban planning; they are more like Slavonian village lanes, popping out one after the other like sausages: Kuta, Legian, Seminyak . . . I was after 47 Raya Seminyak Street. It turned out that street numbers, if there are any, don't mean a thing. Raya Seminyak Street actually has two number 47s, and for some reason none of the local residents, not even the traffic police, seem able to mentally internalize house numbers. Places are remembered by their function: one of the number 47s was some kind of store, the other a massage parlor.

This type of thing, like many other things, is the stuff of life off the resort. Because on Bali you have life on the resort and life off the resort. Tourists live on the resorts, the Balinese off. The Balinese go around grinning like Cheshire cats, while tourists' lips seem firmly jammed together by invisible pegs; you first have to take the peg off and return the smile, which is pretty tiring if you're out of practice. On Bali there's a "Center for Laughter," opened by a former-tourist-turned Bali resident. The woman decided to recoup the money she had invested in annual holidays and transform her annual holiday into a lifelong calling, passing on her smile know-how to incurable sourpusses. Bali is the "Island of the Gods," and many here have experienced similar enlightenment, including Elizabeth Gilbert, author of the global bestseller *Eat, Pray, Love*—six million copies sold and counting. When the film version hits the cinema, a lot of women are going to be hurtling off to Bali in search of their happiness—and their Javier Bardem.

Joss sticks burn everywhere, and yearning for any kind of sensation, physical, emotional, spiritual, financial, everybody burns with them. The locals' lives revolve around tourists, something I know a little about from my former homeland. I once saw a little boy in a small Adriatic town holding a plastic yogurt container with some water and a jellyfish in it, hollering: "Buy the jellyfish that stung you!" There are similarly ingenious hucksters here too. In a large opening in the rocks near Tanah Lot, an enterprising Balinese dressed as a Buddhist monk offers tourists their chance to stroke the head of a bulging, allegedly deadly, serpent-like creature. Like many tourists that day, I too stroked the head of the docile slow worm, leaving his owner a few rupees.

Balinese supermarkets reminded me of early communist supermarkets: frozen fish and meat, "Nivea" cream with the kind of obsolete packaging that's no longer sold in Europe, a handful of symbolic products—English biscuits well past their expiration date, inedible Japanese rice crackers—just enough to satisfy a tourist who needs a fix of nutritional nostalgia. The cosmetics section, with all its skin-whitening creams and potions, was disconcerting to say the least.

Indonesia had its place in my childhood imaginary, albeit a humble one. As a little girl I eloquently pronounced the names Sukarno, Nasser, Nkrumah, Nehru, and Sirimavo Bandaranaik; sarongs, skull-caps, and flowers in my hair were part of my childhood landscape. How so? Because of the Non-Aligned Movement. The Non-Aligned Movement brought exotic images to Yugoslavia—either *they* came to us, or Tito went to *them*—and Indonesian, Egyptian, Ceylonese, and Indian children waved their miniature flags, just like me.

There is a small well-integrated community of former Yugoslavs on Bali. Some came as hippies, others as hippies who missed the party the first time, and some as eager entrepreneurs. A woman from Korčula opened a sandwich shop, a guy from Belgrade is involved in tourism, and there are a few young Slovenians living as surfers, actively practicing life as permanent holiday. "Even God forgot me," said one of my countrywomen who has lived here for the past eighteen years. Given where we were (Bali is the "Island of the Gods," right?), the melancholy of her sentence was hard to process, particularly in light of Elizabeth Gilbert's diametrically opposed experience.

In complete contrast to Elizabeth Gilbert, I didn't go to Bali for self-discovery, but to briefly forget who and what I am. I didn't experience self-discovery in the form of a charming Brazilian businessman like she did, but self-discovery didn't completely pass me by either. Each to her own, I guess. My self-discovery was waiting for me on the hotel courtyard's bookshelf, which was full of books other guests had left behind. Seeing the covers, with their large embossed gold letters, I didn't hold out much hope of finding anything to read, let alone one of my own books. Dan Brown, Elias Khoury, Danielle Steel . . . there were also a few Russian books by writers I'd never heard of, which just means that the Russians had made it to Bali too. I took out Dmitri Gluhovski's novel *Metro 2033*. The entire world is in ruins, humanity is devastated, Moscow polluted by radiation and inhabited by monsters. The few surviving humans hide in the Moscow underground, where terror and hopelessness reign. Artiyom, the hero, makes his way through the entire underground in order to save his metro station, and perhaps the whole of humanity with it.

On the last page of the book—I only managed to read a small snippet—I stumbled upon a written appeal. The book's publisher and members of the Russian PEN organization announced the establishment of a "Warm Heart" fund and asked readers to send in donations to support down-and-out contemporary Russian writers. *They desperately need your help*, the appeal read. There are well-known authors among the writers, war veterans (from the Second World War), and former camp inmates who these days literally can't put food on the table. By my reckoning, half a million readers would have read the appeal, about the same number as the book's print run. Optimistically, I thought that if those half-million had left the book behind somewhere, on a park bench, in a café, in the metro,

or in a resort like this one on Bali, the real numbers could be off
the charts.

To cut a long story short, I jotted down the bank account number.
Instead of buying Elizabeth Gilbert's illuminating chronicle of self-
discovery, I decided to send the equivalent sum to the writers who've
discovered the very bottom of their useless profession. Because I also
have a "heart." What's more, it seems that it's still "warm."

June 2010

BATTLE ROYALE

The word impossible has been and must remain deleted from our dictionary.
—*Ingvar Kamprad,* A Furniture Dealer's Testament

Everyone understands the IKEA thing: you get caught once, you'll go back to the scene of the crime. Somebody calculated that no one has ever been to IKEA and walked out with less than five items. I tried it once. Before heading in I swore to myself that I wouldn't buy anything, but I ended up at the check-out with a candle, two small wooden hooks, a packet of paper serviettes, a rubber placemat, and a little green plastic flower. I felt like a kleptomaniac. Even if I'd have gotten past the check-out empty-handed, I would have caved at the little food section near the exit and bought a jar of Swedish cranberry jam, dry Wasa crackers, a bad coffee from the machine, and the kind of crappy hotdog I only ever buy at IKEA, and in the streets of New York, which is of course a completely different story.

What's so irresistible about IKEA? Some guru pretender said that IKEA is *about being, not buying*, and it's true—IKEA is set up like a cozy simulation game for adults. Parents can leave their children in the IKEA playground, have something to eat in the IKEA restaurant, stroll through the enormous display rooms, and then there are the ubiquitous pencils, pads, and tape measures, which transform potential buyers into master craftsmen and craftswomen, measurers of length, width, and height, into builders and designers. There are those well-marked arrows on the floor, gently coaxing us through the IKEA labyrinth to the exit. Admittedly, there are no signs for shortcuts; they're for our sense of orientation to figure out. From the display rooms we automatically end up in the IKEA self-service warehouse, pushing shopping carts that are just waiting to be filled, all the while following the guiding arrows to the check-out and exit. At IKEA everything is welcoming and accessible; IKEA doesn't rub our social status in the dirt. At IKEA we buy the feeling that things are under our control—we do the measuring and choosing, we assemble the furniture, we take the responsibility. IKEA doesn't underrate our intelligence; IKEA makes us an equal player: IKEA gives our self-confidence wings. At IKEA we don't feel disqualified for a second, with IKEA the word *impossible* is eternally deleted from our dictionary.

The game is, without doubt, deeply embedded in our brains, our instincts, reflexes, and behavior; that's why we buy toys, proudly showing them off to one another. This reflex—visible even in one-year-old babies, who'll push every button they can find—remains with us until our last breath. We adults also push buttons on a daily basis: on the remote control, television, radio, VCR, computers, elevators, home intercoms, ovens, lamps, mobile phones, and bank machines. We've wised up: we know that as soon as we forget to push a button, that's when the trouble starts.

That's why today's banks look like Internet cafés. That seems to be why ABN-AMRO, the biggest Dutch bank, refurbished its branch in downtown Amsterdam: there are no tellers or employees anymore, just computers—every client serves him- or herself. Today, we serve and look after ourselves in all kinds of ways: we organize our own travel, book our flights and hotels, do our own banking, pay our bills, make our own diagnoses, figure out on our own whether garlic or green tea is better for reducing high blood pressure. We pick out and try on clothes ourselves, because there's no one to give us any advice; we are left completely to our own devices when we buy technical gadgets, the youthful assistants usually clueless. We communicate with invisible service centers, which then refer us to their websites to find the information needed to solve our problem. We've become *self-sufficient*, the term has entered our dictionaries and it's intent on sticking around forever.

The greatest erosion of our self-confidence and our strongest internal protest are not caused by our social, sexual, racial, national, physical, age, fashion, or any other kind of incompatibility, but by a button, the symbolic button that—if touched incorrectly—will disqualify us from the game. We didn't make it into the packed tram; we locked our keys inside, having slammed the door behind us; we forgot to charge our mobile phones; we didn't bring our glasses; the key got stuck in the lock; we didn't turn the alarm on; we don't know how to turn the alarm off; we parked the wrong way, and there's a ticket waiting for us on the windshield; the computer crashed and we didn't back up in time—all of these, and thousands of similar details, result in internal emotional upheavals whose intensity is completely disproportionate to whatever provoked them.

At the beginning of January 2011 I was supposed to travel to New York and participate in a roundtable discussion. New York is a city

I love, I've been there numerous times, and from the moment I land at John F. Kennedy Airport I enjoy every second.

At Amsterdam's Schiphol Airport, checking my passport and ticket, the check-in person asked me:

"And where's your ESTA form?"

It turned out that the ESTA form—Electronic System for Travel Authorization—is a new bureaucratic obstacle to be negotiated in order to gain permission to travel to the USA. The clerk advised me to complete the form on the special computers there at the airport. Filling out the form on a pokey little screen, with a ball-shaped mouse that was hard to move and kept getting stuck, following less than clear instructions, and anxious that I'd be late for my flight, it was no walk in the park. The guy at the computer next to me seemed to be making good progress.

"How's it going?" I asked, hoping he might help me.

"I've been hunched here for an hour and I'm still at the beginning," said the man jumpily.

I approached the airport's KLM hostesses.

"The machines aren't under our jurisdiction," they said.

"Whose jurisdiction are they under then?"

"The Americans'."

"Is there anyone who can help me?"

"No, the details you enter on the form are strictly confidential," they said.

"How can they be confidential when I've got to supply them when I check in?!"

"Yes, but you've got to fill the form out yourself, unassisted."

"Like packing my own luggage, you mean?"

"Exactly."

Although I knew negotiations with these Dutch clerks would come to nothing, I persisted.

"What if the person traveling is blind, illiterate, or has never seen a computer screen in his or her life?

"Those kinds of people don't usually travel," the tall blonde KLM hostess brushed me off.

I gave filling the form in another two or three tries, then gave up and headed home. The organizers kindly agreed to change my flight to the following day, so I sat down enthusiastically at my computer, found the ESTA form on the American Embassy's website, breezed through filling it in, and paid the requisite fee by credit card. A slightly worrying message appeared on the screen saying that I'd get an answer within seventy-two hours, but sometime after midnight the permission arrived.

In the morning I set off again for Schiphol. The check-in clerk went through my documents.

"You've put your passport number in wrong!" she said.

And really, a mistake had snuck in.

"What shall I do?"

"Try to correct the mistake on the computer . . . let's hope it'll be entered into the system before check-in closes . . ."

Sweat ran down my spine, my heart pounded. The ball-shaped mouse was unresponsive and a message kept popping up saying that my session had expired. The program kept sending me back to the beginning, deleting everything I'd entered in the process. The young guy at the computer beside me was sweating through it too.

I replayed these twin episodes in my head, hoping I might find a detail to reassure me that it wasn't entirely my fault. But it was: I was the one who didn't find out about the new rules on time; if I had, I would have known that I couldn't travel without authorization, and then, when given a second chance, I was the one who filled out the form incorrectly. I felt hopelessly disqualified. The KLM staff were right: such people don't travel. Crestfallen, I went home. The organizers didn't get in touch again, and even my closest friends felt no pity for me. A logical and justifiable disqualification had come my way.

In totalitarian systems nothing was tailored to the individual, nor did the system depend on him or her, a hostile, invisible state apparatus controlled everything. The individual navigated through his or her little life by making adjustments, by cunning, hypocrisy, corruption, haggling, compromise, bribery, and God-knows-what else. The individual could blame all his or her troubles on the cruelty of the system. What's more, in totalitarian systems disqualification was often fatal. People lost their lives in prisons and camps, and their being "unaccommodated" also often meant the suffering and death of those close to them.

The controversial and unrelentingly brutal Japanese film *Battle Royale* (2000), directed by Kinji Fukasaku (based on the eponymous novel by Koushun Takami), is set in a Japan of the future, which is in the throes of a severe economic crisis. As part of the state's economic revitalization program, the army kidnaps a class of Japanese secondary school students and takes them to an abandoned island, which serves as the setting for a monstrous "Battle Royale."

The students, who had set off thinking they were going on a class trip, are forced to participate in a game on which their survival depends. Fitted with dog collars, which are both listening devices and timed explosives, they are given "survival kits," some of which contain useful objects such as a knife or a revolver, while others include little more than a saucepan lid. Whoever eliminates all the other players wins the game, which is being monitored on army computer screens. One couple, a boyfriend and girlfriend, disqualify themselves from the game by committing suicide. Some kill to defend themselves or their partners, and others discover that they enjoy killing games. The teacher, murderer, and, obviously, creator of the game, leaves the students a simple ideological message: *Life is a game!*

In non-totalitarian systems everything is transparent and tailored to the individual. Accordingly, the individual only has him- or herself to blame for their personal failures. Disqualification from the game is, of course, *temporary*. The fact that there are millions of disqualified people in the world doesn't make our hearts bleed, and in any case, why would it? We haven't been eliminated from the game, they have. We're in there, boxing along, surfing and navigating, our computers sending out little bleeps to announce new messages. Our telephones and PINs are fully functional, money machines spit out fresh bills at the touch of a button, our answering machines are switched on, agencies send us ads for cool holidays, we get invitations to do this or that, department stories send us stuff about upcoming sales, hotels offer cheap off-season deals, our diaries and day planners have our dental hygienist appointments, hair appointments, and yoga lessons, our mobile phones buzz impatiently, our fingers caress the little buttons. No way, we're not disqualified, the race is still on, the game still in play . . .

January 2011

ASSAULT ON
THE MINIBAR

I'll put my cards on the table: over the years my statistical sample has become a substantial one. I can reliably claim that in the matter to follow, the quantity of experience really does determine the quality of the assessment. Every new experience just reconfirms the rule—and I had a new experience recently . . .

At the reception desk I filled in all the necessary details and got the key. Before I headed off to my room the receptionist asked:

"Would you like to open a hotel account?"

"What's that?"

"It means that you don't have to pay for everything you have or use in the hotel immediately, you just give your account number."

I declined. What do I want with a hotel account? I'm only here for three days. Breakfast is included, and most of the time I'll be out and about.

The room was large, luxurious, and had that fresh new smell. The furniture was certainly brand-new, the bathroom enormous, and the heavy windows opened gracefully with the touch of a button.

I hadn't even gotten around to unpacking my things when I heard a knock at the door.

"Can I help you?" I asked the young porter.

"Sorry, but I have to lock the minibar."

"Why?"

"Because you didn't open a hotel account," he said, before heading for the minibar, locking it, and leaving.

All of a sudden I felt the blade of the invisible sword of injustice pressing on the back of my neck. I don't even use minibars. Alcohol doesn't agree with me; I don't like greasy stale crisps; I hate any kind of peanuts; candy bars of uncertain origin aren't my thing; random bottled liquids inevitably give me heartburn; and carbonated non-alcoholic drinks are just plain bad for your health. The bottom line is that a minibar doesn't have anything I'd ever want. So why did I feel so humiliated? Just because the bellboy locked the minibar? Did he put a padlock on the shower, the bathroom tap, the TV remote, the toilet seat? He didn't. Rationalizing it, comforting myself with thoughts of the palatial bed or a hot shower, nothing helped. I was inconsolable. It was just the hopeless sense of deprivation.

They say that a German company called Siegas first manufactured the minibar. But apparently we've got the visionary mind of hotel executive Robert Arnold to thank for its ubiquity. As Wikipedia reliably informs us, Arnold was on a Thai Airways flight from Bangkok to Hong Kong in 1974 when he spotted miniature bottles of alcohol for the first time. Arnold ordered a supply of the bottles and his employer, the local Hilton, took a gamble on the honesty of its guests. *Honesty minibars* are what they called them. A few months later, word spread in the hotel world that the minibars in the Hong Kong Hilton had increased turnover on alcoholic drinks by about 500 percent, and from then on minibars were part of the furniture in every hotel in the world. All thanks to Robert Arnold and an epiphany inspired by a quick glance at a tiny bottle. It might seem by the by, but similar miniature bottles were sold in the watering holes of my former homeland. Their devotees lovingly called them "kiddies."

And this is actually the point: love. Minibars are all about love. Let's think about it: What is, in actual fact, a minibar? A minibar is designed as a dollhouse for grown men. Men love their "kiddies." A hip flask, the teenage dream of today's seventy-year-old, was known as a "buddy." Kiddie, buddy, minibar—they're all diminutives for a guilty something. Guilt in the diminutive is not guilt; it's the simulation of guilt. And therein lies the unique psychotherapeutic effect of the minibar.

For many a lonely businessman, the minibar is a symbolic substitute for home. Getting back to your room, opening the little fridge door, popping open a bottle of beer, flopping down into an armchair and putting one's feet up on the table—it's a ritual deeply ingrained in the imaginary, even of those who don't come home, open the fridge, and take a beer.

The minibar is also designed as a first-aid kit. Even if you've never used it, the thought of your home first-aid kit makes you feel safe and protected. That's why some minibars also have condoms. "Buddies" to protect you from "kiddies."

The minibar is also a kind of temple, a place where we come face-to-face with the metaphysical. In a hotel room you wake from a nightmare. Surrounded by the indifferent darkness, there's no one to hug and comfort you. The minibar gives off a dull (transcendent) light, bottles and bags stand contritely upright, as if in a chapel. The minibar radiates serenity. In the terrifying darkness of the hotel room this lit-up display acts like apaurin. Everything is OK, I'm back in reality—the nightmare is over.

This psychodramatic riddle—home, guilt, first aid, temple—is solved at the reception desk when you check out. The answer is the final and finale-like question that every receptionist asks every guest in every hotel of the world: "Did you have anything from the minibar?" At that moment the guest senses the painful prick of metaphysical guilt. *An honesty minibar?* In some hotels the maids audit the contents of the minibar every morning, restocking it as they go, making the question superfluous. Nonetheless, all receptionists ask it—and they all ask it with that same snippy interrogative tone. The guest's rage begins to swell. Not only did you pre-pay for the room, not only did you pay for overpriced coffee in the hotel bar, not only did you pay for this, that, or the other thing, but you then have put up with a lowly receptionist humiliating you with an honesty test. Nothing's free in life. No argument there. But why oh why is the cost so high?!

The minibar is an expensive escapade, just like a psychoanalytic séance. The minibar perpetuates the same psychoanalytic model. Hence the receptionist's authoritarian tone, hence the sniffing around your room and inspection (of your minibar!) in your absence, hence your righteous rage at this mind-numbing display of power. In this psychoanalytic séance the receptionist turns into an authoritarian mother or father, into your boss at work, the police, an institution of power with which there can be no negotiation. For God's sake, you could pinch the towels, the bathrobes, the table lamp, remove the hand basin and shower taps, and make off with the lot scot-free, but the thought doesn't help. They pin you to the wall over a piddly bottle of bad vermouth and a rancid bag of crisps.

I don't know whether hotel staff read Internet forums. It's enough to type in "minibar" and private armies of the aggrieved assemble, many waging personal guerrilla wars. Did you know that there are people who pee into empty beer bottles, jam the lids back on, and put them back in the minibar? Did you know that some people plaster the base of bottles with hairspray, stick them back down in the fridge, and leave the next person to desperately try to pry them loose? Did you know that if you don't check the minibar as soon as you get into the room, they're likely to sting you for a half-empty bottle of beer someone snuck into your fridge? Or how's this: There are even minibars with built-in sensors that clock every movement and change in weight, so that if you don't put the bottle or the chips back within ten seconds you have to pay for them, no matter what. I mean, who wouldn't get in a huff? They're busy trying to pull a quickie on you, while, at the same time, demanding *your* honesty. They've got it in for you in advance—you're a thief, a grifter, and a boozehound. The minibar is a symbol of the totalitarian world. And by the way—can you be sure that at the pearly gates St. Peter isn't going to welcome you with the question: "Did you take something from a minibar and not pay for it?" and then, depending on your answer, send you to a heavenly hotel with one, three, or seven stars?

In my native language the word "minibar" contains a number of other words. Two of them are critical here: *rab* or *rob*, which means "slave," and *mina*, which means "mine"—as in "land mine." The minibar is a psychoanalytic minefield, for as soon as you cross its path you've immediately become a slave. Today, when almost every totalitarian system has exploded (OK, fine, it's more that they imploded), the minibar is totalitarian shrapnel snugly nestled into a cosy space that's devoid of all ideology—the hotel room. The minibar is the last bastion of totalitarianism, its invisible nest. Struggle against the minibar is possible, but only as a personal guerrilla action.

So, getting back to the hotel I mentioned at the start, this is my confession: I launched the assault on the minibar in room 513. I wrestled it into the bathroom. I defaced it with the hotel key, scratching *Death to the Minibar!* into its smooth surface. I threw it in the bath tub, and I turned on the tap. And finally, when the receptionist asked, "Did you have anything from the minibar?" I replied: "I wouldn't be caught dead!" We need to put our heads together. If hotels know how to put sensors in their minibars, they'll soon figure out a way of charging us for the mere thought that we might fancy a little something.

And that's why, next time around, I'm planting a mine under the minibar.

January 2010

3.

WITHOUT
ANESTHESIA

NO COUNTRY
FOR OLD WOMEN

As an emotional phenomenon, patriotism belongs to the psychopathology of human behavior. Its perversity is shared by only one other phenomenon, namely love of God, because paraphilia, among other things, is defined as "love for a non-human object." In this case the word *love* implies the impulsive and obsessive sexual excitement that a given non-human object stimulates in the paraphiliac. Many psychiatrists spent years challenging the negative connotations of the word *paraphilia*, and so it is that nowadays, the general consensus appears to be that paraphilia should not be treated as a mental disorder unless it causes direct harm to the individual or those around them.

Love for one's homeland is an emotion an individual feels for a "non-human" object. Until recently at least, love for non-human objects was classified as a mental disorder.

This raises a few questions: How is it that no other psychopathological activity has succeeded in establishing itself as socially *normal*? How is that no other form of mental disorder has been legalized and institutionalized? How is it that no other disorder wields such enormous social power, or can boast such a long and rich history? How did such a turn of events come about? How did the semantic transition occur? How did something that is fundamentally abnormal somehow morph not only into something that is normal, but into something that is actually desirable? It's simple. We just put a little effort toward humanizing the non-human object and our love becomes normal and understandable. This is why, among other reasons, believers swallow the host, a floury substitute for Jesus's abstract body, and drink red wine, a liquid stand-in for Jesus's abstract blood. Given to us to sniff, nibble, and lick, God's mysterious spirit will come one step closer.

Right there we have the one and only reason the abstract homeland is most often portrayed as a mother in popular iconography. Hence the multitude of paintings in which the homeland-as-mother suckles her many children at her voluptuous bosom. Hence the gigantic sculptures scattered everywhere that represent the homeland-as-Motherland. In every former Soviet capital, there was at least one gigantic mother: Mother Russia, Mother Armenia, Mother Georgia, and so forth. While the homeland is represented by the figure of the collective mother, the state is most frequently represented by the figure of the Father. The whole thing inevitably ends in a symbolic sex scene: in the tangled embrace of Mother and Father.

I underwent a patriotic initiation when I started primary school. The initiation uniform was a short navy-blue skirt, a white blouse, a little navy-blue Tito-style cap with a red star on the front, and a red Pioneer scarf that I wore around my neck. Believing every word, I repeated the sacred text of the Pioneer's pledge (*Today, as I become a Pioneer, I give my Pioneer's word of honor that I will work and study*

hard, and be a good comrade; that I will love my homeland the Social-
ist Federal Republic of Yugoslavia, that I will guard its achievements,
spread brotherhood and unity . . .). The Pioneer's greeting with which
the oath concluded—*With Tito for the homeland! Onwards!*—was the
socialist replacement for the sacred *Amen!* The truth is that children
make the greatest patriots, most devout believers, most diligent
conservationists, and most loyal consumers. State ideologues, politicians, priests, and the canny manufacturers of children's products
know this only too well. At the occasional school function, I recited
a whole repertoire of patriotic verses, although I don't remember ever
writing a single one down. The phrases promising that I will *guard
the achievements of my homeland* and *brotherhood and unity like the
apple of my eye* have remained forever engraved in my memory. The
Yugoslav anthem "Hey, Slavs" makes my skin tingle. I learned the
Latin and Cyrillic alphabets; I knew Slovenian, Croatian, Bosnian,
Serbian, Macedonian, and Montenegrin songs; and I also knew a
handful of ethnic jokes about representatives of the Yugoslav nations
and nationalities. I learned geography, developed a good ear for all
Yugoslav languages and dialects, and made my own the conviction
that *fascists* are bad guys and anti-fascists *good guys.*

The above could be taken as the abridged contents of my first homeland package. Nevertheless, as a child I still had mixed feelings
about my homeland, because my mother had a different homeland to
me. My first encounter with her homeland, and another language—
I was seven at the time—raised the confusing possibility that there
were lots of homelands, and that homelands could also be replaced.
My mother had two: the one she was born and grew up in, and the
other, which she chose out of love. Out of love for this homeland?
No—out of love for my father. Truth be told, a child—the future
me—was also on the way.

Yugoslavia helped constitute my Yugoslav identity. Its disintegration, the war, and my new Croatian identity, not to mention the bureaucratic ritual of changing passports—the old Yugoslav one for a new Croatian one—destroyed every shred of belief in the seriousness or genuineness of identities that are tied to homelands. The phrase from the Pioneer's pledge about guarding brotherhood and unity like the apple of my eye was suddenly turned on its head, becoming a snake devouring its own tail, a hook on which many necks hung, a silver bullet that ripped apart the "vampiric" heart of federal Yugoslavia. Former brothers rushed to gouge each other's eyes out. Patriotism suddenly appeared as a divine promise; one merely needed to make a choice—and the majority chose correctly. Everyone became patriots. For some, the less agile, patriotism simply meant a guarantee they could stay where they were; for the more agile, it brought pennies from heaven. The homeland was a goldmine—and those who understood the metaphor literally rolled in it. On the back of a verse written to the glory of the homeland, people became ambassadors overnight; on the back of public declarations about the glory of the homeland, others became government ministers. Denouncing a neighbor who didn't love the homeland could mean an unforeseen extension of one's apartment—into the neighbor's of course. Patriotic commitment brought hotels, companies, ministerial chairs, and directorships to the committed. Patriotism was even a currency: entire factories could be bought with a heart-rending patriotic word. It was enough to place one's hand on one's heart, turn on the tears, sing the anthem, curse the enemy, and there you go, people became political power-brokers: one a TV bigwig, another a hospital boss, one the ambassador to Malaysia, another to Washington. Overnight, frogs turned into princes. People understood that it was a once-in-a-lifetime opportunity and made their play to woo the homeland. The deposit was peanuts, the profit enormous. Thanks to the magic power of patriotism, people who hadn't even been to university became university professors, public opinion-makers who held forth on anything and everything, local stars, desirable lovers, owners of villas with swimming pools. Patriotism was hard to resist and had the same effect as Viagra. Patriotism was like a magic shirt, the kind that in Russian fairytales protects the hero against every evil, and helps him vanquish the serpent and win the princess, the kingdom, and the crown. The other truth is that in the race for patriotic gold, in the race to defend the honor of the homeland, some lost their lives. Surviving defenders of the homeland's honor were generously compensated in their place.

My third initiatory homeland package is almost empty; there's just a passport and a tax number. My new homeland doesn't want my love, and neither does it promise to love me. We don't have any mutual illusions in matters of the heart. I've heard it said that new Dutch citizens attend a low-key ceremony, during which they are presented with a Delft-style china potato, as well as a passport. I got a passport, but not a potato. In any case, unlike for the first two, I am bound to my new country by choice. Half-hearted or unequivocal, confused or clear-headed, good or bad, hasty or considered, it doesn't matter, the choice was mine. Sometimes, when coming in to land at the airport, I look out at the surface of my new homeland, so skinny and pressed up against the sea. And I feel a sympathy I can't quite articulate. In these moments, in my imagination, I put my finger in the hole of a dike to save it from imaginary floods.

In the forests of the Amazon there are little birds called "architects." During the mating season, the males, the "architects," build nests of various shapes with incredible inventiveness, decorating them with forest berries, little feathers, and leaves. Every nest is a miniature architectural masterpiece. Then a female appears, and she carefully inspects each nest before finally settling on a single one. The chosen "architect" wins the right to mate—in another words, to continue the species. In an ideal world, it would be the same with homelands. We should be able to take a quick look at each, check it out, and give it a grade, and then, if we must, choose the best—the best being the one which secures the future of our descendants.

Homelands should promote themselves like tourist destinations, something which many countries actually do. Croats themselves have declared Croatia *paradise on earth*, and *a little country for a big holiday*. Tourist agencies, of course, lie. You pay for a hotel with five stars, and you get a wonky bed, a shower that doesn't work, and a pool that leaves you with a fungal infection as a memento. Many states are cunning; they know that free choice could be damaging, so they come up with laws, visas, passports, an entire system of complications, which prevent open inspection and free choice. In this way, many states turn their citizens into hostages, and so the majority of us—citizens—mate in the nest in which we're caught. What's more, this nest is where we find our own greatness, particularity, identity, strength, and glorious history: Hey, it's the same nest where our parents, grandparents, and great-grandparents mated! We derive perverse satisfaction from the thought that our children will also mate in this same nest. We'll warble away, inventing legends about how our nest is the most beautiful on the planet. We'll force ourselves and those around us to love our nest. We'll declare our neighbors' nests filthy and hostile. We'll decorate our nest with crests and flags, surround it with wire, see our love for it blossom, force children to love it—we're ready to defend it to the death.

Asked what communism is, a child replied: "I don't have communism because I drink my milk regularly." Asked how I feel about patriotism, as a woman I could cite Virginia Woolf and her famous line: "As a woman I have no country. As a woman I want no country. As a woman my country is the whole world."[1] However, as the gossip rags have it, Angelina Jolie has that quote tattooed on her body. As a writer, I unfortunately can't quote private tattoos. So, all things told—how do I feel about patriotism? I don't have it: I drink my milk regularly.

February 2010

---

1   Virginia Woolf, *Three Guineas.*

OLD MEN AND THEIR GRANDCHILDREN

One hundred and one old men

Over the weekend of July 19th and 20th, 2008, the town of Key West in Florida played host to 141 Ernest Hemingways. Hemingways from all over America gathered in Key West in a competition for the greatest degree of physical resemblance to the famous writer. This year the winner was Tom Grizzard, in what is said to have been a very stiff competition. The photograph that went round the world shows a collection of merry granddads, looking like Father Christmases who have escaped from their winter duties—in other words, like Ernest Hemingway. The old men, who meet every year in Key West on Hemingway's birthday, also took part in fishing and short story writing competitions.

Another old man . . .

The following day, newspapers in Croatia carried a photograph of an old man who has no connection at all with the 141 old men from the previous article. In Croatia on July 21st, 2008, Dinko Šakić died, at the age of eighty-six. Who was Dinko Šakić? Šakić was the commandant of the Ustasha concentration camp of Jasenovac, where Jews, Serbs, Gyspies, and communist-oriented Croats were efficiently executed. After the war he managed to escape to Argentina, and it was not until 1999 that the Argentinian authorities handed him over to Croatia, where he was sentenced to twenty years in prison. At that "historic" moment, many Croats saw the sentence of Dinko Šakić as an injustice—for them that same Independent State of Croatia (in which Dinko Šakić had killed Jews, Gypsies, Serbs, and unsuitable Croats) was "the foundation of our present Croatian homeland," as the local priest, Vjekoslav Lasić, put it on the occasion of Šakić's death. The priest was in fact merely expounding a thesis put forward by Franjo Tuđman, the first President of Croatia (since Ante Pavelić), and the "father of the Croatian nation." "That is why every decent Croat is proud of the name of Dinko Šakić," announced the priest Vjekoslav Lasić, adding that he was "proud that he had seen Šakić on his bier dressed in an Ustasha uniform." The funeral of old Dinko Šakić at Mirogoj cemetery in Zagreb on July 24th, 2008 was attended by some three hundred people. Even aged criminals have friends. Three hundred people is not a bad number.

And yet another old man . . .

On the day of Dinko Šakić's funeral, another old man rose from the grave in Croatia. Zvonko Bušić Tajko—*the Croatian Mandela, or the most renowned Croatian émigré* (as some Croatian newspaper headlines put it)—landed at Zagreb airport on July 24th, to an enthusiastic reception by a crowd of some five hundred people. Bušić was returning to Croatia metaphorically from the grave, but in fact out of American prisons where he had spent thirty-two years. Way back in the 1970s, with his American wife, Julienne Eden Bušić, and a few friends, he had hijacked an American airplane on its way to

New York, because "he wanted to draw the attention of the world to the unjust position of Croatia in the former Yugoslavia." This gesture of "political activism" (as the Croatian papers defined Bušić's terrorist act) ended ingloriously—Bušić's explosive device led to one American policeman being killed and another losing an eye, and Bušić and his wife ended up in prison. Julienne was released on the eve of Croatian independence; she got a job in the Croatian Embassy in Washington, and later in Croatia, in Franjo Tuđman's personal security service. The Croatian army built a villa on the Adriatic coast, so that she would be able to dedicate herself fully to writing her autobiographical novel *Lovers & Madmen* and to her political activities, lobbying for her husband's release from prison. Among those gathered at Zagreb airport were Croatian politicians, patriots, pop singers (Marko Perković Thompson, for example), priests, children sitting on their fathers' shoulders and holding their welcome banners up to the cameras, young people shouting Ustasha slogans (*"For the homeland ever ready!"*) and singing Ustasha songs. "The Croatian Mandela" made a patriotic speech and quoted a verse from Gundulić's poem *Osman*, which every Croatian primary school pupil knows by heart:

> *The wheel of fate spins about*
> *Round and about ceaselessly:*
> *He who was high is cast down*
> *And who was below is now on high.*

Zvonko Bušić added that, thanks to the good Lord and free Croatia (*"At last I am in my free homeland!"*), he had climbed *high*, while, according to the logic of the wheel of fortune, his enemies had fallen. The only person to comment briefly the following day on Bušić's resurrection was the Croatian President Stipe Mesić (*his motive could have been patriotic, but the method he applied was the method of ter-rorism).* Zvonko and Julienne Bušić told the newspapers that they wanted a little peace, although Bušić's lively speech, his evident excitement at finally finding himself "among his own people," and the five-hundred strong crowd seem to indicate the opposite.

Doctor Velbing and Mr. Hide

On the July 21st, 2008, the day Dinko Šakić died, all the world's newspapers carried a photograph of an old man with a long white beard and white hair, coquettishly gathered on the crown of his head like a kind of diminutive Samurai pigtail. This old man had no connection whatever with the Hemingways of Key West, nor with the late Dinko Šakić, nor with Zvonko Bušić, who was to land at Zagreb airport three days later. This old man looked as though he had fallen out of the file of some Hollywood agent: like a third-rate actor who specialized in playing Merlin and Gandalf in film fairytales. The old man was arrested in Belgrade by the Serbian police just as he was getting into a number 73 bus. It turned out that the old man was called Dragan Dabić, or rather Dragan David Dabić (3D), or rather—Radovan Karadžić. From the moment of the arrest of Radovan Karadžić, the Balkan *butcher* and European *Osama Bin Laden*, the media were flooded with numerous farcical details: Karadžić's unsuccessful attempts to get involved in football and his derisive nickname "Phantom"; his statement that *Yasser Ara-fat was first an international terrorist, then twenty years later he was awarded the Nobel Prize* (an echo of Tuđman's claim that someone who knew about the Nobel Prize had once flattered him: "*If you were not a Croat, General, you would certainly have received the Nobel Prize*"); Karadžić's frenetic 1968 student speech from the roof of the university; his activities as a police informer; his financial fraud and embezzlement; his collection of children's verse, *There Are Miracles, There Are No Miracles*; his alleged mistress who also has two names; his online shop where you can buy a little *"velbing"* (from *well-being*) or a "cross-shaped composition of the smallest *velbing* for your personal protection to be worn on the chest" or a large *"velbing* or spacious cross-shaped composition which harmonizes a whole space"; the decoration on his website, a Jewish three-branched (!) menorah, which is in fact the Orthodox three-fingered blessing in disguise; his cheap aphorisms, which seem to have been copied from Paulo Coelho (*"Man is the most perfect instrument!"*). Commentaries circulated on the Internet and in private emails. They included mention of the film *The Hunting Party*, set in the forests of Bosnia, through which Richard Gere hunts the notorious Bogdanovich, played in the film by the Croatian actor Ljubomir Kerekeš . . . And then a friend of the author of these lines dug up a You Tube video clip from *Barbarella* in which Dr. Durand Durand (3D!) sets his *Excessive machine* in motion and performs his *Sonata for the Executioner of Various Women*. What possible connection can there be between Barbarella and Karadžić? None whatsoever. Apart from the fact that the Irish actor Milo O'Shea, who plays Dr. Durand Durand, is extraordinarily like Ljubomir Kerekeš, that is to say Dr. Bogdanovich, from the film *The Hunting Party*, in other words like Karadžić before his complete *makeover.*

Despite everything, this heap of trivial rubbish circulating in the media served Karadžić himself well, it transformed him from a notorious murderer into a clown and placated a potentially hostile crowd. Intrigued by the farce of his disguise, many people forgot that this same Karadžić-Bogdanovich-Dabić is sitting on a pile of anonymous human corpses, and that there is a large, silent, nameless heap of witnesses, including the women of Srebrenica, for whom this whole media circus that surrounds Karadžić is like salt on an open wound.

The truth will out . . .

Pawel Pawlikowski's *Serbian Epics*—the best and fullest portrait of Karadžić to date—was made as long ago as 1992. Everything in the film is so clear and explicit that this documentary on its own could serve as an indictment against Radovan Karadžić.

In the intervening years, Karadžić's criminal file has become notoriously public, and the new details which have flooded the media since his arrest have merely confirmed what we all knew: that Karadžić is a murderer, sitting calmly on a pile of the corpses of people whom he himself killed, and the only thought buzzing in his head is—how to survive. An enormous human mechanism has been keeping Karadžić alive, the same mechanism that preserved Milošević for years: servants, like-thinkers, admirers, assistants, petty and large-scale criminals, the police, the state apparatus, politicians, murderers, fighters, patients, women, friends, priests, the church, believers, dealers, people—both sick and quite ordinary.

At this moment, many Serbs are lighting candles and praying for their man in prison in The Hague. Ordinary citizens, aging rockers (Bora Đorđević), members of the ultra-right group "Honor" (Obraz), Serbian radicals, supporters of Šešelj, Nikolić, Karadžić, with children at their head—a boy and a girl—they are all marching at this moment through Belgrade, shouting slogans of support for Karadžić, threatening the Serbian government, The Hague Tribunal, the world. Many Serbs—who otherwise have no idea what to do in the face of a sudden "blow" in their household, when, for example, there's a faulty tap in the bathroom, or if their wife ends up in hospital—suddenly display supreme organizational skills and political agility:

Karadžić has been arrested—a heavy "blow" has been struck against their "Serbdom." Every *blow against Serbdom* has the effect of an adrenaline injection.

Following the false news of Karadžić's arrest in 2001, "defensive" meetings were instantly organized in Karadžić's native village and some other places in Montenegro.

Supporters from Montenegro and Serbia gathered, Chetnik songs rang out, priests waved censers around. Karadžić was proclaimed a "haiduk," "poet," "fighter," "saint" and "symbol of Serbdom." People fell into poetic raptures (*"We will not hand Karadžić over!" "Wake up Serbian fire! Radovan is a spark in the rock. Whoever betrays the spark be damned!" "And may all belonging to the traitor be damned a thousand times!"*) Those present were given masks of Karadžić's face. The Montenegrin backwoods sent a message to the world: *"We are all Radovan Karadžić"*; in other words the people behind the masks brazenly admitted their complicity in genocide, both real and mental. The main slogan of the Chetnik organization "Honor" is: *"Every Serb is Radovan!"*—and it could be seen in recent days again in the streets of Belgrade. Is Karadžić, Radovan, really an exclusively Serbian monster? Let us not forget the fact that Karadžić easily crossed the borders between such "irreconcilably different" peoples as the Croats, Serbs, Bosnians, and Montenegrins; he spent his summer holidays in Croatia (making only a single linguistic error, the experts maintain). In the end, if for no other reason than because of Karadžić's longevity and his ability to rise up again like a phoenix, one might ask: How many citizens of the former Yugoslavia were Radovan Karadžić!?

Children, grandchildren, mutants
The lack of a symbolic lynching of Karadžić—now that it is possible—demonstrates that the problem is deeper and harder, and

that it is not after all confined to "Karadžićes": swindlers; prophets and profiteers; doctors of the human soul; grudge-bearers who
drag their personal affronts out of dusty chests and transform them
into ideologies; necrophiliacs; bone-diggers; bullies; exterminators;
murderers; drummers-up of collective hysteria; local "butchers" and
"vampires" for whom many citizens of the former Yugoslavia have
been obediently stretching out their necks for two decades now. The
problem is that all these servants of fascism—like Karadžić—do not
excel in the quantity of evil they produce, but in an invisible form,
in the seed they leave behind them, in their children, and their
grandchildren.

And those children, grandchildren, mutants, have sprung up, healthy
and handsome, in the course of these last twenty years. These are
the children with Chetnik caps on their heads, who demonstrate
throughout Serbia against Karadžić's arrest. Or Marija Šefarović
whose three-fingered sign of the cross spread throughout Europe,
although she was unable to explain its purpose (*"In the name of
mother, father, and you know . . ."* she tried irritably to explain to a
Dutch woman journalist), and who, when she won the Eurovision
Song Contest, did so as she put it herself, *"for Serbia"*. These are the
enthusiastic supporters of the "granddads," of the Serbian radical
Tomislav Nikolić (the author of the statement, *"God created the world
in six days, and it took me two to send it reeling."*); these are the bullies
who beat up Gypsies and homosexuals in the streets of Belgrade;
the drunken, ecstatic crowd at concerts by Ceca Ražnjatović-Arkan.
These young mutants are from Bosnia; they go on the rampage
during football championships and wrap themselves in Croatian,
Serbian, and Turkish flags as if in a protective placenta. They are
secondary-school children from Makarska who recently had themselves photographed for their school almanac with a swastika in the

background, "for fun" ("*It's not a swastika but an Indian symbol of love and peace*", a pupil explained meekly) and strutted about wearing T-shirts bearing the slogan *Über alles* ("*We meant that we had matriculated, it was over, we were above all others*", explained another even more meekly). These are the children who appear at concerts by Marko Perković Thompson in Ustasha uniforms and raise their right hands to the level of their noses, while their granddads—Croatian academicians, writers, journalists, doctors, generals, philosophers, and publicists—write open letters of support for Thompson, the illiterate, third-rate turbo-folk singer, defending his right to the expression of uncensored Ustasha ideas in *our free Croatian homeland*. They are the young members of obscure pro-fascist parties in Serbia; children with tattoos, whose bodies display Pavelić's face; customers in shops freely selling fascist souvenirs; the "brave" attackers of tourists, foreigners, homosexuals, and Gypsies. These are children who wear crosses round their necks, who regularly attend Catholic and Orthodox churches and Muslim mosques, who hate each other, or some third party, and all join in hating Gypsies, Jews, Blacks, and homosexuals. These are young contributors to chat-sites who, I presume, know of their brothers: the young Hungarian fascists (*Magyar garda*), who rose up to defend "Magyar values and culture"; the young Bulgarian fascists of *Bogdan Rassata*, who "defend Bulgarian values and culture" and for ideological reasons beat up Turks and Gypsies; the brutal Russian children, who beat to death anyone whose skin is darker than Putin's; the eco-fascists of the German radical right . . . They are members of "Honor" and similar ultra-rightwing groups who lure children with the cheap glue of *love of God and the homeland, Serbian Serbia, gallant armed forces, the crucified fatherland*, and *the suffering nation (We need new heroes, Obilićes, and new Maids of Kosovo!)*. These children are young Croats, Serbs, Montenegrins, and Bosnians who use both open and closed web forums to sow and graft their hatred and proclaim that *the war is not yet over* . . . And they are not alone (there are their grandparents, their parents, their families, Serbdom, Croatdom), nor are they original: fascism thrives among servants and in serving. The local press, local authorities, and local politicians do not pay attention to the "children," "cases," "hooligans," "troublemakers," "unpleasant, but understandable incidents" in what is otherwise the successful daily life of transition.

Meanwhile Radovan Karadžić can stroll peacefully in his Hugo Boss suits into the Hague courtroom. His work is done.

A procession of collective shame

The job of the Hague judges is to prove individual guilt in the war crimes committed on the territory of the former Yugoslavia, and they, the judges, will be the first, I presume, not to agree with the emotional and hazy thesis of collective guilt. It seems, however, that the mere trial of war criminals does not have the power to bring about a real catharsis or to set in motion real social changes. For without the admission of collective responsibility there can be no successful de-Nazification. For many citizens of the former Yugoslavia, regardless of the actual scale of their responsibility and guilt in the recent war—which, we emphasize, is not equal or the same—those who are to blame for everything are always the others: for the Croats it is the Serbs, for the Serbs the Muslims, the Kosovo Albanians, the Croats, *the whole world* . . . All of them blame the communists, Tito, and the Partisans for everything. And then the "Americans," the "Russians," "Jews," "Europe," "the world," unfavorable stars, destiny. All, without distinction, insist on interpreting the events—which they themselves initiated, which they failed to prevent, or in which they themselves took part—as natural catastrophes in which they are exclusively the victims. In that sense Karadžić's schizophrenic fragmentation—into a *gusle*-player, a psychiatrist, would-be footballer, ecologist, police informer, Chetnik, murderer, politician, would-be Nobel Prizewinner, thief, poet, tutti-frutti guru, Orthodox mystic, into Radovan Karadžić and Dragan David Dabić—is a typical local sickness, the result of a general social lie, a profound moral and mental disturbance, a madness which their milieu continues persistently to treat as though it were normal.

There is a hope that, with the arrest of Karadžić, by contrast with the messages of the young mutants, the war will finally end. There is a childish hope that we will one day come across the following little newspaper announcement: *On the 21ˢᵗ of July 2018—the day of the arrest of the criminal Radovan Karadžić, sentenced to a hundred years in prison for genocide in Bosnia, in the Montenegrin town of Meljina, which is known for its traditional festival of* gusle-*playing—there took place a "procession of collective shame," consisting of 141 old men. The old men had false beards and false white hair gathered on the crowns of their heads in pigtails, and they exposed themselves voluntarily to being spat at by the crowd, which this year had gathered in large numbers in order to participate in the ritual of repentance. In this ritual "the old men" (every year there are new volunteers—everyone has the right to participate in the ritual only once, so that all interested volunteers can have their turn) express their awareness of the crimes committed, of the fact that these crimes were committed in their name, with their full knowledge or even their participation, they confess their responsibility for their crimes and apologize wholeheartedly to their victims.*

July 2008

A QUESTION OF
PERSPECTIVE

1. Without Anesthesia

I met Ryszard Kapuściński in Berlin in 1994; he was there on the same scholarship as me. Kapuściński asked me why I had left Croatia, and to avoid telling my story, I spluttered out . . .

"Do you remember the Andrzej Wajda film *Without Anesthesia?* The one about the journalist, you know, foreign newspapers stop arriving at his office, and then one thing leads to another, and he loses his job, his wife, everything . . . ?"

The thing was, I could only vaguely remember the film, and I already regretted such a clumsily chosen example.

"I remember," said Kapuściński. "I was the journalist."

2. The Professor Thumbs His Ears

It's an icy January in Amsterdam, unusual for the wet Dutch winters. In the warmth of my writing room, I perform my morning ritual—flicking through the online newspapers, Croatian ones among them. My eye lingers on a particular photograph: an old man with a naughty-little-boy expression on his face, looking straight at the reader, and "thumbing his ears." To thumb your nose at someone, you put your thumb on the tip of your nose and wiggle your fingers. Thumbing your ears is the same, but you use both hands; thumbs in your ears, you wiggle your fingers like a monkey. Both gestures are infantile and mocking, on a par with poking your tongue out at someone. Both went out of fashion years ago.

I know the smile. The smile signals that the smiler is conscious of having "misbehaved" (maybe he's lied, stolen, cheated, hit someone, tripped someone up, or even "broken wind" in someone's presence), but he still tries to mollify the victim. The smiler doesn't consider his smile an apology, but rather a victory. Hence the cheeky shine in his eyes. It's not the smile of the culpable, but of the self-assured master of the situation; it's the smile of the putative servant who is in fact served by others. It's the smile of the swindler giving you the finger, his hands buried in his pockets.

Many of the men in my former homeland smirk like this. It's the way the men of the Serbian parliament sniggered at the beginning of the war (I'm sure there's a video somewhere). Obviously bored, one threw a paper ball at another's head, and suddenly it was laughs all around. The TV cameras started rolling, the ball was thrown on, and for a brief moment the parliamentary session resembled a rowdy schoolroom, full of little boys. But outside those walls, because of those same little boys, little boys grown fat, old, and gray, a war merrily raged.

The interview with the old man, a university professor, was the five-minute media crown placed on his head by the Croatian weekly *Globus.* From the interview we learn that the professor is a Pole by birth; that he came to Zagreb with his family in 1931; that his mother was Polish and was forced to convert to the Orthodox church; that he was baptized in an evangelical church in Zagreb (his mother thus making amends); that he had come to love Croatia; that he'd joined the Partisans, capturing two Germans; and that during the war he had a Jewish girlfriend (*which wasn't easy*, he says), for whom he acquired papers and helped out of Zagreb to the safety of the Adriatic coast. Last but not least, the respected professor of Russian literature signals his disdain for "demanding" literature (*let the super demanding readers read Krleža for the hundredth time, let them read the pick of the foreign writers*), explaining that he'd rather read local Croatian "neighborhood" literature, that intended for the mainstream reader, among whom the professor counts himself (*we, mainstream readers*).

What do these few details tell the hypothetical foreign reader? Nothing in particular. To be fair, the more sensitive foreign reader might find the old professor's bragging about having saved his Jewish girlfriend a little suspect. After all, it's what would be expected of any decent person, particularly given the professor's admission that he was in a position to obtain the necessary documents. It might also occur to our hypothetical foreign reader that the professor was actually signalling to the Croatian public that he himself isn't a Jew, something the politically correct foreigner, unlike the average Croat, might also think a little tasteless. But what do these few details tell any Croatian reader of middle age or older? A lot.

Self-positioning is one of the most vaunted skills in both Croatian media practice and Croatian everyday life, the expression "he's done well for himself" a kind of verbal medal bestowed on the best of the best. Politicians, journalists, writers, and other public figures seem most proficient in doing well for themselves. However, this impression of excellence is only created by virtue of them being public people. Other people get by the best they can.

The professor is the son of a factory owner, but the *Bolsheviks* destroyed the family plant, a fact that automatically elicits compassion in the average Croatian reader (Oh, c'mon: Bolsheviks, Russians, Serbs, they're all the same communist bandits!). By mentioning his baptism, the professor tips his hat to the masses of Croatian Catholics. And as a Partisan in the Second World War, his capture (just capture, not execution!) of two Germans—a feat he puts down to his fluency in German (a little show of erudition!)—positions the professor as a goodly and Godly humanitarian—among the Partisans.

Why does the professor reveal these details so publicly? The timing is completely understandable—he recently published his autobiography. But the reason? Today, these kinds of details are acceptable. Fifteen years ago they weren't. Every public mention of Partisans and anti-fascism provoked an outcry, until a newer government, embodied by the recently-retired Croatian president, changed the tune a little. Of course, the professor didn't mention that he was also a member of the Yugoslav Community Party, as this might still enrage Croatian readers, many of whom were members of the Communist Party themselves, but who, in accord with the times, have diligently deleted this fact from their biographies. Of prime importance is that the professor is a Croatian patriot, and that Croatia is now his true homeland. The professor goes on to boast of a minor, albeit "courageous," bit of mischief in which he was involved: At a student meeting in 1968, he put together a resolution. But he skips over the long "Yugoslav" years after the Second World War. *Every-body knows that as you get older, you increasingly look back and recall the years of your youth, forgetting the more recent ones*—he declares. No one would dispute that one. Old people also forget what they've read over the course of their lives. It's a pity the professor didn't at least remember his countryman, Czesław Miłosz, and his remarkable *The Captive Mind*, or his other countryman, Miroslav Krleža, and his equally remarkable *On the Edge of Reason*.

3. What bugged me?

What bugged me about the interview? And why the ill-tempered objections to an old man basking in a deserved flash of media attention? I know the person in the photograph. I understand his language and recognize the nuances and tones. I catch the scent of every word. I know the local Croatian newspeak, which can change in a split-second, depending on the occasion, and which every once in a while undergoes institutional changes. I react like a finely-tuned sensor, I know that every word is there to nuzzle one ear and inflame the other, that every sentence, even the most banal—whose absence of ambiguity the innocent reader doesn't doubt for a second—is just a new layer of powder on its owner's face.

Why did I take on the dreary task of "unmasking" a completely inconsequential newspaper story? The text is, in any case, untranslatable, and it's untranslatable because it is so deeply contextual. In such a case, attempting translation is like going into battle against Hydra—the translator masochistically agrees to losing in advance.

Try to imagine a situation where a woman who has just been raped tries to give an account of her ordeal, but rather than via the usual channels (the police, the courts, the legal system) is forced to tell her story using the only channel remaining—the "broken telephone."[1] The desperate woman whispers into the ear of one of her neighbors: "They ravished me . . ." The whisper is passed from ear to ear, before the last person in the chain boldly declares: "They lavished me!" Everyone bursts out laughing. The woman tries again, and every time new words pop out the other end. Everyone's having a rollicking time. "You're monsters!" the distressed woman screams. "You're bonkers!" yells the last person in the chain, and everyone again roars with laughter.

The metaphor of the "broken telephone" can be used in regard to all countries of the former Yugoslavia. Having entered every sphere of life, the language of the "broken telephone" is omnipresent: in the media, institutional life, politics, the way people think, their interpersonal relations, their everyday lives. As a result, many crimes remain un-investigated, many victims have been rendered silent, many criminals declared heroes, many thieves business people, many idiots intellectuals (and the odd intellectual an idiot), many perpetrators victims, many victims perpetrators, many crazies normal, and many normal people crazy. As we speak, Radovan Karadžić is playing "broken telephone" at the Hague Tribunal. He brushes off words as if they were pesky little thistles. Every word of the indictment that sounds like *ravish*, he coolly transforms into *lavish*.

The headline of the interview with the professor also reads like it came out the end of a "broken telephone." It says: "Dubravka Ugrešić

---

1   A game also known as Telephone, Chinese Whispers, Grapevine, Whisper Down the Lane, Gossip, Le téléphone arabe, Stille Post, and Gioco del Telefono.

Wasn't Chased Away." But what's my name doing there? And what's with the verb phrase "chased away"? (My first association: to *chase away* pigeons . . .) While the old man is thumbing his ears at me (shoo, shoo, shoo!), the headline is telling me the exact opposite, that I wasn't *chased away*. What kind of nightmare is this?!

I feel as if someone has forcibly catapulted me from my current safe distance in space and time in Amsterdam, January 2010, back into another space and time, to the years 1991, 1992, 1993 . . .

4. Why I Leave the House without an Umbrella

I don't know whether everyone has his or her own personal "inadequacy," but I certainly have mine. I carry it like a birthmark. I'm not even sure that *inadequacy* is the right word; it's more a question of perspective, a way of seeing. Perhaps that colleague, a fellow writer, who long ago brought my "optical deformation" to the attention of the Croatian public, was right. We're inclined to interpret this type of internal failing as the assembly of a conspiracy of details against us; details which over the course of our lives coalesce like little magnetic puzzle pieces, forming our secret parallel biography, an illegible psychogram, an internal map which—in our minds at least—doesn't bear any resemblance to our actual paths in life. This hidden, parallel biography consists of several ambiguous, yet inevitably similar, frustrations or fascinations—a hard-to-trace unease brought on by the same situation and same people; a glow induced by the same gesture or smile; the same small mistakes, obstinacies, and fears . . . As a I child I was always afraid of stairs. Going up wasn't a problem, but I never knew how to go down. Of course I've learned since then, but whenever I look down that childhood fear is always there, lurking somewhere inside me. Little niggling details, nothing too much. Why do I always take the same circuitous route to a particular point in the city? Why is it that this route and not some other remains so stubbornly stuck in my head? Why is it that when I recall certain people I consistently forget their names yet remember details: the way they bow their head, how they worriedly raise their left eyebrow, which gesture follows which particular expression? Why do I persist in going out without an umbrella when it's perfectly obvious that it's going to rain?

5. The ABCs of War

At the beginning of September 1991, my neighbors and I would head down to the cellar of our five-story Zagreb building as the air-raid sirens resounded above. Unlike my neighbors, I didn't take the alarms too seriously. Today I wonder where this "lapse" came from, this arrogance that doesn't take danger "too seriously"?[2]

At the time I firmly believed that the majority of people wouldn't follow their caricature-like leaders, wouldn't destroy everything they'd spent years building together, and wouldn't cast their childrens' futures to the wind. Maybe this belief was to blame for my "lapse." I refused to believe what my impaired vision had witnessed

---

2   Sometime later, the mayor of Zagreb from the time confirmed that the alarms were just a sort of drill to mobilize the people against the enemy. The mayor's casual revelation never reached the collective ear, and to this day, like many other such revelations, it remains forgotten. Why? Because in other places, the alarms were for real. People in Zagreb obviously didn't want to hear that the "threat" they took to be real was in fact a simulation game. The warnings in the daily papers that people be on the lookout for Serbian snipers were a part of this same game. The snipers would apparently ring the doorbell disguised as postmen, or peer from the roofs of Zagreb, disguised as chimney-sweeps. Not a single one was ever caught, neither did any evidence (even false!) of their existence ever materialize. This is but one example of the sea of lies that swamped us. But by the time the lies were finally exposed, no one was prepared to believe the truth anymore.

over the preceding few years. And so it was that in September 1991 I refused to believe the evidence that was right in front of me. Maybe it was actually down there in the cellar, with a small human sample for company, that I should have allowed the dirty little thought to sink in: that many people were actually turned on by the war. New, sudden thrills filled the vacuity of their lives; overnight, personal frustrations found an outlet, personal losses could be made good, personal intolerances hung out to air. There, in the cellar, an older neighbor with rat-like features scurried into my "deformed" field of vision. People said he had illegally moved into the five-bedroom apartment of an old woman who died soon afterwards. The square meters of the apartment thus became his. That very first day in the cellar, he appeared wearing a red armband, a pistol buried in his back pocket. Nobody asked him about the armband or what it meant, or where he got the pistol; we listened intently to his garbled instructions. The very next day the neighbor had a deputy, complete with matching red armband and pocket pistol. The young deputy was unemployed and married to a diligent and hard-working neighbor. At some point her biological clock had started ticking, so she found the young man and bore him three children, after which he'd served and exhausted his purpose. The armband and the revolver gave the jerk his dignity back. Until then, he didn't even know what dignity was.

Switching the volume off, I looked at my neighbors. Then in some small recess of my brain, thanks to my deformed vision, the near future flashed before me: I felt I knew who would be first to sink his teeth into the enemy's throat, who would spend the war in front of the TV, who would rush to denounce his or her neighbor, who would tend the wounds of the inevitable injured, who would lose themselves to depression, who would rouse the rabble, and who would find their way to the money that was to be made. Maybe it was there, in the cellar, that one should have learned the ABCs of war. I, however, threw my fleeting apparitions to the wind like cancelled banknotes.

6. American Fictionary

At the end of September 1991, I hopped on a train for Amsterdam. There I obtained an American visa and headed off to the States to take up a guest lectureship. Getting the visa in Amsterdam proved fortuitous. In Zagreb the embassies, banks, and airport were closed. In New York the realization that my disintegrating country was at war hit home for the first time. For this new misstep, my "deformed vision" was again to blame: what was at that moment so far away suddenly came unbearably close, and I had trouble making out what was right in front of my nose. I was struck down by "cognitive fever," and I exorcised my fears (completely inappropriately) by watching hours of horror films on TV in the small New York apartment where an acquaintance had let me stay. Whenever I actually did venture out of my New York "shelter," I assuaged my fears by meeting up with my fellow countrymen. Most of us were middle-aged, some had come to stay forever, and others, like me, were just passing through. It was a powerful *after-life* experience: there we were on the other side of the world, as if in some nightmarish Mad Hatter's tea party. Actually, not one of us knew for sure what we were going to do with ourselves.

American Fictionary,[3] the book that emerged in those few months,

---

3   Original published as *Americki fikcionar* and published in English as *Have a Nice Day: From the Balkan War to the American Dream*, translated by Celia

was born of my "impaired vision," a series of columns about the American everyday written for a Dutch newspaper.

I didn't ask myself too many questions about what a Dutch reader might make of it all. The authorial situation in which I found myself was at any rate doomed to be a fiasco from the outset. The essays were written in a nervous internal double-voice—one contradicted the other, one supplemented the other, and one bled into the other. In any case, it seems that at least for a moment my *faulty* vision helped me put things in their *right* place.

I returned to Zagreb in June 1992. My feeling of internal "inadequacy" became acute. I again saw everything in duplicate, triplicate, as a copy and in the original. Nothing fit anymore. Titles didn't correspond to images, and the sound was out of synch too. It was no different in the surrounding reality. Familiar streets now had unfamiliar names, familiar faces no longer spoke the same language. People who had been friends until recently contorted their mouths into the strange smile of an unknown other.

At the beginning of September I returned to my regular place of work at the Institute for Literary Theory, which was part of the Faculty of Arts at the University of Zagreb. At first, nothing seemed different, but threatening cracks soon appeared in collegial relations. My colleagues seemed like extras to me, as if they were playing returnees from the front in a third-rate theatre show.

"Leave them, it'll all pass . . ." said a female colleague who had

Hawkesworth (London: Jonathan Cape, 1994; New York: Viking Penguin, 1995).

been in America at the same time as me. "You know, they've suffered, we haven't."

I agreed, although the word "suffered" rung a little hollow, like
the fall of a plastic coin on a plastic surface. I chalked that hollow-
ness of tone up to my "aural deformation."

Over the summer I wrote a short essay entitled "Clean Croatian
Air."[4] At the time souvenir tin cans could be bought at Zagreb
souvenir stands, and this became the essay's central metaphor. The
cans bore the Croatian coat of arms and the slogan: *Clean Croatian
Air.* I made a tally of what and who in Croatia had been cleaned up
by the can's fastidious spirit—Mr. Clean, or Meister Proper. With
the title "Saubere Kroatische Luft," the essay appeared in the October 23rd edition of the German newspaper *Die Zeit,* and a short
while later as "The Dirty Tyranny of Mr. Clean" in the English
Independent on Sunday. It never occurred to me that this short essay,
which I thought had about as much explosive force as a New-Year
firecracker, would actually explode like a bomb in Croatian public
life, or that the tin can metaphor would tighten the noose around
my neck.

7. Croatian Fictionary

In front of me sits a bulging file containing a mass of Croatian
newspaper cuttings from the early 1990s. The newsprint has yellowed a little, the paper become thin. In one breath, it seems this
indifferent heap of newsprint has absolutely nothing to do with me;
in the next, the old paper cuts like a razor. For a moment (just a

---

4   The essay was published in my book *The Culture of Lies* (London: Weiden-
feld and Nicolson; Pennsylvania: Penn State Press, 1998) the first edition of
which appeared in Dutch as *De cultuur van leugens* (Amsterdam: Nijgh & Van
Ditmar, 1995), which was followed a year later by the first Croatian edition,
Kultura laži (Zagreb: Arkzin, 1996).

moment), fresh blood runs from the wound. Then I get the feeling that I'm reading the obituaries, seeing the faces of so many who are no longer among the living. I'm amazed that others are still alive; some people are like tinned goods with no expiration dates, I think. I wonder whether I exist myself, and who's observing whom here: *they* me or me *them*. Then, like an uncoiled spring, a detail I'd never noticed before jumps out at me. With a confidence seemingly backed by hard science, some of the stories point the finger at my ethnic background, others hysterically demand that I *finally* declare it myself. Then my focus switches to dates, and the dates get to me. What at the time seemed like a spontaneous eruption of journalistic vilification of my person now merges into a more consistent story. I bang my head against the paradox as if against a wall: the more consistent the story becomes, the more difficult it is to tell.

My vigilant fellow citizens quickly "cracked" the essay published in *Die Zeit*. The first to denounce me was a journalist employed in the ruling party's "deratization" task force (she later spent many years as the chief editor of Croatian national television), who declared me a *denouncer of the homeland*. A mere two days after my media promotion to "traitor to the homeland" came an attack from the pen of a well-known Croatian writer. My fellow writer not only produced a raft of accusations and general derision aimed in my direction, but also a type of open-ended indictment, suggesting that I was *an internal enemy of the young Croatian state*. With varying degrees of personal creativity, my future media executors would later duly complete it.

Soon after my fellow writer's attack, the president of the Croatian PEN association sent an angry fax from Rio de Janeiro, where the World PEN Conference was being held. The president had gone to

Rio on a crusade, the aim of which was to convince the International PEN committee to nominate Dubrovnik as the venue for the following year's conference. I can only assume that someone there pointed out that it might not be the smartest of ideas to hold the congress in a war zone, but for the audience back home the affronted president decided to translate this detail a little more dramatically. An American writer had apparently raised the question of freedom of the press in Croatia and, again apparently, had also expressed concern about the fate of five (female) "journalists." The very same day, an article entitled "Lobbyists Lose their Voices"[5] appeared (whose author is today the editor of a prominent cultural program on Croatian television), in which five women were accused of conspiracy against Croatia, of attempting to "mine" the future Dubrovnik World PEN Congress, and of deliberately concealing Serbian war crimes, specifically, the rape of Muslim and Croatian women. The World PEN Congress was held in Dubrovnik the following year, and the name of the concerned American writer was never revealed. Why?

---

5   At the time, the Croatian media had individually attacked the journalists Vesna Kesić and Jelena Lovrić, the journalist and writer Slavenka Drakulić, and a professor of philosophy, Rada Iveković. Apparently wanting to conserve energy, they soon came up with a joint indictment for the "five Croatian witches" (me being the fifth). The media haranguing was aimed at convincing the Croatian public that a dangerous feminist-terrorist "cell" was at work, and of the need for unity in the struggle against the internal enemy. We, however, weren't a "cell." Each of us coped with our professional lives and the consequences of our intellectual and moral choices as best we could. In this essay I mention my colleagues only sparingly for two reasons: first and foremost, each of them has the right to tell her own story; secondly, mentioning them would force me to use the pronoun "we," and doing so would mean (inadvertently) contesting their version of events in advance, not to mention dissipating the individual character of these events. This was itself the very aim of the media haranguing—to reduce us all to "broads persecuting Croatia." My reluctance to use the pronoun "we" in no way signals any lack of solidarity with my colleagues, nor, as is my deep conviction, their lack of solidarity with me.

Because the concerned American writer never existed. He or she was a product of the zealous imagination of the president of the Croatian PEN association and his assistants.

The avalanche was triggered. The "case" was crowned by an article in the influential *Globus* weekly, the article being attributed to "the Globus investigative team." Five women—Slavenka Drakulić, Rada Iveković, Vesna Kesić, Jelena Lovrić, and I—were declared "the Witches of Rio." In addition to the story, a table was published containing our dates and places of birth, our educational backgrounds, our ethnicities, our professions, our marital,[6] familial, and employment statuses, details of the real estate we owned, periods we'd spent abroad during the war, "anti-Croatian" quotes taken from our publications, and evidence (or lack thereof) of our membership in the Yugoslav Communist Party.

Although the Globus media fabrication was an incomparably stupid and amateurish piece of work (real experts would have nailed it!), it nonetheless achieved its goal.

When the media lynching had reached its most vicious height, a neighbor stopped me and asked:

"Well then, neighbor, when are you getting **out**?"

The "**out**," I assumed, referred to when I was getting out of Croatia.

---

6   One of the most amusing accusations of the "investigative team" was that we "witches" had generally chosen Serbs as our partners. As they write: "It would be immoral to mention had it not now become clear that what we are dealing with is systematic political choice, not chance coincidence in matters of the heart." ("Hrvatske feministice siluju Hrvatsku" [Croatian Feminists Rape Croatia], *Globus*, December 11, 1992).

"Why should I be getting out?" I asked.

"Well, you keep writing those lies about us."

"And you've read what I write?"

"Why would I? Are you saying that everyone else is lying!?"

And there was nothing you could do about it. Every call to reason led to a more violent madness. In response to the media barrage, I published an essay entitled "Goodnight Croatian Writers,"[7] in Croatian, and in Croatian newspapers. Nobody commented, but two weeks later, like in a game of "broken telephone," the *Globus* investigative team sent the collective response. The confederacy of dunces poked out its tongue and thumbed its monkey ears at me.

My sensitive literary nature can't resist exhibiting a selection of the insults (which refer both to me and the *witch's cell*) proffered by Croatian journalists, writers, and critics, the literati among the literate. I recognize that any psychoanalyst could here accuse me of taking exhibitionist pleasure in the repeated—and this time voluntary—exposition of public insults. But you know what? "Victims" also have a right to narrative pleasure—particularly so if narration is their profession. All in all, in my fellow writers' scribblings I am described as:

A woman with "deformed vision";

A woman who has no understanding for a "people celebrating its own state and freedom of speech";

A woman who has "neither taste nor sense of proportion";

A woman who has opened her mouth "in the wrong manner, the wrong place, and at the wrong time";

---

7   Dubravka Ugrešić, "Laku noć hrvatski pisci" [Goodnight Croatian Writers], *Nedjeljna Dalmacija*, February 25, 1992.

A woman with a "limited perspective";

A woman writer with a "specific talent," whose writing is "scrappy knitting";

A "murderess of the Croatian nation who kills with her pen";

A "broad persecuting Croatia";

A broad who "big mouths, gossips, and denounces";

A woman worthy of "contempt";

A woman in need of a Croatian bonfire "to warm her heart";

A member of "one of the organizational nuclei of international resistance to and defamation of the Croatian Homeland War";

A member of a crew of "slightly unhappy, and at any rate frustrated women";

A "dirty liar";

A "Yugonostalgic";

A "national Daltonist";

A "salon internationalist";

A "spleenful and spiteful surveyor of freedom";

A "squealer offering recipes for freedom from the long-tainted kitchens of the European pseudo-left and pseudo-right";

A woman with "mental problems";

A woman who is "mixed-up";

A woman who "drops her dress in a storm";

A woman ready to "sell her homeland for a hundred German marks";

A woman who for "a little cash, but with obviously great joy, denounces and spits on her homeland";

A "plume of the failed communist regime";

An "informer for the European Community";

A "carefully chosen interlocutor of Brussels and the European Community";

A woman of "dubious repute";

A person "not in the least subjected to harassment";

A "homeless intellectual";

A "grande dame of Croatian post-communism";

A self-immolator (who if she returns to Zagreb "needs to be immediately surrounded by a dozen fire engines, have 300 hoses aimed at her, and whose every word needs to be doused in water");

A "furious woman";

A "Yugo-nostalgic sicko";

A woman who was ready for "a better psychiatric clinic";

A member of a group of "exalted daughters of the revolution";

A "traitor to the homeland";

A "lobbyist who has lost her voice";

A woman "conspiring against Croatia";

A "feminist";

A "feminist raping Croatia";

An "anti-Croatian feminist";

A member of a group of "self-centered middle-aged women who have serious problems with their own ethnic, ethical, human, intellectual and political identities";

A "public enemy";

A woman with a "miserable destiny";

A woman who has "committed moral and intellectual suicide";

A "witch" . . .

Looking back, many of the accusations seem laughable. They weren't at the time. The media recruited people for the war effort day and night, every volunteer was welcome. Ducking out to a neighborhood green grocer's in the summer of 1992, I couldn't take my eyes of a guy in line in front of me who was anxiously buying bananas. It was hot, and he'd stripped down to a singlet and shorts, with a pistol poking out of one of his pockets. Bananas and revolvers—that was a pretty accurate picture of the Croatian everyday at the time.

It was a time when you could buy weapons through newspaper ads, sellers advertising "mother hens," "chicks," and "Kinder Surprises." Mother hen was a synonym for revolver, chicks for bullets, and Kinder Surprises for grenades. There was no accounting for the direction in which a weapon might go off, something I understood best when I saw a newspaper report about a young guy, a returnee from the front, who let off a "Kinder Surprise" in the yard of his former primary school. The darkness of the time swallowed people in different ways.

8. The Dark Corridors of the Arts Faculty

My job at the Institute for Literary Theory was on a multi-year research project entitled *Glossary of the Russian Avant-garde*. The project leader was a professor of Russian literature, who, given his scholarly reputation, had managed to assemble an expert team of contributors from several European countries. The proceedings of our annual scholarly conferences were published in a multi-volume series under the project name, co-edited by the professor and me.

When the aforementioned Croatian bard publicly weighed in on my ethnic, ethical, and literary acceptability, my status at work quickly changed. Having read the guild's evaluation of my case in the news, the very next day my colleagues stopped saying hello or calling in to the Institute's office. Even the professor stopped coming in. My colleagues started meeting in the office after I'd gone home for the day. At first I didn't really understand what was going on; then in time we arrived at a form of unspoken agreement: when I left, they'd come in; when I came in, they'd leave. A colleague and friend, one of the few people to stand by me, witnessed this game, which was, by turns, childish, nasty, and exhausting. He'd often wipe an invisible gob of spit from his face, which, although originally intended for me, every now and then caught him.

Sometime in March or April of 1993 I was supposed to go to New York and give a lecture at NYU. For the first time, approval for a few days leave suddenly became a problem, and at the request of the Dean, I had to produce a written synopsis of my intended lecture. There was nothing about this in the Faculty regulations; it was made up on the fly, expressly for me. Despite that, I still refused to believe that my colleagues and friends believed in the "justice" of the media lynching. Somewhere deep inside I was ashamed both *for* and *instead of* them.

Those few months I worked on arrangements for our regular annual conference, which that year (1993) was held in May, the theme of which was totalitarianism and art. It seemed deeply ironic to me that my fellow scholars were writing papers about a time in which literature and art were subject to strict ideological diktats—about socialist realism, censorship under Stalin, and the lethal absurdities of totalitarian thinking—when, at the same time, fresh fascist and totalitarian fragments from the Croatian everyday slunk by in front of their noses. It was a time in which a notoriously soc-realist exhibition by the now forgotten sculptor, Kruno Bošnjak, was honored and lauded, when books by "unsuitable" authors (Serbs, communists, non-Croats, Yugoslavs, and so forth) were consigned to the scrapheap. It was a time when stickers with a traditional three-strand pattern were proudly affixed to books by "ethnically clean" Croatian writers, when media censorship, particularly on radio, television, in schools, and the publishing industry, was the rule, not the exception. At the time, Vinko Nikolić, a returnee from the diaspora, former member of the Ustasha government of the Independent State of Croatia, and architect of the pamphlet *On Ustasha Literature*, was one of the most prominent figures in Croatian cultural life. Mile Budak, a minor writer, and the architect of the racial laws in Ante Pavelić's same Nazi state, was the literary discovery of the season. It was a time in which black and white propaganda-like texts were everywhere, and the figure of Ivan Aralica, a Member of Parliament and Croatian President Franjo Tuđman's favorite writer, established the new Croatian literary canon. It was a time when witches burned on media bonfires, when the Minister of Culture declared that only ethnically pure Croats were eligible to teach Croatian literature and the Croatian language. And it was a time when many street names were changed, and when renaming the street on which the Faculty of Arts was located became the subject of serious debate. Named after an "unworthy" Partisan hero, it was to take the name of the "worthy" Mile Budak.

I commented on all of these things, and a few other things too, at our conference on totalitarianism and art. The professor, as if he'd been personally wronged, responded that it was absurd to draw comparisons between Stalinism and "Croatian patriotism brought on by Serbian aggression." Or words to that effect. A female colleague suggested that the things I was saying in front of the foreign fellows were deeply inappropriate, because at that moment *our boys are dying at the front* . . . That phrase, *our boys dying at the front* was the moral chewing gum of the time. "While our boys are dying at the front, you were reading your paper on Bulgakov, and now you're about to head off for dinner with our foreign colleagues," I replied. Or words to that effect.

I didn't go to the dinner. In giving my "inappropriate," "wrong place, wrong time, wrong means" presentation, I also gave myself the sack. It'd been kicking around inside me for months. Actually, when I think about it, I didn't give myself the sack, but sacked them, my "guild"—intellectuals, humanists, professors of literature. They deserved sacking for any number of reasons, but one was enough. At the time, in accordance with instructions from the Croatian Minister of Culture, libraries were cleansed of ideologically "unsuitable" authors and their books. Here and there bonfires burned, often initiated by local librarians, teachers, and pupils.[8] According to the rare journalistic investigation, the books of Ivo Andrić, the only Yugoslav to win the Nobel Prize, were found in the rubbish, as were the books of Thomas Mann. Cult books from my childhood such as Branko Ćopić's *The Hedgehog's House* joined them, and my books kept them company. My colleagues, professors of literature, didn't say a word. Not one of them even batted an eyelid.

When I left the university, a long-time co-worker had the following to say:

"The whole time we actually protected you."

"What do you mean?"

"We could have attacked you, but we didn't, right?"

My co-worker was telling the truth. Really, at the time they were in a position to do all kinds of things, but there you have it, they

---

8   The November 2003 edition of the *Prosvjeta* journal entitled "Bibliocide-Culturcide" was dedicated to the bibliocide that occurred in Croatia in 1991 and 1992, the title a clear allusion to Heinich Heine's famous line, "Das war ein Vorspiel nur, dort wo man Bücher verbrennt, verbrennt man am Ende auch Menschen." (That was only a prelude; where they burn books, they ultimately burn people.)

didn't. Nobody put a bullet in my forehead. In other words—they protected me.

Before leaving, I published an article in the local papers that was ironically entitled "The Right to Collective Censorship."[9] Like my "out-of-control" appearance at the Slavic conference, the article was a final attempt to establish public dialogue. The article was greeted with silence. Playing "broken telephone," retelling and mangling my essays published in newspapers abroad was sweeter and deadlier than open confrontation. The very act of engaging in dialogue presupposes a modicum of respect for both one's interlocutor and for dialogue as a form of communication. The refusal of dialogue means ridicule of the other, their irrevocable human and professional disqualification.

When I told the professor, my long-time collaborator, that I was leaving the university, he said:
   "That's the best thing you can do."
   Not a word more, not a word less. And never another word after.

9. A Special Assignment

The *Globus* magazine's fabrication about the Croatian witches was not "Croatian journalism's most shameful moment," as several journalists (much, much later) labelled it—as it had nothing to do with journalism. It was, rather, a special assignment, and *Globus* was but an obedient solder in the battle. All Yugoslav media, Serbian, then Croatian, worked tirelessly on fueling hatred, on quickening the

---

9   Dubravka Ugrešić, "Pravo na kolektivnu cenzuru" [The Right to Collective Censorship], *Nedjeljna Dalmacija*, June 16, 1993.

ethnic pulse of the slumbering masses, and when the war erupted, they performed "special assignments" with distinction. Openly admitting that they were lying, the media adopted a Croatian journalist's declaration that *where the homeland's concerned, I'm prepared to lie* as their general moral slogan. When Franjo Tuđman came to power in 1990, his party, the Croatian Democratic Union, took control of the majority of media organizations. A number of journalists were fired in the process, while others, the loyal, were rewarded with directorships, editorships, and correspondent postings. Young storm troopers who didn't have any moral dilemmas about their profession were recruited in place of those who had been let go—for these storm troopers had neither morals nor a profession.

Very soon, the media itself circulated lists of people who were intended for media execution. My name was among them. Often telephone numbers would appear alongside the names, a weapon offered to small, anonymous citizens. My personal statistics suggest that my patriotic countrywomen were the biggest fans of the telephone as weapon, their anonymous messages littered with vulgarities about sex with "Chetniks." The calls had an "emancipatory" character for my countrywomen, and many distinguished themselves with their verbal creativity, as if their own erotic phantasies on the given political-military theme were in question.

In this special war the media got a dirty job done, and people suffered and died . . .

Because they had the wrong ethnicity;
Because of their Serbian ethnicity;
Because of the absence of an ethnicity;
Because of a mixed ethnicity;
Because of their Yugoslav ethnicity;

Because of a grandmother who was a Serb;
Because of a grandfather who was a Serb;
Because of a father who was a Partisan;
Because of a mother who was a Communist;
Because of an aunt who was an Anti-Fascist;
Because of their ideological beliefs;
Because of their lack of ideological beliefs;
Because of the absence of religious beliefs;
Because of the wrong religious beliefs;
Because they'd stepped on somebody's toes;
Because they owned a villa at the seaside;
Because the villa caught someone's eye;
Because of a job that caught someone's eye;
Because they were Albanians;
Or Roma;
Or Yugoslavs;
Or "unadjusted" Croats;
Because they were successful;
Because they lacked the will to take sides . . .

These were the sweet strategies of fascism. And from behind the media smokescreen, behind the smoke from the bonfires on which witches burned, the anonymous and unfortunate lost their jobs and homes. Some were beaten black and blue, others killed. Many passed through everyday life as if through a hail of invisible bullets.

The question of media guilt has never been seriously asked. The majority of the journalists from the time—employees of the Croatian media's hate industry—are still in their jobs today. It's true, the language has changed a little, and the strategies are less visible. In any case, today one doesn't need to lie to "defend the bleeding homeland." These days one defends what was acquired over the previous twenty years: property, jobs, a secure retirement, or more simply—a decent biography.[10]

---

10 Celebrating the 500th episode of the program *Pola ure kulture* [Half an Hour of Culture], in the April 2, 2010 issue of the *Globus* weekly (that magazine again!) an interview appeared with the show's host, Branka Kamenski. In the interview, Kamenski speaks of Hloverka Novak-Srzić as her *best friend and ersatz sister*. Novak-Srzić helped Kamenski move from journalist on the *Večernji list* daily to host and editor of what is arguably the only cultural program on Croatian television. Kamenski also recalls her intimate relationship with the Croatian writer Antun Šoljan (*who was one of the most important people in my life; I feel privileged to have known him*, says Kamenski). She also recalls her most important interviews, such as that with the aforementioned Vinko Nikolić, in the course of which she came *face to face not only with Croatian history . . . but also with Nikolić's piercing and incredibly blue eyes*.

Branka Kamenski's "sister" Hloverka Novak-Srzić was the first to denounce me ("Denunciranje domovine" [Denouncing the Homeland], *Glasnik*, November 9, 1992). Two days after Novak-Srzić declared me a "denouncer of the homeland," and a person of suspicious ethnic background (which meant a Serbian background), an article appeared by the previously-mentioned Croatian bard, Antun Šoljan ("Dubravka Cvek u raljama rata" [Dubravka Cvek in the Jaws of War], *Večernji list*, November 11, 1992). (Translator's Note: the title of Šoljan's article is a play on the title of Ugrešić's highly-popular short novel *Štefica Cvek u raljama života* ["Štefica Cvek in the Jaws of Life," 1981], the metafictional chronicle of a klutzy and lovelorn typist's quest to find Mr. Right—and thereby "get a life." The implications of Šoljan's wordplay would have been crystal clear to his Croatian audience.) Šoljan, let's not forget, was one of the most important people in Branka Kamenski's life. Three weeks later, two articles by Kamenski herself appeared ("Lobistice promukla glas" [Lobbyists Lost their Voice], and "Ćorak u Riju" [Dud Bullet in Rio], *Večernji list*, December 5, 1992), which officially opened the media pack hunt on the five Croatian witches. In her *Globus* interview, Kamenski also talks about tennis, her favorite hobby, and there is a photo featuring her favorite tennis partners. In addition to her *ersatz sister*, a man called Slaven Letica is in the line-up. Slaven Letica really has done it all, from being a personal advisor to Franjo Tuđman to himself standing for President as an independent. Among other things, he was also the initiator and author of the *Globus* fabrication,

Sitting pretty with their sinecures, and fêted with local literary prizes, the lions and lionesses of Croatian literature have today expropriated the "witches' discourse," retrospectively touching up their images in the process. They know people have short memories, and the truth is, they're right—they live in an amnesiac society and they know it. These people (the majority of whom are men) held their tongues for twenty years, yet today boldly recycle the "witches' letter," nullifying its original authorship, and in doing so, effectively complete the work of the "witch-hunters" of yesterday.

10. The Fairytale of the Small-town Croatian Patriot

The objection of my colleague, the well-known Croatian writer, that I could have shown more *understanding for a people celebrating their own state and freedom of speech* really doesn't stack up. At that moment I understood the so-called "people" better than I understood myself. I know the biographies of dozens of "small-town" Croatian patriots; I'm intimately familiar with the psychogram that creates yes-men. I've learned when, why, and who will make a grab for the flag,

---

Globus, December 11, 1992), published only six days after Kamenski's early efforts.

Today, eighteen years later, Branka Kamenski claims that: *On television we were the first to address the question of dissidents in the new Croatian state, Dubravka Ugrešić, Slavenka Drakulić, Slobodan Šnajder. It was 1996 . . .* Referring to me she adds: *I particularly admire Dubravka Ugrešić, I think she's one of our best writers and it's regrettable that during the war she wrote essays like "Clean Croatian Air." I like books that I remember, and hers are such.*

The contents of this footnote could create the false impression that the "Witches of Rio" affair was simply the concoction of a homespun "cottage industry," of a group of people who enjoyed media power at the time (which they still enjoy today). The witch-hunt, however, was but one example of a strategy designed to silently and systematically cleanse Croatia of all manner of "internal enemies." The refusal to acknowledge this fact is still in force today.

who'll be first to scramble off in defense of their country, defending it as if their personal dignity were at stake. Because for many people, the homeland is a synonym for personal dignity; particularly for those who have nothing else.

I knew Ivica (let's give him a common Croatian name) from high school. He was two or three years older than me, and had he not suddenly re-entered my life, I would have completely forgotten him. Who knows, maybe back in high school I accidentally stepped on his toes. Ivica fell into that category of losers who everyone gave a clip around the ears.

Ivica later studied History at the University of Zagreb, eventually finding work as a secondary school teacher. When I happened to run into him many years later, my heart ached. His status obviously hadn't changed much. Scruffy, with a wispy beard (completely unfashionable at the time), wearing a suit that was several sizes too big, hair thinning despite only being in his thirties, a black public servant's briefcase in hand, Ivica perfectly fit the stereotype of the teacher whose pupils stick funny notes on his back. At the time he was living in a rented apartment and whined about his measly pay and rowdy pupils.

But then, at an international history seminar, he met the woman of his dreams, the beautiful daughter of a pair of doctors from an Eastern European capital. Blonde, translucent, pale, with dark rings under her big green eyes, she looked like she'd grown up on cocaine, not kefir. Ivica, like a hero from a Russian fairytale, crossed seven state borders and seven bureaucratic valleys, before finally bringing his blonde-haired beauty back to Zagreb. Fortune had smiled on him, his school came to the party and gave him an apartment, a child was on the way, and even the rowdy kids at school learned a few manners. But when the child was born, his wife filed for divorce. Ivica, it seems, was for her but a first step on the stairway of her life's aspirations. So Ivica exited his recently-acquired familial bliss and returned to the lonely life of a tenant.

And then, like a surprising burst of sunshine after the rain, like hitting the lottery jackpot, She, the Homeland, appeared. And Ivica promptly signed up, stood in the first rows, bowed to the great leader of the Croatian people, and hustled his way into parliament. Along the way he publicly lobbed several gobs of spit at me. Here, with all my heart, I offer him my forgiveness. What's more, for his personal happiness, I am also ready to turn the other cheek.

The Homeland gave him a new, spacious apartment, and—people say—a personal chauffeur, although it's possible the chauffeur is simply a product of my empathetic imagination. He had everything now. He just didn't have a wife, and for a Croatian politican and a Catholic, this was a not insignificant obstacle to a more serious career. So Ivica (I mean, what else could he do?) proposed to his "cocaine blonde" for a second time, and there you go, the smart woman accepted. From then on we saw her on television every time an Eastern European delegation was in town, serving as President Tuđman's personal translator.

And then Ivica's numbers again came up in the Homeland lottery, and he was awarded an ambassadorial posting in—oh, what a surprise—his wife's Eastern European capital. I imagine his first ambassadorial reception: Ivica, the child of a Croatian peasant, being welcomed by his father and mother-in-law, the doctors. I imagine how all those bumps and bruises vanished in the air. I imagine the in-laws, the doctors, diplomatically bowing and curtsying to their son-in-law. Instead of snotty wee Ivica, a weedy Croatian peasant from the backwoods, they were being received by the Croatian ambassador. The pauper, to whom they had so clumsily abandoned the one-and-only apple of their eye, had become a prince!

I don't know how things ended up, but it seems that Ivica is no longer an ambassador. Maybe he is still warming a chair somewhere, but in any case the TV cameras have moved on. The Croatian state apparatus is slowly ridding itself of its storm troopers. Storm troopers, they say, destroy the image of Croatia as it seeks to enter the European Union. Ivica is an almost textbook case of an ur-fascist psychogram. And people with these kinds of "valuable" psychograms are never put out to pasture; they're just put on ice.

11. Mom

I resigned from the Faculty of Arts in June 1993 and spent the autumn in southern Germany. The following year I was to take up a scholarship in Berlin, but what I'd do and where I'd go after that, I had no idea . . .

Although I had left Croatia, Croatia had difficulty leaving me. It kept boomeranging back, hysterically reminding me of the fact that I belonged to her, meaning that I would always belong to her, and that it was up to her to decide whether she would *ravish* me or *lavish* me. All over Europe the tribe shuffled along behind me, sitting in on my literary readings, bickering and squabbling, hurling caustic remarks, crudely interrupting my appearances with the same accusatory repertoire. The tribe would appear in the guise of a grey-haired old man in Vienna, scribbling in a notebook like an old-school police informant; as a highly-strung woman in Copenhagen, who waved an invisible thermometer tkaing the temperature of my patriotic commitment; as a young teacher of Croatian in Bonn, who (having first proudly declared that she hadn't read a single one of my books) accused me of using too many Serbian words in my writings; as the haughty representative of the Croatian Catholic community in Berlin, who at (my!) literary readings accused me of destroying the Croatian tourism industry. Of course, none of these people ever gave their first or last name. The tribe introduced itself with the pronoun "we."

Sometimes Croatia would perfidiously follow me around in the form of nasty gossip, as a wave of letters to the *Neue Zürcher Zeitung* from Swiss Croats, who, encouraged by the slippery Croatian cultural attaché in Zurich, vented their rage every time I published an article. Sometimes Croatia would show its institutional face, such as when the Croatian embassy in Sofia approached my Bulgarian publisher with an offer to buy the entire print run of *The Culture of Lies*. At the time the Croatian ambassador to Sofia was a fellow writer, a poet; he knew best what my book was about. Sometimes Croatia would appear at a book fair, where **they**, Croatian writers, would stand on one side and **me** on the other. My colleagues would perform their complicated pantomime, walking past *as if they didn't see me*, while at the same time letting me know that *they didn't see me*.

My mom was my biggest supporter. After I'd already left Zagreb, anonymous fellow-citizens would terrorize her on the telephone.

"Is that Mrs. Ugrešić?"

"Yes," my Mom would reply.

"The mother of the writer Ugrešić?!"

And when my naïve mother would proudly answer that it was indeed "Ugrešić-the-writer's mom" on the line, they'd launch into

the most vile diatribe imaginable. Once, a self-declared representative of the small town where I was born announced to her that *they*,
the townspeople, were *disowning* me.

"How can they disown you, they're not your mother!" she joked
to me.

Other times she'd grumble . . .

"Stop with all that 'writing,' they'll take my pension away because
of you," she'd protest.

"Would you rather they take your pension away or see me at a
reception for Tuđman?" I asked, putting her to the test.

"I'd die of shame if I saw you on television with Tuđman, which
wouldn't be a bad thing, because then I wouldn't need a pension any
more," she'd reply, and we'd both burst into laughter.

Sometimes I'd get down about everything, not knowing how to
cope with others' hatred.

"Imagine how you'd feel if they loved you!" mom would cheer-
fully console me.

And then sometimes she'd again get down, grumpily asking herself why fate had given her, of all people, such a stubborn daughter.

"Imagine what it was like for Joseph Brodsky's parents!" I'd blurt
out.

"Yes, but you're not Brodsky!" she'd shoot back.

And we'd both break into mutually reassuring laughter.

Now, from that mess—where on one side "the facts" take the form
of a nonsensical heap of newsprint, and on the other sits my "deformed" memory—my mother emerges as the rare face of common
sense. And if someone were to push me up against a wall and force
me, after so many years, to respond to the nonsensical question of
whether I have a Croatian homeland at all, I'd respond that I do,

that it is my mother, a Bulgarian. To my deep sadness, mom recently departed the world of the living.

12. Pigeon Chasers

Let's go back to where we began, to the photograph of the professor thumbing his ears at me, and the headline letting me know that I wasn't "chased away." Asked whether he follows what I write these days, he responds, "Since she's been abroad, no. On the one hand, it's a question of personal relationships, and on the other, the fact that she willingly left here. She wasn't expelled, nobody drove her out, she left to take up a scholarship . . . I wasn't prepared to accept her essayistic work. We parted company the very moment she started to think of it as her 'war' abroad, and began promoting herself as a dissident, an exile."[11]

The professor could have responded to the question by simply admitting that he wasn't familiar with my work since I went abroad. It would have been a less than flattering response for a professor of literature, but an understandable one all the same. Although they didn't ask him whether I had *willingly* left Croatia, whether I was *expelled* or *driven out*, he felt the need to lie. He qualifies my literary work as *essayistic* (how would he know if he hasn't read it?) and says that he parted company with me (falsely implying that there had been a dialogue) the moment I started thinking of my essayistic work (unworthy of intellectual attention) as a war conducted from abroad (I shot from the pen hunkered in a foreign bunker). In the considered opinion of this respected expert in the literature of the

11 "Dubravka Ugrešić nije otjerana" [Dubravka Ugrešić Wasn't Chased Away], *Globus*, January 22, 2010.

Russian avant-garde, I apparently promote myself as a dissident and exile (my position is, therefore, fake, inauthentic).

Why does the professor get off on all of this? How is it that, after a good eighteen years, when the bonfires have already gone out, he suddenly plucks up the courage to publicly strike a match, employing the same rhetoric as his predecessors? Of course, back then he secretly blew the flames, but only now has he decided to break his silence. The professor knows only too well that he lives in a milieu where people have no moral principles, but, that said, they do have the milieu. As Miroslav Krleža put it, *it stinks among the people, but at least it's warm.* And the professor prefers the warmth. Fear of exclusion from the group is evidently one of the most powerful human fears, such fears being inculcated when one is first excluded from a children's game, a children's birthday party, or left out by one's classmates. Fear of exclusion from the group is the basis of every fascism. No one is exempt from this fear, and the professor is no exception.

Why did *Globus* choose the headline "Dubravka Ugrešić Wasn't Chased Away"? *Globus* needed the professor's authority to confirm that eighteen years ago its investigative team really was in the right. But why now? A short time before the interview was published, *Globus* lost the lawsuit that it had dragged out for a full seventeen years. Apart from having to pay out a small amount in damages for "burns" I received in the media bonfire, the terms of the settlement also obliged *Globus* to publish the judge's decision in full. Publishing the ruling would mean a public admission of moral defeat, something *Globus* has successfully avoided for years. Instead, *Globus* published the interview with the professor. The headline—"Dubravka Ugrešić Wasn't Chased Out"—rings out like a definitive verdict, letting everyone know who wears the pants in the Croatian home.

In the very act of expressing public contempt for his former student and long-time collaborator, the elderly professor dispatched a hoary pedagogical message: every individual act of disobedience (she left *willingly!*), every rebellious voice must be punished. The milieu is good and righteous, and its prodigal daughters and sons (essayists, dissidents, exiles) deserve every reproach. The elderly professor— the editor of an anthology bearing the inspiring title *Heretics and Dreamers*, a promoter of Russian avant-gardists and the literary term *the poetics of dispute*—sadly missed his mark. Rather than a moral arbiter, he served as a mere pigeon chaser. A pigeon chaser?!

My Zagreb apartment had a large balcony, which, being constantly overrun by pigeons, wasn't particularly attractive. My neighbors had the same problem. No one had any idea of how to get rid of the nuisance. One day an injured pigeon appeared on my neighbors' balcony. The neighbors felt sorry for it and nursed it back to health, and in return, the pigeon, a female, became as loyal as a household pet. Then one day she brought a "boyfriend" home to the balcony. The neighbors also accepted the "boyfriend" and regularly fed the couple. As a sign of his gratitude for the regular crumbs, the "boyfriend" became a "policeman," diligently expelling other pigeons from the balcony. The elderly professor threateningly gnashed his blunt beak in my direction, feebly flapping his wings. He did so in return for a few empathetic crumbs thrown to him by the hand of the warm Croatian hearth.

There is another interesting pigeon-related coincidence to speak of here. After my *willing* departure from the university, the *Glossary of the Russian Avant-garde* changed its name to the *Zagreb Glossary of Twentieth Century Culture*. Why the change? I'm certain the professor initiated this little repositioning. In the political context of the time, *Russian Avant-garde* had an irritating ring. For Christ's sake, somebody might think that an elite group of international Slavic scholars was scheming its way around Croatia, advocating the return of communism, revolution, the avant-garde, lobbying for the Russians and who knows what else. At the time, Croatia was screaming into the ether that it was a European and a Catholic country, that it was the sacrificial shield defending European culture from the hordes of invading Orthodox barbarians. Naturally, the scholarly team and its field of research remained the same, only the name changed. The eventual danger that someone might have lumped the professor in with the "Eastern bandits" because of Bulgakov-the-Orthodox-Christian or Malevic-the-Serb was skillfully averted. There was one other significant innovation. A certain Ivan **Golub** (which in Croatian means "pigeon" and is a fairly common name), a theologian, lay minister, and poet, was tasked with writing the customary introduction to the *Zagreb Glossary of Twentieth Century Culture*. How did Ivan Golub manage to join a team of scholars working on the Russian avant-garde? Ivan Golub symbolically performed the same role as the ever diligent Croatian priests of the day (a role they still perform today): he poured holy water over everything—newly purchased hospital equipment, new kindergartens and schools, newly-asphalted roads, new tractors, newborn babies. In his introductions (not lacking in expertise I might add), Ivan Golub blessed and poured holy water over this literary and scholarly anthology, exorcising all manner of impurities, not to mention "witches" of all stripes. All things told, the professor found a priest, the priest found a professor, and together they were stronger.

13. Bizarre News from the Third World

At a September 2009 meeting in Geneva, United Nations officials, individual country representatives, activists, and NGO workers expressed their concern at the increasing prevalence of witch-hunting in poor, mostly rural areas of India, Africa, and Asia. Most of the victims are women and children.

Although experts maintain that reliable statistics are hard to come by, according to Indian sources in Asam and Western Bengal, an estimated 750 women have been killed since 2003. Suspected witches are terrorized by members of their own communities: they have their heads shaved, are stripped naked and forced to walk through the village, are beaten with sticks, branded with hot irons, buried alive, tied to trees, set on fire, and forced to endure deadly tests. One of the tests, a *pareksha*, involves a woman being forced to pick up a coin from the bottom of a pot of burning oil: if her hand comes out unscathed, it means she's not a witch, if it burns, she is. As a practice, witch-hunting usually has hidden pragmatic motives. In India the burning of witches is a local form of geronticide, a way for the community to eliminate a mouth that is no longer capable of earning its bread. Studies show that in India witch-hunting increases in years of drought. Accusing the witches of having cursed the crop, the community—the collective executor—rids itself of its "useless" elderly members. In places such as Tanzania and Congo, victims are also most often elderly women from poor rural households.

The practice of witch-hunting has recently experienced exponential growth in Papua New Guinea. The country is home to ninety percent of all AIDS sufferers in the Pacific islands, and recently surpassed Uganda in total numbers of those infected with the virus. The island nation's inhabitants blame witches (who they refer to as *sangume*) for the spread of the disease, subjecting them to terror that most often ends in murder.

A particularly worrying trend is the increase in child molestation, where children, irrespective of their gender, are proclaimed witches by their communities. Estimates suggest that tens of thousands of children live on the streets of Kinshasa, the majority of whom have been disowned by their parents on the suspicion that they are witches. The real reason is poverty, and the accusers are parents who are unable to care for their large broods. A leading role in the brutal practice is played by local priests, who conduct hearings (determining who's a witch, and who's not) and perform torture in the form of exorcism, which involves forcing children to drink nitric acid. Needless to say, the priests are paid for their services.

African albinos are also an endangered group, as it is believed that certain parts of their bodies serve as antidotes to witches' spells. Children are particularly vulnerable, and the terrifying practice of live organ harvesting is not uncommon, the organs being ingredients in a purported anti-serum.

In witch practice there is also a phenomenon known as *koro* or penis snatching. The phenomenon was first documented in China and other Asian countries, but the more recent examples can be found in Africa (Congo, Nigeria, Cameroon, Ghana, Gambia). Men occasionally become engulfed in the collective hysteria, believing that their penises have disappeared. Anyone can be accused of penis theft: "witches," "black men"(!), people wearing a "gold ring," "the devil's right-hand," a mysterious "stranger." The penises of the affected supposedly disappear after they have shaken hands with any such person. Enraged, the "dismembered" men physically turn on the "thief." An unfortunate Sudanese accused a "Zionist agent who was sent to Sudan to prevent the procreation and propagation of our people" for the theft of his penis.

Witch-hunts involve two kinds of participant: accusers, or *witch-smellers*, and executors. Although banned, in some African cultures (the Bantu culture, for example) the practice of witch-hunting is yet to be eradicated. Dressed in ceremonial clothing, the witch-smellers, usually women, perform a ritual designed to flush out the witch or witches. Members of the tribe sit down in a circle and, accompanied by rhythmical handclaps, begin a hypnotic, ritualistic chanting, until at a given moment the witch-smeller goes into a state of trance. Whomever the witch-smeller touches in her trance is deemed to be a witch; it could be one or many people. Their fellow tribesmen drag the accused from the circle, summarily executing them. Sometimes the rituals go on for days, and sometimes they end in a tribal self-slaughter. Animals can also be witches. The accuser, the witch-smeller, eats raw animal flesh in order to enter the animal's spirit and refine her hunting instincts.

14. Accusers and Executioners

Today, almost twenty years later, I see many similarities between the living tribal practice of witch-hunting and my own "witch" case. In the early nineties, the Croatian tribe fell into a state of collective trance. Shamans, tribal leaders, and the media, beating their drums day and night to the rhythm of "the-nation-endangered," led them into the trance. The shamans (ritually draped in the Croatian flag) called their fellow tribesmen to the hunt. The people ate raw meat to refine their instincts, their appetites only increasing when they saw they would go unpunished, and that the other side was doing the same. Their snouts now sophisticated, they became either accusers or executioners. The yellow witch fever dimmed the lights in many people's heads. A handful of disobedient women were the first to be publicly denounced; others had their turn later. The women were accused of colluding with the devil, of casting spells and betraying tribal custom, spoiling the harvest and spreading illness, and were deemed responsible for the tribe's misfortune. As punishment, the Croatian witches were subject to public humiliation, media terror, intimidation, contempt, verbal attacks, ostracism, slander, and vicious gossip. They were stripped of intellectual employment, the right to dialogue, and as public figures—actresses, professors, journalists, and writers—removed from public life. Their families were subject to harassment and intimidation, and collective and personal letters were sent to foreign universities, journalists, writers, and translators, all with the express purpose of denying the women access to a public platform or any kind of professional opportunity. It's true, not one of the accused women was beaten or killed. But far from the media storm, other, anonymous people were. The "witches" served as media surrogates, as fairground attractions, as free dartboards erected on town squares, as the cheapest way to homogenize the people against "internal" and "external" enemies.

Having become shamans, arbitrators, and *witch-smellers*, my fellow writers and scholars bit into my flesh. In their patriotic trance they denounced me, and then it was open season. At the start—when many came running to burn me on the media bonfire; when the telephone rang at all hours of the day, vomiting threatening messages in my ear; when those same writers and scholars performed their pathetic, third-rate pantomime (a head that turns away in disgust, a glance suddenly lowered on meeting mine), demonstrating—less to me, and more to the milieu—that I had been cast from the circle; when everyone sought a way to perform his or her loyal duty to the new regime, and it was easiest to spit on a "witch"—I still interpreted their hatred as an indirect call for dialogue. But pragmatic, powerful, and efficient, the machinery of hate picked me up and launched my broom on a powerful tailwind. And I flew.

Today, like a dreary re-run twenty years later, everything has been reduced to a photograph of an old man monkeying around and thumbing his ears at me. Now I finally understand: my "deformed perspective" was to blame. I overestimated my "milieu." Its volume is much smaller and its substance less distinctive than I thought. I underestimated its resistance: it's much stiffer and stronger than I thought.

So, what really happened? I *abandoned* my milieu, I left *willingly*, and it poked its tongue out at me, the only thing it knew how to do. It didn't bother reading my books—that would have meant dialogue, and I might have believed that, in spite of everything, I'd actually managed to "knit" something its size. But it had always valued its own "mainstream," oral literature, and that's why it believed the rumors produced in its own factory. So, really, nothing happened. And not a damn thing is happening—even that telephone is always broken . . .

So, my fellow tribesmen, let's give it one more try, loud and clear this time: Yes, I left *willingly*. No, you didn't *chase* me away, I *abandoned* you. No, you didn't *part company* with me, I did with you. You didn't *disqualify* me, you disqualified yourselves. You didn't *fire* me, I fired you, yes, *you*. And Professor, as far as you're concerned, I have no qualms in saying what you somewhere already know yourself: No, I didn't fail the exam; you did.

In the twenty intervening years many people have disappeared, many have had their biographies burned, many live elsewhere, many lives have been stolen, many lie under the earth, many live buried alive, many of the guilty still walk free, but the majority of my fellow citizens are still around. My fellow citizens still pick their noses and "break wind," still sit around in cafés, slag off and suck up to one another, drink their coffee, spend their Saturdays loafing about the town square, which has of course changed its name, but even that doesn't really change anything. They scuttle to the market, bargain and barter, buy fresh cottage cheese and cream, read the papers, blink in the sun, mix and mingle, flip each other the bird, nod their heads, exchange air kisses, and good-naturedly feed the pigeons that are strutting around the square. For a few crumbs both people and pigeons are ready to get off their backsides, flap their wings and flash their beaks, all for a crumb more. But that's nothing new; life continues on much the same as it always has.

15. Penis-Snatching

Sometimes I have a laugh imagining how I'd respond if my former immolators—professors who thumb their ears, colleagues, merry rodent exterminators, jokesters, intellectuals, rabble-rousers, witch-smellers, armchair critics, informers, ridiculers, smart-asses, amnesiacs, patriots and patriotesses—would just ask . . .

"Why did we singe you a little back then?"

And I think about how to respond; I'm a writer, I should know what might inflame the ears of my pyromaniac people.

"You'd fallen into a national collective trance. *Koro* . . ." I whisper into the ear beside me.

"Koro!?" the person frowns.

"In some parts of Africa men succumb to a collective hysteria. They're convinced that their penises have disappeared, that someone stole them. And so the angry mob of supposedly dismembered men sets off to hunt down those who are suspected of mutilating them."

"I don't understand a word you're saying. What have Africans got to do with you? Or with us?!"

"I'm speaking in metaphors. Back then, twenty years ago, you accused me of making off with your collective, national thing. Your symbolic thing, naturally . . ." I whisper to the person beside me.

"But it can't have been just about men? What about the women?"

"As protectors of the national virtue, the women were also involved in stringing up the suspected thieves."

The people in the chain start to grumble.

"C'mon, get it together! We haven't got all day!" they yell impatiently.

"Well, what shall I tell the person beside me?" he asks, genuinely confused.

"Now I don't even know anymore . . ."

"Why did you end up on the bonfire? Tell me, just make it quick," he said.

"Because I stole your penis," I whisper.

The owner of the ear nods his head, he understands, and he tells the person next to him, and the words are whispered from ear to ear. It's a long chain.

"Because I stole your pride!" yells the last person finally.

It seems that the only remaining channel of communication—the broken telephone—actually still works.

"Yes, because I stole your pride," I confirm.

My pyromaniacs almost laugh their heads off.

The wind gently licking my face, I take my broom and silently steal away. I look down and my countrymen wave happily, their smiling leaf-like faces turned skywards. From this height they look like cabbages left to grow in an abandoned field. Beneath them, in the dirt, human corpses are rotting. They help the cabbages grow bigger and shinier. Or is that just how things appear to me? I admit, it's all a question of perspective, and we're all responsible for our own. And, light as a feather, I ride the wind.

April 2010

4.

THE COOKIE THAT MADE A FRENCHMAN FAMOUS

THE FLY

1.

It was like a mystical revelation. I remember it. Having cleared passport control, I was sitting in a café at the airport in Budapest waiting for my flight. OK, let's not get carried away, it wasn't a revelation, let alone a mystical one—more like the gentle prick of an acupuncture needle, the prick of recognition. Glancing idly at the contents in the display cabinet—sandwiches trying to become "European" and cakes fortunately trying to remain "Hungarian"—I saw it: a fly languidly meandering along the inside of the smeared plastic. The imaginary acupuncture needle hit a random spot and provoked a mental twinge, which sent the untranslatable Russian word *rodnoe* (roughly meaning kindred, close, familiar) flashing across my internal screen. Russian words don't usually happen upon me out of the blue. This one dropped from my internal thesaurus like a burly winter fly.

Communism had fallen; Hungarians had flocked to newly-opened shopping centers; IKEA furniture had begun its occupation of

Hungarian homes; the grand houses of Budapest had ditched their dilapidated façades and slipped on crisp new ones; unsightly communist sculptures had been shunted to the distant Memento Park. But the fly, it was as if the sprays of transition hadn't even come close. It sauntered past like a middle finger aimed at transition enthusiasm. I hate insects, the lot of them, but contemplating this Hungarian fly, a *légy*, I felt a wholly ambiguous feeling of conciliation. I swear it was only later that I read somewhere about the fly as protector of the balance of Mother Nature, and about the special place it occupies in American Indian mythology.

Not long afterwards I traveled to Warsaw. Once again at an airport café, my gaze wandered over the food display, and there it was: this time a Polish fly, its little legs languidly crawling along inside the plastic cabinet. *Myxa, moucha, mucha, muva, muha* . . . Sofia, Krakow, Prague, Warsaw, Belgrade, Skopje, Moscow, Zagreb, Sarajevo . . . With a practiced eye, I now searched it out in the cafés of Central and Eastern European airports, and each time I spotted it, I'd feel the same ambiguous sense of relief. Eastern Europe is not lost. The fly is here. Everything is in its place. Something like that.

2.

Literary festivals criss-cross the European continent. Today, even the smallest European towns and cities have their own literary festival, and every writer in Europe, whoever he or she may be, is deluged with invitations. Even if a writer decides not to attend, sending off polite refusal letters takes more time than grabbing a suitcase and jetting off for a couple of days in Köln, Mantua, or Ohrid. Festival organizers treat writers like penniless tourists, or at any rate, like people who are happy to flit from one place to the next in search of a little gratification. Festivals are a chance for writers to get out from behind their desks, or to spend a few days somewhere they'd never go of their own accord, or to meet readers and do a little work on their chronically tattered self-confidence—or, as is most often the case, all of the above. At literary festivals the writer is putty in the hands of the youthful organizers, who, kitted out with mobile phones and little headsets, can barely remember the writer's name. So writers wander around with little name badges pinned to their lapels. With a well-practiced eye, your interlocutor's gaze flicks down to your name tag, snaps your surname in a second, and then glances back up, looking at you like you've known each other forever.

All the activities at literary festivals are geared towards festival visitors, the potential reading public. Random people come up to you with a photo they've downloaded from the Internet asking for your autograph, although, incidentally, you barely recognize yourself. The photo was of course taken and uploaded by some chancer who had never entertained the idea of asking permission. You wonder why they want the autograph, and what any of this has to do with literature, so at first you refuse, but a second later you reproach yourself for your arrogance, and resignedly sign your name. And then there are the autograph cranks with their bits of paper, notepads, and programs: Yes, there, please, next to where your name is printed, yep, below's fine too. During your appearance—either on your own or as part of group, where you have two minutes to explain who and what you are, and five minutes to read something—the mobile phone generation sit holding their phones above their heads, and snap away at random, taking pictures of who knows what and God knows why. Then, transfixed, they start fiddling with their slinky toys, caressing the display, tapping away as if they're solving a mathematical puzzle, flashing pictures to each other for a quick peek. Then there are those who come up holding a copy of your book. You're nicer to them, like a teacher with her star pupils, only to realize in the next breath that they've got you mixed up with someone else. If you correct them, an apologetic, slightly derisory smile flickers across their faces: They never thought you'd be so sensitive!

The majority, however, just come to check you out: what you look like, how you speak, how you hold yourself, whether you match the picture they've created of you—assuming they even have one at all. Some come to learn a little about where you're from, others to reminisce about a distant holiday (*Yes, we went there one summer, a beautiful island, Hu..ar! Hvar? Yes, yes, Hvar!*). Some of them gawk at your shoes, others at your outfit. With all the staring, you feel a dizzy spell coming on and clutch at a copy of your book, as if it were a railing that could save you from a possible fall.

Most people attend literary festivals out of a childlike curiosity about creativity (*How does that work, you just sit down and write a novel?! What inspired you to become a writer? Are you more creative in the morning or in the evening? How long does it take you to write a novel?*) You and your writerly persona are second fiddles; it's all about the secret of creativity, whose chance flag bearer you are—I mean, you've got the proof, haven't you? For crying out loud, it's right there in front of your nose, bound in your book.

The secret of creativity is where the fundamental misunderstanding between writer and festival visitor lies. As Joseph Brodsky wrote, "seen from the outside, creativity is the object of fascination or envy; seen from within, it is an unending exercise in uncertainty, and tremendous school for insecurity." [1] And there, right there, is where the

---

1   Joseph Brodsky, "A Cat's Meow," in *On Grief and Reason*.

mutual disappointment lies. A writer doesn't appear at a literary festival out of geographical curiosity, but is driven by an internal search
for the ideal reader, one whose words will salve, who'll say that the
architectonics of her novels leave him or her as breathless as the
Hagia Sophia; that her dialogues are more graphic than Carver's;
that the dynamics of her novelistic texture are awe-inspiring, on a
par with the overwhelming awe one feels at the sight of New York's
Grand Central Station. But instead of the desired ego-stroker, the
writer encounters a shrinking violet who thrusts a bit of paper under
her nose in the hope of receiving a lame autograph. It turns out
that he or she, our festival visitor, wasn't on a desperate mission to
meet a writer, but someone whose words would salve, who'd say that
every life, however insignificant it seems to its owner, is worthy of
description; that each of us has a hidden creative wellspring, we
just need to let it flow; that life's truths are more important than a
writer's bag of tricks. Instead, the festival visitor encounters a person
who is evidently insecure, who clings to his or her own book like
a handrail, and who obviously hasn't seen a fashion magazine in at
least fifteen years. And on that subject, it's high time he or she got
a new haircut.

3.

Romanians, both young and middle-aged, like to wear their hair
tied back in a long ponytail. My translator, an anorexic thirty-something, had a silky blonde one. Rake-thin, he rolled matchstickish
cigarettes, chain-smoking one after the other, his English that of a
born and bred American. Parading his feathers in front of me, this
young man was well-informed about everything and anything, as if
he'd spent the past few months glued to the Internet. Yet for all his
eloquence, there was also an old-fashioned jitteriness there, a kind
of "tubercular" excitability. He dusted the general dreariness of the

surroundings with words, as if his mouth were a snow machine. I spent the two days at a Bucharest literary festival surrounded by a similar crowd. But looking past their faces, eyes, shoulders, and voices, I managed to catch a glimpse of other chance details: the ramshackle streets, peeling façades, the ubiquitous and nonchalant packs of stray dogs who gave the impression that they, and not humans, were the true masters of the city.

I also felt a strong yet vague sense of absence. Of what I wasn't exactly sure, but it felt like I was walking around a graveyard that was just pretending to be a city. Being in Bucharest was like finding myself in the not-so-distant past, in the already-vanished Eastern European intellectual everyday, a world permeated with tobacco smoke, alcohol, intellectual excitability, and the inevitable bitterness; a world where the smell of betrayal, like naphthalene, hung in the air, but also where people still dreamed dreams of art that would change the world. The faces around me were shot through with the sum total of despair, because everyone carried his or her own, a world of sudden ascents to arrogance and headlong falls into inferiority. I didn't understand the language, but knew well what people were talking about.

On the last day of October, sitting in an airport café in Bucharest and waiting for a flight to Istanbul, I spotted it again out of the corner of my eye. A *muscă*, a fly, crept along my chair and jumped onto the rim of my coffee cup, anchoring itself there, frozen. It was early in the morning, and my lower back hurt from sleeping in a guesthouse bed so low and narrow you would have thought it was for a child. Even the bathroom mirror was hung lower than normal. In my nostrils I could still smell the old sewers and the sulfurous stench that had filled my room.

Why, today, more than ever, does Eastern Europe really look like Eastern Europe, as if it was trying to fit the stereotypes others have created of it? The further it moves towards the West, the more it remains in the East. Or is it perhaps the other way around? Does the East today look more like the West than the West is prepared to admit? And is my gaze an eastern or western one?

I wandered, dazed and confused, around the vanished system of co-ordinates. East and West definitely no longer exist. In the meantime, the world has split into the rich, who enrich themselves globally, and the poor, who are impoverished locally. A well-heeled English friend of mine recently spent a summer holiday on an exclusive Thai island. The nature over there, he said, really is pristine and untouched, but the island itself is overrun with wealthy Russians. "It was great," he said. "I got to brush up my rusty Russian."

I proceed towards the boarding gate for Istanbul. From the lip of my coffee cup, the *muscă*, the fly, watched me leave. Or maybe that's just how it seemed to me.

4.

Insects creep merrily through the literary, musical, and visual texts of the Eastern European cultural zone as in the delirium tremens of a chronic alcoholic. Kafka's emblematic *Metamorphosis* doesn't even scratch the surface of the insect-inspired artistic corpus: cockroaches, fleas, bedbugs, and flies are everywhere. For a start, there's Maya-kovsky's drama *The Bedbug* and Dostoyevsky's novel *Demons*, from which Captain Lebyadkin's poem "The Cockroach" (*'Tis of a cock-roach I will tell* . . .) was later set to music by Dmitri Shostakovich. Sticking with music, there's also Nikolai Rimsky-Korsakov's "Flight of the Bumble Bee" and Béla Bartók's "From the Diary of a Fly."

In the area of poetry, generations of Russian children know Korney Chukovsky's "The Clattering Fly" (*Mukha-Tsokotukha*) by heart, not to mention his short story "The Giant Roach" (*Tarakanishche*), in which the "roachzilla" title character is actually thought to be Stalin. In Vladimir Dudintsev's novel *White Robes* (*Beliye Odezhdi*), a character named Xavier appears as a cockroach, while his more contemporary countryman Victor Pelevin has a novel entitled *The Life of Insects* (*Zhizn' nasekomyh*). Long before Pelevin, the Čapek brothers, Karel and Josef, wrote the allegorical *Ze života hmyzu*, itself often translated as *The Life of Insects*. Even when "Easterners" switch cultural zones, there's absolutely no guarantee that they'll shake their fascination with flies. The Serbian-American poet Charles Simic published a memoir entitled *A Fly in the Soup*.

Ilya Kabakov's *Life of a Fly* project consisted of sketches, albums, and installations on the theme of the fly. It also included an authorial hoax, which included brief notes on the role of the fly in art, politics, economics, music, and philosophy and the fabricated comments of fictitious visitors to the exhibition. One of the installations is entitled "My Homeland" (*Moya rodina*): in a cavernous empty space a swarm of flies buzzes through the air towards the ceiling.

Culturally and linguistically (at least in Slavic languages) the fly carries any number of negative connotations: the fly is insignificant (*I'll squash you like a fly!*); hasn't a shred of dignity (*Where can a fly go but to the shit!*); is stupid and irrational (*He goes around like headless fly!*); is ubiquitous, annoying, and boring (*Boring as a fly!*); and is inevitably associated with poverty, decay, and chaos. As Boris Groys writes, although Kabakov sees Russia as "a country of rubbish and flies" ("*strana musora i muh*"), he leaves the symbolic nature of the fly open. For every negative connotation, a fly could equally serve as a symbol of freedom, "soul," and spirituality (an angel in the diminutive?). It could be an "archeologist;" a guardian of memories and of continuity (because wherever there are "rubbish" and ruins, there are also flies); an emissary between worlds; a comic symbol of the relativization of all values (it sits on both the dung heap and the Czar's crown); a standard-bearer for the re-evaluation of closed meanings, clichés, and hierarchies; a constant human companion who sees through non-human eyes.

5.

The Istanbul festival set was worlds apart from its Bucharest counterparts. Young management and translation studies students, volunteers, hovered everywhere. I was involved in two events: the first was in a restaurant with a spectacular view of the Bosphorus, where we sat jammed in a corner doing our best to ignore the encroaching restaurant noise. The festival organizer read excerpts from our books in Turkish, each writer getting about two or three minutes. Apart from the student volunteers, there were actually only two spectators in the audience, although I couldn't help thinking they might be the organizer's mother and aunt. The other reading was in an Istanbul literary café. The audience of volunteers, relatives, and friends was almost identical. The two Turkish writers, one on either side of me, were particularly impressive. In his black Armani suit and black T-shirt, the shaven-headed young guy looked like a male model, his young countrywomen, a new corporate literary star— Manolo Blahnik shoes and frosted-blond Hilary Clinton hair—the perfect match. Both of them had a superior stage presence, but the enviably muscular self-confidence of the young Turkess set her apart. Everything was the way it should have been: there were writers, local and foreign, the odd literary agent, the odd publisher, the odd ambitious and American-educated local editor. The event had everything—except an audience, mutual curiosity, books, and literature.

An old Russian writer and I sat in the hotel lobby kvetching about it all.

"To be honest, it's really all the same to me," he said.

"What do you mean?"

"I'd just like to keep traveling while I still can, to write this or that while I've still got the juice in me . . ." The phrase *while I've still got the juice in me* had an indecent, almost pornographic, ring. I didn't respond. With a flirtatious kick, he got up and hobbled off towards the lift.

At an alfresco restaurant near our hotel a Bulgarian writer friend and I sat down and had a kvetch about it all too. He showed me a gorgeously illustrated picture book for which he'd written the text. It was the story of a fly that buzzed about everywhere, for the most part through European historical epochs.

"We wanted to capture a fly's distinctive perspective," said the friend, referring to himself and the illustrator.

"If it's a fly's perspective, then why is it making a school primer out of European history? It's as if the fly is the class geek, and not a fly . . ."

He shrugged his shoulders.

"That aside, do flies really land on masterpieces of European art like Leonardo da Vinci's *The Last Supper*? I mean, as a fly, surely you could've chosen something else, right?"

"It landed on a plate on the table . . . there it is, there . . ." said my friend sheepishly.

"Flies are conformists . . ." I said, taking a mollifying tone. "But why then would you want a fly's perspective!? Isn't a fly just a means of transport for your perspective?"

It was a sunny day, Istanbul was experiencing an Indian summer, we were eating baklava, the golden wasps of Istanbul buzzed overhead.

6.

"Hey, pretty lady, stop a while! Come and take a look at my rugs . . ." shouts the broad-smiling squirt of a man beckoning me into his shop. I don't have the slightest intention of stopping; I'm on my way back to the hotel after a day spent playing tourist. I'm exhausted, and can hardly wait to get under a hot shower and into bed. Besides, I know the whole bazaar hustle: if I even think about stopping, it'll be tough to wriggle out.

No, please God, no way—I find myself obediently stopping, as if someone had zapped me with the TV remote.

"You don't have to buy anything, come in, take a look around, we'll have tea . . ."

The Turk was in his thirties, and I wouldn't have remembered him had it not been for the floppy dumbo ears planted on either side of his shaven head.

"I can come in, but as I already told you, I'm not going to buy anything . . ." I say, though I hadn't actually told him anything yet.

The Turk lifted his arm protectively as if he was going to wrap it around my shoulder, leading me into a spacious and elegant rug shop. He sat me down on a cushion-laden sofa, clicked his fingers, and voila, a cute little boy sprang out from somewhere with a tray carrying small glasses of Turkish apple tea.

"You really are very gracious, but I'm not a buyer . . ." I said.

Not batting an eyelid, the Turk again clicked his fingers, pointed to one of the shelves and nodded his head, yep, that one. The boy pulled out a rug, skillfully unrolling it. For a moment I thought we were all extras in an ad or an Orientalist film.

The Turk lets his rug story unfurl. He tells of rugs from the Balkans to Pakistan, the differences between Bulgarian, Turkish, Armenian, Persian, Egyptian, Israeli, Jordanian, and Indian rugs, of styles, shapes, stitches, knots, and fabrics, of wool, cotton, and silk, of thickness, length, and lustre. The boy is as agile as a gymnast, unrolling and re-rolling rugs in silence.

"There's no point going to any effort, I'm not going to buy anything . . ." I repeat.

"This is a magnificent, handmade piece . . ."

"I doubt it's handmade," I said, slightly irritated.

"How do you know it's not?"

"You can see from the underside . . ." I bluff.

"You're wrong, madame, you're so terribly wrong. My mother wove this with her own hands," said the Turk in a pained voice, as if I'd insulted him.

Choosing to let it go, he continued spinning a yarn about his mother who lives in a small village (his mother being a weaver, an artist, and the cornerstone of the family), about his brothers and sisters, about his family, family values, and his family lineage whose honesty is known far and wide.

"We're in a recession—even if I wanted to, I couldn't buy one," say I, in lieu of an apology.

The Turk agrees, nods his head, turns the mother and family channel off and changes tack. Of course, yes, the recession, but you know a recession is exactly the right time to invest in things of lasting value; gold, paintings, precious rugs, that sort of thing. Rembrandt, Picasso, precious silk rugs, they're all works of art . . . And if you can't afford a Picasso, why wouldn't you buy yourself a rug?

"I know, but I'm not buying . . ."

The Turk looks at me silently. I squirm on the sofa.

"I can't . . ." I add.

"And what, madame, do you do?"

Of course I hadn't the slightest intention of telling him. Why would I tell him? I could invent any profession I like—tell him I was a waitress, for example.

"I'm a writer . . ."

The Turk stops for a second and, for the first time, frowns a little, as if this wasn't the answer he was expecting. With a theatrical wave of the hand, he dismisses the assistant.

"Do you write for a newspaper?"

Yes, I think; maybe it's better to tell him I write for a newspaper . . .

"I write books."

"What kind of books?"

"Well, you know, novels, stories, and stuff . . ."

He frowns again, as if rocked by unpleasant news, but recovers in a second and jovially declares . . .

"I love novels too, and stories . . . books should adorn every home, like rugs."

"My book is in every bookstore in Istanbul; it's been translated into Turkish," I reply in a single breath, as if someone were forcibly dragging me along by my tongue.

"Bravo! Give me your name and the title, and I'll buy it . . . but did you know that rugs are books too?"

"No . . ."

"All those fairytale heroes on flying carpets are actually flying on books, because actually, books are 'the wings of imagination,' are they not?"

The Turk hits a button on his invisible remote again. The boy reappears, unfurling rugs as if they were papyruses, laying them at my feet.

"There we go, madame, now tell me what they say," the Turk demands.

"How am I supposed to read them?!"

"They're all stories written by your sisters. And women being women, your sisters have woven all sorts of things into these rugs: young girls their dreams of love and marriage, young married women their dissatisfaction with impotent husbands and evil step-mothers, old grannies memories of their youth. Rugs are women's diaries, you just need to know how to read them. But I see you're illiterate in this area. You say you're a writer, but you don't know the alphabet."

"Well, the script is different . . ." I say.

"Look, this is bird, this is a wolf's muzzle, a scorpion, a comb, an eye, a star, a snake, a burdock, an amulet . . . Fruit usually means fertility, this zig-zag line denotes water and eternity, this eight-pointed star is divine, this Z-shaped line is light, a snake is wisdom, and a rose, as you know, usually means love. Having a rug with a tarantula in the house is excellent protection against all kinds of insects . . . A horse means freedom, a peacock is a holy spirit, although truth be told, I can't stand the bloody things. A camel is just another symbol of wealth and happiness, and a dog is a protector of the home, but that one you could've worked for yourself.

"A hen-pigeon, this one here, is an SMS from God, a snake usually means a win of some sort, and a fish happiness . . . Of course, every symbol, every line and color can also mean something completely different. There's no firm collective agreement on coded language. Because then it wouldn't be coded, would it?"

"Of course not . . ." I say.

"I hope your need to read all the feminist books in my shop is now clear?! Starting with this little pure silk rug—look at how it shines! And I'm going to give you an exercise to help. Just think of it as obligatory reading. It's easy to carry, and the text is short. I won't tell you what it says of course, you'll have to work that out for yourself, but take my word for it, pretty lady, it's perfect for you, perfect. If you don't figure it out, use it as a mouse pad, put it on the wall, polish your shoes with it, do whatever you like, but buy it you must!" he says, his tone putting a full-stop on our conversation.

Pressed again the wall, I take out my credit card and, what do you know, I pay without further ado. In the shop doorway, the Turk palms his business card off on me.

"Will you write about me in one of your books" he asks, smiling broadly.

"Why would I?"

"So people find out about me and my rugs! All publicity's good publicity."

"I definitely will," I mumble, glancing at the business card. Adem, his name is Adem.

Drained, I set off for the hotel. All I want is a hot shower and to slip into bed. On the way it occurred to me that he'd forgotten to ask for the Turkish title of my book. Oh Adem, you sly dog, you.

7.

That evening in the hotel room I unrolled the little rug of pure silk. I looked for the symbols and tried to crack the coded language. I couldn't see a thing. I even gave it a little shake, thinking a message might fall out. I didn't expect fortune-cookie-type wisdom, actually; I would have been happy with the standard, *We're sorry, all of our operators are currently unavailable.* The rug, however, didn't say boo. It was like a mobile phone with an empty battery. I flipped it over a few times, seeing if it would do the shiny trick. It didn't. Adem was the battery charger, without him it simply didn't "work." I folded it up (it was about four A4 pages in size) and stuffed it in my suitcase. I paid 250 euro for a Turkish apple tea and a one-on-one literature lesson from an Istanbul rug merchant.

In the morning, at Istanbul Airport, waiting for a flight to Zagreb, I tried to piece together the random details of my travels (my fly's hop: Bucharest-Istanbul-Zagreb). The pieces didn't fit. I tried stitching them together with the metaphorical thread of the fly, but that didn't work either; the thread broke, and the pieces flew everywhere. I thought about the navigation of reality; about how we interpret reality, stitches, colors, threads, and symbols; about how we read people, situations, and details; about perspectives; about how the language of reality, in which we normally swim like fish in water, can in a flash become terrifyingly unintelligible, and then, in another, worryingly self-explanatory. I kept thinking of Adem, the prince of liars, the teacher of optics and holograms, the master of now-you-see-it-now-you-don't tricks, the philosopher king: Yes, madame, each of sees as much as we are given to see . . .

Suddenly a Turkish fly landed on the edge of my coffee cup, a *sinek*, and I felt a strange sense of relief. I just sat there and watched it. I thought about the fact that I hadn't managed to capture the substance of my travels, and I conceded defeat. Then I reassured myself with the idea that, who knows, maybe the point of everything we do isn't in the capture, but rather in the hunt. And then, as unexpectedly as an unannounced fly, I remembered the lines of a Croatian nursery rhyme:

> *Three butchers tried to skin a fly's hide*
> *But hopping here, then hopping there,*
> *The fly left them to chide and stare.*

And as I headed off towards the gate for Zagreb, from the edge of the coffee cup, the *sinek*, the fly (an angel in the diminutive?), watched me go. Or maybe that's just how it seemed to me.

December 2010

DANGEROUS
LIAISONS

Upton Sinclair, author of the novel *Oil!*, would have stayed a half-forgotten American literary classic had there not been a film adaptation of the novel *There Will Be Blood* (2007), with the entrancing Daniel Day-Lewis in the main role, which briefly blew the dust off of Sinclair's name.

Having seen the movie, I thought back to the shelf of books in my mother's apartment and the book cover of the first Yugoslav edition of *Oil!*, which was titled *Petrolej*. There were pencil drawings all over the inside: those, said my mother, were my first childish scribblings. It was the time of post-war poverty, and the cover of a book doubled as a drawing pad. Upton Sinclair's novel *Oil!*, Maxim Gorky's *The Mother*, and Theodore Dreiser's *American Tragedy* were not, perhaps, my mother's favorite books, but they sold in the bookstores of post-war, socialist Yugoslavia. These and a few others were the first titles in the home library of my young parents.

I don't remember whether I ever actually read *Oil!* Probably not, but if I did, back when I was a student—earnestly dedicated to comparative literature—I wouldn't have dared say so out loud. At that time, defense of the "autonomy of the literary text" was something nearly sacred to every student of comparative literature, and I certainly perceived myself as battling on the front lines. In my student days "literary autonomy" was closely tied to values and literary taste. In simple terms, we felt that good writers did not embark on politics— or write about life in overly real terms. Real life was left to the bad writers and those who flirted with politics. "Literary" literature was "in." The Yugoslav writers were never seriously infected with the virus of socialist realism, which does not mean, of course, that there weren't those who compromised. But resistance to the tendency to ideologize and politicize in literature, despite the occasional line penned to glorify Tito, lasted unusually long after the enemy, socialist realism, was dead and buried. There were many good writers, thanks to this, who wrote fine books. There were bad writers, on the other hand, who were labeled "good" because they "didn't get caught up in politics"; just as many good writers were deemed bad because they had no bone to pick with the regime, or at least didn't do so publicly; just as there were bad writers who were deemed good only because they had taken a public stand against the regime. The fine Croatian writer Miroslav Krleža, long since dead and buried, bears a stigma even today for his friendship with Tito.

Today, of course, I know that the connection between literature and "ideology" has been around since the beginnings of literacy. The Bible, the cornerstone of the European literatures, is not just a grandiose work of literature, it is a grandiose work of ideology. The history of the bond between literature and ideology is long, complex, and dramatic. Because of the written word, writers have lost their lives and been put to death. The history of the relations between emperors and poets, between leaders and court fools, between those who order literature and those who comply with the orders is too gory, the episodes of book burning and censorship too frequent, the number of writers' lives given for the freedom of speech, for an idea, or even just a dream is too vast to allow taking this fatal historical combination lightly. The notion of literary autonomy served too often as an alibi for it to enjoy full validity: when they thought they had something to gain by it, there were writers who stepped into politics; others took on politics even when doing so led to symbolic or real suicide. Some, when they were looking to save their skins, sought the shield of literary autonomy, while others paid for their literary autonomy with their hides.

The tension between the two opposing poles—the political engagement of a writer and a writer's autonomy—was particularly dramatic in the literatures of the former Eastern Europe, and even today, surprising as this may seem, it has still not lost its hold, although the context has changed in terms of the politics, ideas, and culture. The Eastern European literary environments were much more rigid than the Western European ones; in the Eastern European literary zones careers were destroyed because of the written word or, conversely, the writer was promoted to government minister. This is no different today, it seems, though it may seem to be different: state institutions continue to play the part of literary patron, albeit a bad and stingy patron, but there is barely any independent territory left. The writer in small post-communist states is still treated as the "voice of his people" or as a "traitor." Why? For the simple reason that communism in transitional countries has been replaced by nationalism, and both systems have their eyes on writers. The literary marketplace is too small for the writer to maintain his belief that he is independent.

As I watched the movie *There Will Be Blood*, I thought back to the soc-realist Yugoslav design of the book cover for *Petrolej*. I tried to bring to memory the many Yugoslav writers who were not fortunate enough to survive the shift from socialism to nationalism, to reposition themselves nationally, thereby ensuring themselves a place on the bookshelves of the national literature. Some of them tried, and survived a year or so longer, slipping through the eye of the needle. Many of the losers, along with their collected works and mountains of scribbled pages, however, sank into the dust of oblivion. Young writers, and with them the young literary critics and theoreticians, showed no compassion; they must have figured this wasn't their story. Today is, after all, another time, life is proceeding at a rapid clip, literature is a time-investment which for most of us does not provide anything more than aching joints and bankruptcy, but it is a lottery which brings the lucky winner the jackpot. The young rush out to buy lottery tickets and don't ask too many questions. How is it, for instance, that the writers who were dissidents in their communist states, are so quick to accept posts in ministries, embassies, or elsewhere in the new democra-tatorships? How is it that today, in one way or another, everyone continues to live on government handouts? How is it that those who once pressed so fiercely for autonomy in literature are now demanding that their state institutions underwrite culture (hence literature), thereby implicitly agreeing that they won't bite the hand that feeds them.

All in all, culture in small countries was never viable on the market, nor could it have been. That is why writers from small countries, whether they like it or not, are condemned to act as representatives for their country, whether the state be Croatia, Serbia, Estonia, or Latvia; either that or they are labeled "traitors" and live abroad. One often goes hand in hand with the other. Even international literary stars, who have long since left their home literatures behind, changing the language they write in as they go, are not immune to the righteous fury of the homeland. The recent incident with Milan Kundera only confirms that the Czech republic is a small country and that the model for traumatic back-and-forth between literature and ideology is unchanged. The not so distant example of Salman Rushdie confirms that religion can be an equally rigid ideology, and that writers, no matter where they live, are still vulnerable to being branded usurpers of religious taboos, with the attendant life-threatening consequences. And a very recent interview with Ismail Kadare shows the unfortunate duality and hypocrisy of the literary position: every year Albania nominates Kadare for the Nobel Prize, yet Kadare is an Albanian dissident, a writer who denies the connection between politics and literature, and still he himslef comes back to that dangerous liaison, re-warming his own trauma and reinforcing it as his own niche of literary identification.

The question arises: Is it possible to step out of the hellish circle, where the autonomy of a literary text is only another name for politicization, and politicization is only another name for autonomy? How does the relationship to a text change when the context changes?

Exile is literally a change of context. Exile implies the personal experience of every exilee, which would be difficult to subsume under terms that are stubbornly endorsed by literary critics from both worlds, the writer's home base and the host environment. The terms—*émigré, immigrant, exile, nomad, minority, ethnic, hybrid literature*—discriminate, but they are also affirmative. With these terms the home base expels the writer, while the same terms are used by the host environment to relegate the writer to an ethnic niche, and at the same time affirm his or her existence. The home base makes assumptions of monoculturalism and exclusivity, while the host environment make assumptions of multiculturalism and inclusivity, but both are essentially working with dusty labels of ethnicity and the politics of *otherness*. Even if I were to write a text about the desolation of frozen landscapes at the North Pole, I would still be chiefly labeled as a Croatian writer, or as a Croatian writer in exile writing about the desolation of the frozen landscapes at the North Pole. Reviewers would promptly populate the frozen wasteland of my text with concepts such as exile, Croatia, ex-Yugoslavia, post-communism, the Balkans, Eastern Europe, the Slavic world, Balkan feminism, or perhaps Balkan eco-feminism, while journalists would ask me whether I had the opportunity while up in the frozen waste-land to run into the Yugoslav diaspora, and how I perceived the situation in Kosovo from that frozen vantage point. If an English writer writes his or her version of a visit to the North Pole, Englishness will not likely serve as the framework within which his or her text is read. This attitude of the host environment to writer-newcomers springs from a subconscious colonial attitude—just when the larger literary world is doing its best to reject this—in a market which relishes any form of the profitable exotic, what with the always vital relations between the periphery and the center. The concepts of periphery and center are, however, elastic; I am sure that Serbs feel closer to the center than do the Bulgarians, and the Bulgarians feel closer to the center than do the Turks. Feelings, however, are one thing and real relations of power are something else. The real center of power is America, or rather Anglo-American culture, whose cultural domination marked the twentieth century. We are still looking to that center with equal fascination today. Anglo-American culture is the dominant field of reference, while, at the same time, it is the most powerful, if not the most just, mediator of cultural values. In other words, if certain Chinese writers are not translated into English, it is unlikely that any Serbian or Croatian reader, with the exception of the occasional sinologist, will ever hear of them.

The relationship to a literary text changes, of course, with a change of language. There are many examples of writers who embraced the language of their host-country, yet by doing so they did not manage to protect their texts from manipulative readings, but there is an even larger number of writers who, writing in the language of the host country, seek a special ethnic-religious hybrid status for themselves, because only this status will afford them a recognizable, profitable niche. There are also writers who protected their literary text from burdensome and often incorrect readings; they enriched the literary community in which they found themselves, becoming an indivisible part of it. All in all, an opposition asserts itself here, this time the opposition between the autonomy of the literary text and its critical reception and market manipulation (having said that the market is not without its political aspirations) in the new context of the internationalization of literary texts and transnational literature. This is still the realm of literature as we know it, with its tradition, canons, apparatus, institutions, with its system of values. Here we still know, or at least we approximately know, what it is we are talking about when we speak of literature.

The first Croatian-Serbian edition of Sinclair's *Petrolej* is sound asleep on the bookshelf in the apartment of my eighty-two-year-old mother. My mother's grandchildren, of course, have no clue about who Upton Sinclair is. But Grandma knows. Then again Grandma, of course, has no clue who Daniel Day-Lewis is. The grandchildren do. Her grandchildren speak SMS and they mostly read text messages, but they do have a culture of their own. Literature holds no place at all in that culture, unless it's a part of a mass media package. Take Harry Potter, for instance: the movie, the games, the T-shirts, the consumer planet in miniature. As it leaps from the national to the international, literature enters its third context, the powerful global zone of the mass media. In that context literature, or rather its assumptions, dissolves, vanishes, or transmutes into something else. Bookstores are full of books; the chains are reminiscent of supermarkets, there are more translations of books than ever before, more literary awards than ever before; literary festivals are suddenly key points for the popularization of books; there are writers being lauded like pop stars—all of which suggests that things have never been better for writing. However, the culture of the literary form is on the wane. The space in the papers given over to reviews is disappearing, just as the papers themselves are. Literary life is moving onto the Internet. Books circulate through movies (movie screenplays published as books sell better than the books they are based on), through audio recordings, mobile phones. An unruly form of literature is alive and well, democratic, unstructured, extra-institutional, rejecting hierarchy, functioning in the digitalized literary realm, and this powerful literary underground will push literature as we have known it, with all the attendant apparatus, even further out onto the margins. Perhaps, in the digital galaxy, a redefined novel will arise which erases authorship, national and linguistic borders, ethnic identities, hierarchies of evaluation, and literary tradition. Or maybe it won't. Literature is merchandise which, with each passing day, is losing its appeal.

Writers, and the people who publish books, will have to face the change in status. As they postpone facing the music, writers rush off to the last remaining haven, the national Academies of Science and Art, which provide a secure institution for national values and a slightly more secure life in retirement. Such writers are about to become extinct, but they are not necessarily the ones who will lose out in the end. All of us, whoever we are, find ourselves in a new time in which *a premium is placed on being heard rather than listening, being seen rather than watching, and on being read rather than reading.*[1]

Imagine contemporary literature as a mega-marathon in which all the gender, age, ethnic, and racial groups are welcome and, in principle, "equal." An elderly participant runs toward the finish line bearing a porcelain vessel, certain that the vessel holds something precious. The precious cargo, of course, is literature, *literature as art* no less. But it is altogether possible that the race, the exhausting marathon, the symbolic vessel, and literature as art—that these are tragicomically misplaced assumptions. Because it is entirely possible that the marathon runner is running in place without even noticing it, or even going backwards. And even if she does reach the imagined finish line, and delivers the vessel with its precious cargo intact, she may find out that the vessel holds no more than water soup. The only comfort is that all the marathon runners are subject to the same risk.

March 2009

---

1   Colin Robinson, "Diary," *London Review of Books*, February 26, 2009.

THE SPIRIT OF THE KAKANIAN PROVINCE

An Inner Map

Provincial train stations with their apricot-hued façades and window boxes of pelargonia (take a train from Zagreb to Budapest!), architecture (hospitals, bureaucratic buildings, schools, theaters), cuisine (sacher torte, cabbage and noodles, *Kaiserschmarrn*, *Tafelspitz*, dumplings, and poppy-seed noodles), city parks, and the Czech last names sprinkled through the Viennese telephone directory (like poppy seeds on a kaiser roll)—these are not the only ways to recognize a Kakanian landscape.

I am no expert on the Austro-Hungarian monarchy, I hardly even rank as an amateur, but I have a sense that the monarchy stamped a watermark on the souls of its subjects, an internal landscape, the coordinates of periphery and center. The center became aware of itself thanks to the periphery, the periphery grew to know itself thanks to the center. One went from the provinces to Vienna for the opera, to Budapest to buy the latest hats. After all wasn't it a child of the periphery, a postman's son from Sarajevo, who shot Kakania in the head, and afterwards things in Europe were never the same?

The Croatian Kakanian Novel

Croatia lay on the outskirts of Austro-Hungary. I don't know much about the times, but I do recall a few odds and ends from the history of Croatian letters. I remember, for instance, that the protagonists of Croatian novels at the turn of the last century studied in Vienna, Prague, or Budapest, and that aside from Croatian, they used German, Hungarian, or Czech. The detail that a person went off to Vienna to study caught my youthful fancy; it seemed so noble, though it is also true that the characters in these novels could barely make ends meet. And if these protagonists were writers, as some were, their poems were occasionally published in Prague, Budapest, or Viennese publications, to the envy of their milieu. That, too, had a noble ring. The Kakanian metropoli have long since lost their attraction and pizzazz. The center moved elsewhere. I'm guessing that today's writers in Prague, Budapest and Vienna envy the rare compatriot whose name appears as a contributor in the *New Yorker*.

While I was leafing through a few Croatian Kakanian novels (which I'd last cracked in high school), I felt I was working not with literary texts but genes. It was like discovering something we have always known but failed to attend to, like discovering a birthmark exactly where it was on our parents, children, grandchildren. At the same time, the literary critic in me grumbled while reading the ongoing episodes of these provincial literary soap operas, which have been going on for a century. Ah, picking up old books again is so often a disappointment.

I will say something about these novels in thumbnail sketches, as befits them, like the episodes of TV soap operas, or teletext. All the examples come from the Croatian literary canon and are required reading in high school. At their center there is invariably a male protagonist, and his life's destiny is told in first or third person. The structure of the novel follows a type, like the window-box pelargonia of Austro-Hungarian railway stations. These literary heroes are distant relatives of Werther and Childe Harold, cousins to the Russian literary heroes, those who would be dubbed "superfluous" by literary critics after Turgenev's *The Diary of a Superfluous Man*. The type—the high-strung, over-sensitive, educated misfit or outcast—such as Griboyedov's Chatsky, Pushkin's Eugene Onegin, Lermontov's Pechorin, Turgenev's heroes (Rudin, Lavrecki, the Kirsanovs, and Bazarov), Goncharov's Oblomov and others—proliferated throughout the Slavic literatures and is exclusively the characteristic of the male literary lineage. The women in these novels belong to one of three varieties: a) the young, beautiful, noble, and patriotic girl, who is abandoned, as a rule, by the hero; b) the femme fatale (often foreign), who toys with the hero; c) the unloved, quiet "sufferer," who follows the hero faithfully to the end of her days.

The First Suicide

The novel *Janko Borislavić* by Ksaver Šandor Gjalski was published in 1887 (we are already twenty years into Austro-Hungary at this point). The novel is a belated romantic work on "Faustian problems of the spirit," as Croatian literary criticism of the day deemed it. Janko Borislavić is a Croatian landowner who, while studying abroad, is torn by doubts as to his course of study, theology, and returns to his estate in the Croatian Zagorje region. Here he falls in love with charming Dorica, though love, thinks Borislavić, is "fickle," turning a "chaste, holy virgin" into nothing more than a "simple organ for prolonging the species." Possessed by the "intellectualistic" restlessness of the period, steeped in Schopenhauer's philosophy, and, of course, a fear of women, Borislavić in his long internal monologues polemicizes passionately with the books he has read. He leaves Dorica and ventures into the world, where he spends six years, sinking into greater and greater disappointment. Human "stupidity" is "eternal and absolute" and everywhere.

"Ha, ha, for that you, my Diderot, Rousseau and you other unfortunates who were so gifted with human spirit, for this you wrote those volumes of wisdom! In vain your efforts, futile all that work. Ah, so stupid, stupid is the world."

"Compelled by his Faustian nature, his inner fire, to track down the thousands of threads that compose the mysterious source of life," Borislavić travels. He leaves Paris, disappointed ("Eighty years ago you shed so much blood, alas, my Frenchmen!"); he stops briefly in England, where he cannot bear the "stuffiness of human society which lies in wait implacably to thwart all progress and then it serves up peace for the human spirit." From England he goes to America, but there he is put off by the "amalgam of inherited prejudices, the frenzy and struggle of individual wills and desires." Upon his return from America he disembarks in Germany, like "vast barracks of philistine phalanges." Borislavić returns to his native Zagorje, but here, as well, "human malice and stupidity revel in orgy." Again he sets out on his journey, again he returns, he has a "nervous breakdown," slits his wrists, and dies.

A Second Death

A somewhat later novel by Ksaver Šandor Gjalski, *Radmilović* (1894), has a similar plot. Here the hero, Marko Radmilović, is not destroyed by "world anguish" but by the environment of Zagreb, the place Radmilović comes to from the Croatian provinces. Radmilović publishes his poems and short stories in Czech, Polish, Russian, and other Slavic languages, they have even heard of him in Paris, but in Zagreb he is unknown and unrecognized.

"It is sad, so sad that such a writer is unknown! . . . Had he been born in France, Russia or Germany, believe me, the whole world would have known of him. But he is only a Croatian writer, he works on the threshold to the Orient, at the fringes of Europe . . . This could easily happen here with someone like Bourget, or another more vaunted celebrity. There is no such European or world fame which could so easily surmount our high wall, the wall of pervasive non-reading."

Radmilović is insulted by the "cannabilistic persecutions" of his colleagues, an environment which holds that the literary calling is not worthy of respect and where there is no educated readership.

"—So, I tell you, were all our literary institutions to collapse, were all our writers to breathe their last, the gentlemen here would not fall silent for so much as a instant, or even notice that something was amiss! But were the German Leipzig Press to stop coming out, heaven forbid, with its *Familienblatters*, its *Buch fur Alle*, or its pound-a-novel publications such as *Sibiriens Holle*, these men would be despondent . . . How many lovely Croatian women know the names of a Gundulić, a Mažuranić, a Preradović, how many of them would blush if you were to catch them unaware of Osman or Čengić? . . . Ah—yet heaven forbid that you come across a single one who knows nothing of the German Elise Polko or Marlitt!—for this we struggle, day and night, for this we sacrifice peace of mind and a sure existence, health, everything! Oh, Lord, where do we find the will to keep working?—This work brings us no sustenance, gives us no moral or ethical reward, no fame, no benefit to the people. Why keep working at all?"

Radmilović rents a small room in a modest dwelling where a girl named Stanka lives with her ailing mother. Radmilović finds a sympathetic soul in Stanka, but falls in love instead with wealthy, frivolous, beautiful Olga. When Olga becomes engaged to a more profitable life partner, Radmilović plunges into despair. With Stanka's help he completes his novel, *The Sufferers*. Radmilović and Stanka marry, leave Zagreb, and move to a provincial town. Though an attorney by profession, Radmilović finds work at a local attorney's office as an ordinary legal clerk. When a publishing house decides not to bring out his new novel, Radmilović publishes it at his own expense, but the literary critics dismiss the novel with scorn. Radmilović burns his own book in a fit of pique, suffers a nervous breakdown, and soon dies in a madhouse.

The same writer, two of the same endings—a person undone, descending into madness and death. Let us continue on our way and see whether the Kakanian Croatian writers offer us a more cheerful novelistic resolution after the protagonist returns from the metropolis to his native provinces.

Two Worlds

The hero of Vjenceslav Novak's *Two Worlds* (*Dva svijeta*, 1901), Amadej Zlatanić (the Croatian Mozart!), having been left early without parents, finds parental care and support in the local chaplain, Jan Jahoda (a Czech, of course). Jahoda discovers the boy's remarkable musical talent and seeks a scholarship for him through the local authorities, so that Zlatanić can attend the Prague conservatory.

"Among the smaller peoples—and that means you, Croats—such natural talents are often lost both out of poverty and the lack of understanding by those who should be seeing to their education." The local authorities turn down Jahoda's request ("Pane Jahoda, our children are not made for such things. We leave this to you Czechs.")

When Jahoda dies, Amadej sells his parental home for a pittance and goes to Prague, where he passes the entrance exam and enrolls at the conservatory. Amadej graduates from the conservatory with success, and his composition, entitled "Adelka" (the name of the girl waiting for him at home), is performed at the final student recital. With glowing reviews in the Prague papers and his diploma in his pocket, Amadej returns home full of hope and plans. He is given a modest salary as the local chaplain and marries Adelka. He sends his composition "Adelka" to Zagreb, but its performance receives bad reviews ("A homework assignment, in which the mostly familiar motifs have been reworked"). Amadej plunges into despair, his only solace being the appearance of Irma Leschetizky, the wife of a man involved in a future railway line (see, here are Austro-Hungarian railway lines and foreign women full of understanding!). Amadej spends more and more time with Irma. When Irma leaves, Adelka falls seriously ill. Amadej realizes he has been unfair to Adelka, the one person who is truly dedicated to him.

With the intention of relegating to "the shadows all arrogant talents" in town, the authorities introduce Rakovčić, a tambura player. Rakovčić's tamburitza ensemble is far more draw for everyone than Amadej's classical music.

"Mr. Z. played a Chopin piece on the piano which did not warm up the audience. Perhaps this does for the cold north, but in the warm south everything is more lush and heartfelt, even the music."

Amadej loses his job, and it is given to Rakovčić the tambura player. Faced with poverty, Amadej gives private lessons. Irma Leschetizky speaks for Amadej in Berlin musical circles. Amadej is made an offer to sell his compositions to a Berlin publisher, but he must relinquish the copyright. Amadej refuses, but when Adelka's health worsens, he sells his compositions to the Berlin publisher after all ("I go around the world, nameless, hence no one can see me.") Adelka dies, Amadej loses his bearings, the local authorities lock him up in an asylum, and he soon dies.

Vjenceslav Novak develops a similar theme once more, but this time from the perspective of a theory, popular at the time, of heredity. In the novel *Tito Dorčić* (1906) he describes the sad fate of a fisherman's son. Though all the people in Tito Dorčić's family are fishermen, his father compels the boy to pursue a different path in life. He dispatches him to school in Vienna (again Vienna!), where Tito fritters away his days, utterly disinterested in his surroundings and the study of law. His father's bribes propel him, somehow, through his studies, and he comes home and finds work as a local judge. The job does not interest him. His father's efforts are finally undone when Tito, out of lack of ability and carelessness, condemns an innocent man to die. Dorčić goes mad and drowns in the sea, returning to where he belongs.

We can add here that the time of mass suicides in Europe came a decade or so later, inspired by the Great Depression and Rezső Seress's hit "Szomoru Vasarnap." As the story goes, Seress managed to infect not only Central Europeans but Americans with a Central

European melancholy. Supposedly people threw themselves off of the Brooklyn Bridge after listening to Seress's doleful hit in New York.

Another Suicide

Milutin Cihlar Nehajev's novel *Escape* (*Bijeg*, 1909) is thought by Croatian critics to be the finest novel of Croatian Modernism. Đuro Andrijašević, the protagonist, throws away two years spent studying law in Vienna (Vienna again!); he returns to Zagreb, where he enrolls at the faculty and passes all the exams. All he has left to do is his doctoral dissertation. His uncle, who has been sending him monthly financial support, dies without leaving Đuro the anticipated inheritance. Andrijašević is engaged to Vera Hrabarova, but he fears he will lose her because of his unexpected financial woes. The history of Andrijašević's fall begins the moment he finds a job as a teacher in a secondary school in Senj. Andrijašević finds everything in the small costal town boring and strange.

"It's not that the people are bad, they are not repulsive. But they are empty, so horribly empty. And the same—one is like the next. They have nearly identical habits, they even drink the same number of glasses of beer."

Andrijašević is not interested in the school and finds it difficult to write his dissertation. After waiting patiently for several years, Vera leaves him and becomes engaged to someone else. Andrijašević falls further and further into debt, spends all his time drinking and quarreling with a growing number of people, and is ultimately fired. In his last letter, which he sends to his one remaining friend, he hints at suicide.

"The only thing I feel is: I must put an end to this. I should escape altogether—flee from this life, so sickening, so disgraceful . . . Surely you can see that I have always fled from life and people. I've never resisted—I have stepped aside. And when I came in contact with the life of our people, a life in poverty and straightened circumstances, I fled. I fled from myself, not wanting to see how I was plummeting; drinking, awaiting the end."

Andrijašević, who "carries the tragedy of himself and others," ends his life just as his literary predecessor Tito Dorčić did, drowning one night in the sea.

Upon hearing these brief statistics, a naïve reader might conclude that Croats in the late 19th and early twentieth century used the sea for nothing but drowning. Fortunately, tourism developed in the meanwhile, which has truly vindicated the deaths of these fictional victims and reversed the destructive opposition of metropolis—province, at least during the summer months, to the benefit of the provinces. This, of course, happened in reality, not in literature.

The novels *The Return of Philip Latinowicz (Povratak Filipa Lati-novicza*, 1932) and *On the Edge of Reason (Na rubu pameti*, 1937) by Miroslav Krleža are the literary crown of the Croatian Kakanian literary dynasty. The central figure of *Philip Latinowicz* repeats the trajectory of his predecessors: he is a painter, forty years old, who returns to his native region, Pannonia, from Paris after having spent twenty-three years abroad. The hero of *On the Edge of Reason* describes how he is gradually being destroyed by Zagreb's bourgeois environment, just as his literary predecessors were. Krleža's novels can be read in all the Kakanian, and many other, languages, and this availability is the only reason why these lines about him amount to little more than a footnote. Miroslav Krleža de-provincialized Croatian literature, imposing exacting literary standards. These standards were rarely later attained by Krleža's literary progeny, which is one of the answers to the question of why the canonical Krleža is still a despised writer in Croatia today. In an ideal literary republic, all other Croatian writers, including those mentioned above, would be nothing but a footnote—to Miroslav Krleža.

The Provinces—The Metropoli

Why am I dusting off old books that mean nothing to anyone except high-school Croatian-literature teachers? Literature is not a reliable aide in detecting the everyday life of an historical era, nor is that its job. Literature plays within its coordinates, its themes, its genres, its language, and even if readers recognize truth in it, this still does not elevate literature to the role of arbiter in questions of what is truth and what is a lie. All the prose examples given so far nevertheless ring with a strikingly similar tone, the same web of motives about the dislocation of the intelligent individual from the environment and his state of forever being torn between provinces and metropoli. The hero's choice always favors a return to the homeland, the periphery, the provinces.

The stubborn permutation of the theme of a periphery that devours its young is made even more complex if we consider the real historical context, the way Croatia was torn between Austro-Hungary, their dream of independence, and a possible alliance of southern Slavs. Ksaver Šandor Gjalski's now forgotten novel *In the Night (U noći*, 1886) is surprisingly close to the contemporary Croatian political life of these last twenty years. The reader wonders: in 1991, just

as Croatia was becoming an independent state, did Croatian political life truly regress to Gjalski's nineteenth century, or did it simply
fail to move forward?

The self-pitying tone of the provinces resonates to this day. Perhaps the South Slavic states regressed by a century with the collapse
of Yugoslavia, as if they were in a session of regressive psychotherapy.
Or maybe they simply failed to move. They, too, are torn between
options—pro-European versus anti-European positions, the Royalist
versus the Democratic, a willingness to consider stronger alliances
versus a more than glaring affiliation with religion, be it Catholicism, Orthodoxy, or Islam.

The colonized mentality has clearly carried on beyond colonial
times. Sometimes it seems as if a colonizer-boogeyman is constantly crouching among the inhabitants of the former Kakanian
provinces, whether in the form of a Turk with fez and saber, or a
Hungarian, an Austrian, an Italian, a German, a Bulgarian, fascists
and communists, Russians, Serbs, Croats, foreign banks, foreign
capital, domestic capital, the Chinese, corrupt politicians, the geo-
graphic position, loss in the geo-political lottery, fate, or celestial
constellations. The imaginary acupuncture points on the imaginary
national body always seem to respond in the same way. An unending delusion—about independence and freedom, flight from one
trap to another, infantilism, immaturity, aggression, passivity, and
submissiveness (when choosing between confrontation and com-
formism, they choose conformism)—all this situates the periphery
as the historical victim. Seldom can one remain normal with such
a psychogram, the best one can do is to sustain a semblance of
normalcy.

The question remains whether socialist Yugoslavia managed to eman-
cipate and de-provincialize the mindset of its citizens. Apparently it

did. World War II had ended. Yugoslavia had come out of the war on the winning side, a victor, which was already in and of itself enough to help most citizens repair their self-image. Tito said his historic "NO" to Stalin. Unlike their communist neighbors, the Yugoslavs had passports in the 1960s, a better standard of living, and open borders. Free schooling, a university education, and self-betterment as fundamental values, a communist faith that knowledge is power, self-management, the non-aligned-nations movement, tourism, festivals of international theater and film, a lively publishing industry, a number of cultural centers (Belgrade—Zagreb—Sarajevo—Ljubljana), and the general impression that life was getting better from one year to the next—all this was the praxis of de-provincialization. And yet texts that broach the themes of better and worse worlds, the periphery and the center, kept right on appearing in the Yugoslav literatures. And why not add the detail: the passport. In order to contemplate the theme of periphery and center, the author needs a passport that would allow him to cross borders without obstruction. The Yugoslavs had such a passport.

People Who'd Rather Be Sleeping

The novel-essay *My Dear Petrović* (*Dragi moj, Petroviću*, 1986) by Milovan Danojlić consists of ten letters, arranged in chronological order, sent by Mihailo Putnik, a retired returnee from America, to his friend Steve Petrovich in Cleveland. Putnik writes the letters to help Petrovich, who is wondering whether or not he should return to the old country. The letter-writer sits every day in *Domovina* (meaning Homeland) Café, and the name of the town is Kopanja. *Kopanja* is a wooden trough for feeding swine.

"Dizzy from the fact that you aren't needed," in a place where "wasteland enters at one door, and boredom sneaks out another,"

Mihajlo Putnik contemplates civilizations ("You and I no longer live in the same century," writes Putnik to his friend), the backwardness, paralysis, gloom, and lackluster life of the Serbian provinces, claiming that the Earth orbits more slowly where he is from, and that there is a special "delight taken in deadening," a "disease of sleeping," "relish of neglect and deafness," moments when you "forget where you were headed, what you were after, and you don't want anyone reminding you of it."

Putnik dissuades his friend from returning, claiming that what is drawing him back "is best cherished and held as memory."

"There is no real life anywhere for you and me. It is tough there, it is tough here, it is toughest of all with yourself. The trick is choosing the toughness that suits you best right now. As far as I am concerned it would be best if you could stand at the same time in several places, here and there, on your native soil and abroad, in abundance and poverty, in freedom and constraint, and to pass through all that, experiencing the one, while gauging its opposite; to be with your people (because you love them) and yet far away (because you find them disturbing), to serve and be served, to have and have not, never to be in one place with a single, final choice."

Putnik is merciless on the question of emigré illusions of home. He describes his "countrymen" who "seem to enjoy exacerbating their predicament: they aggravate it through laziness and fear, they worsen it by how unaccustomed they are to serious thinking"; their countrymen "would rather have been sleeping, walking in a dream, multiplying and feeding dream-like for fifty or a hundred years." Putnik is horrified by their stupidity, indifference, stubbornness ("Shout, they don't hear, write, they won't read. They have more pressing things to do. They are working to accomplish what they transcended in the beginning"), by their humility and their attachment to authority ("And the ordinary man is always standing with a man who is holding a cudgel"), their coarseness and malevolence.

Putnik furthermore dissects the delusions "our people" cultivate about themselves, tartly describing their traits, their arrogance, which comes from a suppressed "feeling of unimportance." He describes their obsession with death (funerals that, like weddings, last for three days); their penury, and how an entire philosophy of impoverishment has grown out of their poverty, troubles, and ignorance; and "the skills of the poor." The skills of the poor are the "acrobatics of spitting into the wind"; the skill of stealing salt shakers, toothpicks, and napkins from cafés and toilet paper from public bathrooms; the skill of cursing. Fellow countrymen are suspicious of everything and everybody ("He would rather starve than taste something he has never eaten before"); fearful of the cold ("The poor fear chills"); they have an aversion to "fresh air" ("Drafts are, for them, demonic"); they fear exploitation ("Now that's an idea particular to the poor: to think that it is possible to live without spending life"); they are wasteful and rapacious.

"For the holidays, they burst with pork and lamb roasts, stuffed cabbage, and boiled pig's feet. The television and radio programs for those days are like broadcasts from provincial taverns. Truck drivers' songs ring out, hiccuping and burping reverberate, and comedians offer advice for how to cure hangovers. Instead of antacids they recommend brine. Once they've had their fill of food and drink, they strike up a circle dance. The radio and television sets wobble, the kitchen credenza trembles with glasses that are never set out on the table! When Ćira married, he used up a whole tub of lard. For centuries they have been dreaming of a tub of lard, the lard drips down their whiskers, dribbles into their dream."

Putnik holds forth on the servile nature of their "countrymen" and their "terrifying" capacity to adapt to things ("There is nothing they won't learn to live with"). He senses the virulence of hatred ("Their malice has drawn into a clench around their lips, it has settled in their pupils, nestled into their speech"); he is appalled at its force ("Nothing will save you. Not a single public success, no honor, no riches or glory, nothing will give you safe haven"); its longevity ("They have long memories, they are waiting to pay back in kind, they will wait a hundred years for the opportunity. They exact their revenge even from the innocent, only so that they can knock the evil out of themselves"); and the fact that it cannot be rooted out. "The word for hate, *mrzeti*, is too strong. Our people have come up with a word that is more endearing, more heartfelt: *mrzančiti*. I assume you haven't heard it, and I doubt you'll find a true parallel in English. *Mrzančiti* means to exude hatred, to hate in quiet, long, and with determination, in keeping with tradition, for no reason in particular."

The Metaphysical Palanka

Danojlić's novel is close kin to another book, published earlier, the 400-page long philosophical essay *The Philosophy of the Palanka* (*Filozofija palanke*, 1969) by the Serbian philosopher Radomir Konstantinović. While Danojlić's novel is more or less forgotten today, the *Philosophy of the Palanka* was and remains a cult book. Konstantinović promoted a new concept, he gave a new, more complex meaning to the old word *palanka*. The *palanka* is not a village or a city, it is somewhere between the two. The *palanka* is a de-territorialized and de-contextualized place, everywhere and nowhere, a state of mind, afloat between "tribal spirit, as ideal-unique, and world spirit, as ideal-open." The *palanka* experiences itself as cast-off, forgotten, time left out of historical time, and then it bemoans its bitter fate, while at the same time turning this accursed destiny into its privilege. Being closed and forgotten meant being safe, while beyond, outside the circle of the *palanka*, rules the dangerous chaos of the wide world. Rigidity, petrification, a constant readiness for defense, a strong tribal awareness, infantilism, formulaic patterns of thought, fear of the unknown, fear of change, an apology for purity, innocence, and simplicity, the hermetic, a cult of the dead, security, normativity, conservatism, the static, anti-historicism—are only a few of the features typical of the world of the *palanka*. Konstantinović does not see the root of Serbian fascism in imitation of the German fascist model, or of any other for that matter, but instead he sees it in the *palanka*. The *palanka* is the model for Ur-fascism.

The Feast of the Periphery

One of the outcomes of the collapse of Yugoslavia, the wars, and new nationalistic state projects is the destruction of what had been the shared Yugolsav cultural space, the material destruction of culture (schools, cultural monuments, libraries, book burning, etc.), vandal-ism (the demolition of statues), and effacement of cultural segments (for instance, the era of Yugoslav culture). Every state that disap-peared from the former Yugoslavia has reconfigured its own national culture. In the tumultuous process of reconfiguration, there are cre-ative figures, works, opuses that have been dropped, some forgotten, some abruptly jettisoned, others degraded, de-throned, yet others over-valued in terms of the current national ideology and interests. There have been bad writers and artists in this time of over-inflating national culture who have been elevated to aesthetic heights merely because they were Croatian, Serbian, or Bosnian patriots. In the less than twenty years that the new states have existed on what was the territory of the former Yugoslavia, the cultural landscape has grown grayer, it has narrowed, and become provincial.

The dependent domestic media work to regurgitate political clichés which they have retrieved from nineteenth century political dustbins, and the crazed crowd soaks these up as if they are God's own truth. The domestic media and local politicians prattle on in a delirium about the national state, the ethnically pure and impure peoples, patriotism, heroism, defense of the homeland and patriotic honor, the enemy, his crimes against us, the national identity which had always been suppressed. Meanwhile, the foreign media exercise their almost knee-jerk colonialism, cranking out colonial clichés which ring true and convincing to their readers. They write of the terrible, wild, abandoned, uncivilized Balkans, communist repression, the consequence of which is a struggle of the little peoples for national identity and independence, while at the same time reinforcing the old mental divisions of Europe into its civilized western part and its wild, uncivilized eastern part. Here, of course, is the primitive, exotic, and bloodthirsty child—the Balkans.

Hence cultural texts are formed. The cultural text is a construct which assumes not only material factual culture but many written pages and miles of celluloid. The cultural text is a sort of meta-text. Metropoli create large and productive cultural texts. Vienna is one such cultural text. The Balkans are a cultural text. Kakania is a cultural text. The provinces are a cultural text.

The center is inclusive, the periphery exclusive; the center communicates, the periphery excommunicates; the center is multi-national, the periphery mono-national; the center is like a sponge, the periphery like stone. Whatever the case, the provinces are an inseparable part of the story of the metropolis, just as the center is an inseparable part of the story of the periphery. Only together do they make sense.

Fluorescent Fishermen

Some ten years ago, I cannot recall precisely when, I was out strolling along the Donauinsel during a visit to Vienna. The weather was warm, the shore studded with dozens of little restaurants, and the Viennese were out dancing the salsa. The warm summer evening, the swaying bodies, and the sound of Latin American salsa were nicely incongruous with the image of Vienna on the "beautiful, blue Danube." I saw something unusual on the shore: three figures wearing helmets, with beaming flashlights affixed, holding fishing rods and casting fluorescent lines into the water. The image of the glowing figures with their glowing fishing rods struck me, especially because I soon learned that these were my countrymen, just as in the old jokes—a Croat, a Serb, and a Bosnian. It turned out that they lived in Vienna and spent every weekend fishing on the Danube. I nibbled some cheese pastry with them, sipped brandy straight from the bottle (the real homemade stuff, plum brandy). Around us swirled the sensual strains of the salsa.

"Doesn't the noise disturb the fish?" I asked.

"Not at all," confirmed the fishermen.

Vienna suddenly shone with the glow of a metropolis. The salsa, the immigrants dancing with the Viennese, my happy countrymen—these fluorescent fishermen. The tolerant Danubian fish who weren't disturbed by the noise. I remembered that Zagreb is the only city I know which suffers from hydrophobia. While all the other cities I know embrace the banks of their rivers, Zagreb flees from the Sava to the foothills of the nearby hill, Sljeme, which I hope is not being touted as a mountain in all the new Croatian textbooks. As soon as he came into power, Franjo Tuđman proclaimed Zagreb a metropolis. Of course he also proclaimed himself the Croatian George Washington. From his official position, from the mouth of the first Croatian president, poured the language of the provinces with a thundering inferiority complex. Our "little Paris," our "little Vienna," our Croatian "George Washington"—those are the tropes of the provinces. With this rhetorical figure, stuck like a burr to popular references, the provinces do what they can to leap on board the train of history and inscribe themselves on the map.

Culture As Utopia

Most of the culture of Europe came out of the vortex of these fundamental oppositions, from the dynamics of center and periphery, metropolis and the provinces, the *palanka* and the world. Today, at a moment when all the great Utopian systems have come tumbling down, when the political and social imagination has been exhausted, when the idea of democracy is spent, when the gray, cold mechanism of money has replaced all else, at a time when the five-hundred-year-old Gutenberg galaxy is dying while the new, young, omnipresent Digital galaxy is ascendant, at a time of the barbarization of high technology, Culture suddenly looms large as a straw to be grasped at. Culture is suddenly the language, the reason, the goal. Culture has taken the place of the mumbo-jumbo of European political lingo and substance, and, hey, the main substance of European unification has suddenly become culture. Culture is the ideological Euro, the means of communication. Culture is the diplomatic language and the language of diplomacy. Culture is a field of struggle, an exorcism of superiority. Culture is the legal nursery of chauvinism, racism, nationalism, otherness, and supremacy (*Dostoyevsky vs. Balzac*). Culture is a means of transportation (*Only with culture can we go out into the world*) and a way to export value. Culture is a brand, culture is the vehicle of national identity (*If it weren't for Ivo Pogorelić, no one would know a thing about us!*), culture is the tourist industry. Culture is what countries are. Ireland is the land of James Joyce, France is the land of Marcel Proust, Austria is the land of Robert Musil, just as little Klagenfurt is where Musil was born. *These are the people of Ivo Andrić, Miloš Crnjanski*, howled Emir Kusturica at a Belgrade gathering, condemning the proclamation of independence for Kosovo Albanians. And the Kosovars must have separated, of course, only so they could steal culture, *the sacred Serbian monasteries.* James Joyce, who fled from Ireland, was dragged back there after his death and placed on the throne of Irish literature—and Irish tourism. Today his name and face are trapped on souvenir coffee cups. Even little Galway profits from the little house, now a museum, where Nora, Joyce's wife, was born.

So what is culture, then? Culture is a phenomenon that serves for all sorts of things, from money laundering to laundering the collective national conscience, and perhaps a recent event can provide the clearest illustration. Only two days after Joshua Bell, the famous violinist, had performed in Boston at a concert where people paid large sums to come and hear him, he performed the same repertoire at a subway station, except that no one stopped to listen, and he collected only a few coins in his hat.

The Kakania Project

Two decades ago the cultural construct of "Central Europe" surfaced briefly among intellectuals, and for a time academics and writers such as Milan Kundera, György Konrád, Joseph Brodsky, and others wrote about it. This construct no longer attracts interest, but one occasionally comes across mention of the "Kakania," as a half-hearted call for a new republic of writers, or a sense of shared geographical and historical space, or a longing for a new cultural construct. If we play for a moment with the Kakanian literary utopia, we will automatically find ourselves imagining this (and every other) republic of writers as a space of freedom. Why not do the opposite and try to imagine the Kakania republic in other ways: as a space of restriction, or a space of decontamination, or of deprivation, depending, of course, on one's perspective.

So we imagine that at the border of the Republic of Literature of Kakania the imperial officials demand of writers that they leave behind their passports and agree in writing to respect the Kakanian rules of the road. For Kakania is a literary republic, is it not? Aren't writers banned, while dwelling there, from strutting the stuff of their nations, their states (they are not literary soccer players after all), their ethnicity, their religious and political conviction? One must be forbidden from speaking of such things. The only visa for entry to the Republic of Letters should be a literary work.

Let us now try to imagine a conversation between two Kakanians, one who is respecting the rules and another who is violating them.

"So, you, too, are a writer?"

"Yes. Aren't we all?"

"We are, we are, we all put pen to paper, we do little else. But some of us are more successful at it than others. It is not the same if you're English or if you're Macedonian. And, by the way, where are you from?"

"Kakania. Isn't that obvious?"

"Why should it be? I'm betting you're Lithuanian. Come on, admit it."

"No, I am Kakanian."

"OK. Kakanian. I have nothing against it. I am a Czech, my

mother is Hungarian, and I'm not ashamed to admit it. From the cultural and historical perspective, I have more right to call myself Kakanian than you do. But we aren't splitting hairs here, now are we. What language do you write in?"

"Literary."

"All of us are literate, we wouldn't be here otherwise. But whether you write in the language of Shakespeare or some fellow called Costa Costolopoulus matters. Come on, confess, I won't tell a soul."

"Literary language."

"You are really stuck on that. Weren't you baptized? And by the way, do you believe in God?"

"I believe in the muse."

"Jesus, what a stickler! And on top of it you've disguised yourself as a feminist. OK, so that's politically correct. The muses were women after all, so we had to include them in our work. But, do tell, my Kakanian, where do you stand on politics?"

"I believe in humanism."

"Humanism?! Blah, blah, blah . . . I haven't met anyone more boring than you in ages!"

I am afraid such a Utopian Kakania would soon lose its citizens. European writers are too used to lugging the baggage of their states with them, acting as its representatives, espousing its history, its political, national, religious beliefs, its communities and homeland. They are too used to not treating Others, no matter who those others are, as their own. If the Republic of Literature as described above, with all its rules, were to actually exist, it would be a dangerous test for Europe, for its foundations, and its future.

Most writers flourish within their state, religious, political, ethnic, and national communities, within their clans, institutions, publishing houses, readers, academies, their honors, and seldom do they toss out all the medals they have received and go out into the world as beggars, relying only on their naked talent. What happens to art when it is stripped of its context is best shown by the example of Joshua Bell. Everyone will spit at you, or even worse, they won't even see you. In any case your hat will be empty.

All in all, writers are only people, and literature is a complex, multifaceted thing, just as the relations of influence and power, interrelations between the periphery and the center, between the metropolis and the provinces, between the *palanka* and the outside world are complex. The well-intentioned creators of European cultural policy and those who are putting it into practice imagine that relationship as if it were part of a fairy tale.

The prince meets a frog. "Kiss me," says the frog, "and I'll turn into a princess." The prince kisses the frog and, bingo!, it turns into a princess.

But the fairy tale could also go like this . . .
     "Kiss me," says the frog, "and I'll turn into a princess."
     "No, for the time being you suit me better as a frog," answers the prince.

Or, like this . . .
     "I'll kiss you, and you'll turn into a princess!" says the prince to the frog.
     "No thanks," says the frog, "for the time being I would rather stay a frog."

April 2010

THE ELUSIVE
SUBSTANCE OF
THE ARCHIVE

A File-Storm

There's something I need to confess: I've never peered into a real archive, and I don't know how such an archive works. I'm a writer, an archive amateur. My private archive is a hazy, subconscious space in which the camera of my eye has randomly stored dozens of faces, dozens of chance gestures, sounds, and sentences. It's a house that does not exist, but of which I regularly dream, full of staircases, balconies, cubbyholes, cobwebs, and holes in the wall through which a harsh wind blows. This archive is home to the real and imagined conversations I've had, objects and memories of objects, images, scents, and books whose contents resemble the house from my recurring dream. But the thing is, I'm not the one who walks this subconscious archival space picking out files: files rush out at me. They leap from the archive, jostling for my attention, pushing and shoving, hustling, all so embarrassingly "promiscuous": so many things slip into bed with so many other things, and I'm really not sure why.

I recently visited the island of Bali. Night falls early on Bali, and the morning rises late. In the silence of the evening I would listen out for the sound of heavy leaves falling from the trees. Always one leaf after the other, never two at once. The giant ants that would come crawling down the computer screen from out of nowhere, and the books grey with damp, left behind by tourists and stacked on an open shelf for anyone to read, were the triggers for the "file-storm" to come. (I mean, I think they were?) The hotel staff spent the day with brooms and rubbish bags in hand, diligently sweeping up every fallen leaf. They'd even do so when it was windy—actually, especially then—as if they were having a competition with the wind. Other staff changed the bed linen daily, and the hand towels several times a day. I'd wake up at night, sit out on the veranda in a wicker armchair, and stare out into the muggy tropical darkness. Invisible files from my archive would fall on me like leaves, and at times I thought I was going to faint, lose control, and be forever submerged beneath that lush and invisible pile.

My recently-deceased mother was with me on Bali, as was my long-deceased father. The town of Bol on the Adriatic island of Brač also appeared, the place my mother and I spent our last summer holiday together. (Look, there, out of nowhere an image of my mother's clothing pops up: a petite silk blouse and a little straw hat! Had Bali become Bol or Bol Bali?) A few people who really had no business being there also turned up, people who I hadn't seen for more than thirty years, and with whom I've long since had any contact. What do they want from me here on Bali? I asked myself. And what would happen if the hotel staff found out about all the people staying in my room on the sly. How much would that cost? I wondered.

On Bali the locals use palm leaves as miniature trays and every morning place offerings (a flower, some rice, and a joss stick) in front of their houses, food for both good and evil spirits. As I understand it, with this daily religious ritual they pacify the Archive in which the living and the dead, the visible and invisible worlds reside. "You need to feed them, because when they're hungry, man they can have a mean streak," a local taxi driver confirmed.

The Encyclopedia of the Dead

It is said that Danilo Kiš's short story "The Encyclopedia of the Dead" was inspired by a newspaper clipping about a secret Mormon archive in Utah, the Granite Mountain Records Vault. Today, thanks to the Internet, photographs of the archive, its impressive location, and equally impressive information about the archive, are widely available. Thirty years ago, when the short story was written, a small newspaper article about Mormon biographies stored on microfilm in hidden caves in Utah appears to have fired Kiš's historically sensitive imagination. The narrator of "The Encyclopedia of the Dead" is a theatre scholar by profession ("Last year, as you know, I went to Sweden at the invitation of the Institute for Theatre Research"[1]) and narrates her story to an unnamed listener. In Stockholm she is shown a mysterious archive containing the biographies of people whose names are not recorded "in any other encyclopedia."[2] The narrator's experience of the archive is so incredibly romanticized that fragments from a gothic novel come to mind. The narrator is ushered into the archive by a guard "holding a large ring of keys."[3] The

---

1   Danilo Kiš, *The Encyclopedia of the Dead*, trans. by Michael Henry Heim (Evanston, IL: Northwestern University Press, 1997), 39.

2   Ibid., 43.

3   Ibid., 39.

guard—whom the narrator refers to as "Mr. Cerberus"—locks the door behind her, leaving her alone in the library as if in a casemate. In this sense, entry into the library is entry into Hades, into the world of the dead.

> A draft blew in from somewhere, rippling the cobwebs, which, like dirty scraps of gauze, hung from the book-shelves as over select bottles of old wine in a cellar. All the rooms were alike, connected by a narrow passageway, and the draft, whose source I could not identify, penetrated everywhere.[4]

> I therefore started skimming through the paragraphs, turn-ing the open book, insofar as the chain would allow, in the direction of the pale light shed by the lamp. The thick layer of dust that had gathered along their edges and the dan-gling scraps of cobwebs bore clear witness to the fact that no one had handled the volumes in a long time. They were fettered to one another like galley slaves, but their chains had no locks.[5]

The secret initiators of *The Encyclopedia of the Dead* . . .

> believe in the miracle of the biblical resurrection and they complete their vast catalogue in preparation for that mo-ment. So that everyone will be able to find not only his fel-low men but also—and more important—his own forgotten past. When the time comes, this compendium will serve

---

4   Ibid., 40.
5   Ibid., 41.

as a great treasury of memories and a unique proof of the resurrection.[6]

Danilo Kiš's short story was published in 1983, long before the Internet was in widespread use. In skimming the encyclopedia, the manner in which the narrator finds and reads the biography of her recently deceased father is almost a literary foreshadowing of today's navigation of the Internet. The narrator doesn't really *read*, she skims the pages, she *looks* ("Then, as if it were all unfolding before my eyes"[7]), and sees that every detail of her father's biography is intricately bound up with the details of other events.

> For The Encyclopedia of the Dead, history is the sum of human destinies, the totality of ephemeral happenings. That is why it records every action, every thought, every creative breath, every spot height in the survey, every shovelful of mud, every motion that cleared a book from the ruins.[8]

We don't learn anything about encyclopedists, about the archivist, or about systematizers of human destinies from Kiš's story. They remain hidden. Only *The Book of the Dead* (or *The Encyclopedia of the Dead*, or just *The Book*) exists, an all-knowing, all-seeing, and therefore, divine mechanism of memory, one that eliminates hierarchies, which belong to the human world, and restores a higher justice. This supreme mechanism of memory, which thirty years ago emerged from Kiš's humanistic and utopian imagination, and his

---

6   Ibid., 43.

7   Ibid., 42.

8   Ibid., 56-57.

painful firsthand knowledge that the majority of human lives end as anonymous dust, has today, thanks to technology, slipped its ethical, aesthetic, moral, and metaphysical coordinates and become the dominant cultural obsession of our age. Superficially, this obsession is expressed as a mass orgy of self-representation. Below the surface breeds an anxious fear, the fear of death.

The Archive Is Real, Life Is Virtual

The archive (or, more accurately, an archivist) given voice by Pete Postlethwaite is the narrator of the film *The Age of Stupid* (2009). The film opens with devastated symbols of the contemporary world (London under water, the Taj Mahal in ruins, Las Vegas buried under sand, the Sydney Opera House in flames) before the camera leads us out across the oceans towards a giant platform shaped like a flower—a kind of Noah's Ark stranded and suspended above the sea. "Welcome to the Global Archive!" the voice of the archivist greets us. The year is 2055, and with the assistance of a super touchscreen the archivist takes us back to our time, to the year 2008. The film is about global warming and how humankind, instead of salvation, chose suicide. The archive, located in the middle of nowhere, has been left for future intelligent beings as testimony to our existence. The archive, which to the man in the street first prompts associations with a secret police or state archive, and then perhaps a lonely and forlorn gathering place for eccentrics, works its way into the popular imagination as a virtual Noah's Ark—one devoid of specimens of the human species, sent out in an unknown direction to an unknown recipient, like a message in a bottle. I suspect that those watching the film don't actually notice the upended relationship between the virtual and the real worlds, a relationship the authors of this emotionally charged ecological manifesto simply disregard. Relationships are set up contrary to expectations: the archive is a

real place, where real, physical exhibits are housed, and attended to by a **real** archivist. Humankind and its history are virtual, only coming to life when the archivist lowers his finger onto the touchscreen.

How Did That Happen?

For the man in the street the archive is a synonym for the original, the authentic. Whoever controls the archive possesses significant manipulative power. And for this reason the price of the archive on the market of our values is in constantly growing, irrespective of whether we are dealing with the shoes Judy Garland wore in *The Wizard of Oz* or the archives of a writer. Writers who strike a deal on the sale of their archives in their own lifetimes guarantee themselves immortality. Even a certain Croatian poet cottoned on to the connection between the archive and immortality, and he gave his all to outlive his contemporaries. And he succeeded, dying in his one-hundred-and-first year on earth. He spent his whole life carefully building his archive, collecting everything—people say that he even kept his tram tickets. The only thing he messed up, tragically, was the context. He and his archive turned up in the wrong century, in the wrong country, and in the wrong circumstances.

Until the discovery of photography came along, the poor never left any proof of their existence. It was some time before the privileged let the less privileged have their turn in front of the camera, those who only could afford a single, once-in-a-lifetime shot. In Russian peasant huts there was a place called the "pretty corner"—*krassnyj ugolok*—set aside for icons and candles lit to honor God and the family's patron saint. It was also some time before photos of the *pater familias* and other family members made their way into the "pretty corner," before this miniature domestic shrine became a miniature home archive, before family photos made their way into boxes (inevitably shoe boxes), and then finally into family albums, at last uncoupled from God and the saints.

How did it happen, the transfer of power from the archive to the archivist, from the institution to the profession, and then, from the professional to the amateur archivist? The process began, I think, when photos were first placed in the household shrine, and continued with the destruction of the old order, with the deconstruction of systems of power, of institutions of state and religion, of history as a science, and with the emergence of psychoanalysis and the mass repudiation of established beliefs. Art, the Russian Revolution, and avant-garde movements of the early twentieth century, Dadaism and Futurism, and their poetics of subversion of established values—whether aesthetic, moral, or of any other nature—all played their part.

In Russian culture the theme of archivomania begins with Russian realism (with its emblematic scrooge figures). A century later the theme of the archive sprung into life in the novels of Konstantin Vaginov, a Russian writer from the 1930s. Vaginov depicts a world of obsessive, half-crazed collectors and archivists, those who in a time of revolutionary chaos scavenge the flotsam and jetsam of the everyday. Svistonov collects books, newspaper cuttings, and even real-life characters for the novel he is writing. The heroes of *Bambocciada* found the "Society for the Collection of Trivia," while the hero of *Harpagoniana,* a certain Zhulonbin, is a systematizer of all kinds of trash, from chewed pencils to cigarette butts and fingernails. These carnivalesque losers, inhabitants of the world of yesterday, are the antithesis of a revolutionary time (re)constructing life from the very beginning.

Archivomania burst back into thematic life in the 1970s in the artistic program of Russian Soc-artists. Sensing that the Soviet epoch was on the wane, Soc-artists set about defamiliarizing their everyday surroundings. Based on the traditions of both the Russian avant-garde and Pop-Art, Ilya Kabakov obsessively deconstructs the Soviet everyday by simply making it visible. Kabakov's installations bring all manner of things together and to life: social realist imagery, bureaucratic forms, slogans, posters, Soviet school primers, consumer products, and not least, the language of Soviet clichés. Kabakov's projects are tragic archives of the "rubbish" that the Soviet epoch, embodied by a loyal representative—the anonymous Soviet citizen—left behind.

After the symbolic Dadaist gesture of Duchamp's (in)famous *Fountain* and the epoch of the avant-garde, the Pop Art movement, marked by the iconic figure of Andy Warhol and his famous *Campbell's Soup* cans, continued to breathe life into and develop the archival line. Contemporary art practice today is largely based on the idea and practice of the archive; moreover, the archivization of the work in progress is frequently transformed into the work of art itself.

One of the most important figures in contemporary art, Christian Boltanski, was back in the news last year when, in a bizarre artistic gesture, the sixty-five-year-old sold his life to the Australian millionaire and art collector, David Walsh. For eight years, commencing January 1, 2010, four cameras will film (that is, archive) the artist in his studio day and night, projecting this unusual one-man-big-brother-show in a cave in Tasmania. If Boltanski lives for the next eight years, he will receive the full asking price for his life. If he dies within the eight years, he gets nothing. In doing what he is doing,

Christian Boltanski is putting into practice the human archivization on which his own art centers, an art exemplified by his ongoing collection of anonymous human heartbeats. The artist has finally put his head on the block of the archive and symbolically returned the whole endeavor of art to its beginnings—to a cave. (Weren't cave drawings the first archival exhibits?!)

As a longtime archivist of anonymous human destinies, Boltanski has now put himself in the position of the archived object, an act completely in accord with our time, one in which we all, as if in a kind of pact with the devil, are simultaneously archivist and the archived.

Archive Fever

I first showed symptoms of archive fever in 1989, although at the time I didn't pick them up. All of sudden I was overcome by a feeling that the world I knew was under threat from a terrible amnesiac tsunami. A rescue project to save symbols of Yugoslav everyday life and popular culture—an idea that was to become the *Lexicon of Yugoslav Mythology*—was sketched in a document of not more than two or three pages and briefly kept alfoat by the enthusiasm of three people. The common Yugoslav home fell apart barely two years later. When a house is collapsing, normal people look to save life and limb, and rescuing their favorite books is the furthest thing from their minds. But actually, I'm not so sure about that. Warned to take only their most essential belongings, when the air raid signals blared people took the most bizarre things down into the shelters. During the first alarm in Zagreb an old lady admitted to me that during the Second World War she found herself in the basement with an alarm clock in her hand. Why an alarm clock, of all things, was so essential she wasn't able to explain.

Going abroad was like finding oneself an air raid shelter—one only takes the essentials. Most of all I missed my books, my Zagreb home library. The truth is that new books stuck to me like magnets, as if trying to compensate for the loss. I don't exclude the possibility that I made Amsterdam my home just so I could give a home to my books, to both the new and the old, which lay in boxes, lonely and neglected in a friend's Zagreb basement. It was a number of years before I felt able to confront the boxes. During a visit to Zagreb I spent a few days going through them, sorting out the books that I'd one day take to Amsterdam with me. A couple of years later my Zagreb friend offered to pack the books I'd set aside in a combi-van and taxi them to Amsterdam. I planned a welcome reception for their arrival, cleaning up my Amsterdam cellar and having special shelves built. At first I'll put all the boxes in the cellar I thought, and then slowly, one by one, I'll take them up to the apartment. I gave up after unpacking the first few boxes. Holding them in my hands again, the books no longer meant what I thought they would mean to me. Their order had been lost forever; their arrangement in my old Zagreb library impossible to reconstruct; their significance lost along with the codes of memory, as if they were written in a dead, undecipherable language. Ten unopened boxes still languish in my Amsterdam cellar.

In the meantime the *Lexicon of Yugoslav Mythology* has been published as a book and is apparently even in its third edition. A handful of enterprising people copied the online corpus I had begun collecting with my Amsterdam students and gave it a hardcover. These memory fragments of the former Yugoslav everyday assembled by a group of anonymous young contributors don't set my heart aflutter. The authenticity of the impulse has petered out. Because things that I was sure would disappear forever (the Internet was not yet in widespread use), today, twenty years later, pop up like jack-in-the-boxes. Everything the ordinary Yugonostalgic heart could ever desire is on YouTube. There are Internet sites loaded with old Yugoslav films and TV series, sites with ethnic jokes from the Yugoslav-era, virtual collections of objects from the Yugoslav everyday, the packaging of pioneering Yugoslav products, exemplars of socialist design. There are new "Yugonostalgic" souvenirs: men's socks with Tito on them, bottles of wine with Tito's signature, cookbooks with Tito's favorite recipes. Memory of the Yugoslav everyday, which just fifteen years ago was an act of political and cultural subversion, is today just a bit of fun; things once considered irreplaceable relics are today cheap souvenirs. An authentic need to reestablish a brutally broken cultural continuity has been transformed into political kitsch and the cultural program of a well-funded NGO.

Serious and historically relevant analyses of the Yugoslav system have yet to appear. Equally lacking are reliable analyses of Yugoslavia's disintegration. The diligent historians are for the time being maintaining their silence. Tito's monuments have been destroyed, but a cookbook with his favorite dishes is, it seems, a bestseller. The virtual and physically-existing souvenir industry is broadcasting false signals, offering symbolic and high-speed acknowledgement of an unacknowledged history.

I am from the generation born after the Second World War, experience of which I gleaned directly from my parents and Yugoslav post-war culture, one that in spite of its proclaimed future orientation was actually deeply immersed in the wartime past. I am a witness to the recent "Yugoslav" disintegration and war (the war officially ended fifteen years ago), the change of ideological and political systems, and the collapse of a cultural system. I am a witness to multiple strategies conceived to organize the erasure of the past: the burning of books; the deletion of biographies; the rewriting of school textbooks and official truths; the change of languages, flags, and ideological options; the excavation and burial of bones; the fabrication of history; and the renovation and renaming of an entire landscape. I am also a witness to the overnight disappearance of an untold number of people.

In my life experience I also know something of the rapid replacement of technology (and it seems that technology shapes our consciousness far more than ideology). With enviable elasticity I replaced the ink pot and quill with a typewriter, and a typewriter with a computer. I also possess intergalactic experience—from the Gutenberg galaxy I've moved, like or it not, into a digital one. Since achieving mass penetration (and this happened barely fifteen years ago!), the Internet has turned everything we knew on its head. And here an important question arises, one that I suspect has no quick answer. Would Marcel Proust have written *In Search of Lost Time* if he had had a Madeleine cookie on the computer screen in front of him?

Memory Stick

And here we are, in a time in which a Kamchatka pensioner doing the crossword can check the Internet for the image of a cookie that made a French writer famous. We live in a time in which the bizarre collectors of Vaginov's novel, the founders of the "Society for the Collection of Trivia," should be acknowledged as visionaries. A quick Internet search for unusual museums proves the point: Museum of Toast Portraits of Famous People, World Carrot Museum, Virtual Museum of Scams and Frauds, Museum of Odd Socks, Gallery of Obscure Things, Museum of Funeral History, The Trash Museum,

Virtual Museum of Cigar Box Art, Zymoglyphic Museum, Banana Museum, Pretzel Museum, Museum of Toilets, Museum of Modern Madness . . . Theorists of popular culture would no doubt claim that virtual museums are an ironic subversion of the cultural canon, for as we all know, the institution of the museum is there to keep strict watch on the canonical order. But even this is a moot point, because we live in a time in which museum architecture has turned the traditional concept of the museum on its head, a time in which a museum's architecture is inevitably far more important than its contents. Today, museums are rarely built to house art, rather, they are, in and of themselves, works of art. The hypothetical notion—those with art will also need a museum—has today become—those with a museum will get art.

We live in a time of archive fever. We compete with our media gods and goddesses. There we are, walking through the world with our memory sticks around our necks, each of us with our own homepage, each of us with an archive stored on the web. There are also those who wear their archives on their own skin, in the form of tattoos. And we are everywhere: our fingerprints left on scanners at border crossings, in medical clinics and files, on all kinds of cards confirming our membership in different organizations—from fitness clubs to the Subscribers for Posthumous Assistance. We haul our invisible freight through the world, our documents, our power and phone bills, our address books, our bank and business cards. We walk through the world well networked and connected, with MySpace and Facebook, phone numbers stored in mobile phones, family albums stored on the web, with souvenirs and photos of our children in the windows of our apartments (a little Dutch quirk). All of these are our archives. They're how we assure ourselves of eternity. And the more voluminous the archive that trails us, the less of ourselves there is. Yet we head off into battle with renewed energy: with camcorders and digital cameras, recording our voices, our thoughts, our everyday lives down to the minutest of details. In this private big brother show, this public big brother show, we record everything: the hypothetical moment of conception, the embryo, the baby in utero, birth, first steps, first words, first birthdays. And the richer our archives become, the less of ourselves there seems to be. We don't communicate with each other. None of us has the patience for others' photo albums, holiday pictures, or videotapes, which long went out the window in any case. Oh so modern, we put things on YouTube so anyone can gawk at them. We used to send out ghostly signals of our existence, and now we make fireworks out of our lives. We enjoy the orgy of being, twittering, buying new toys, iPhones and iPads, and all the while our hunger just grows and grows. We wear memory sticks around our necks, having of course first made copies. The memory stick is our celestial sarcophagus, our soul, our capsule, our soul in a capsule. One day we will be catapulted into the Great Archive, where someone will find and open us like a black box.

In the meantime, our work will see us turn up in some new place, in a cheap hotel room, with a completely unjustified sense of control over our lives. With indignation we'll discover that the cheap room doesn't have an Internet connection, or a television. We'll try and fall asleep reading a book, but we won't quite manage . . .

> You cannot get to sleep because you lie so narrowly, in an attempt to avoid contact with anything that isn't shielded by sheets and pillowcase. The first sign then, in an excessive attention to the bed, an irresistible anxiety about the hundreds who have slept there before you, leaving their dust

and debris in the fibres of the blankets, greasing the surface of the heavy, slippery counterpane. The dust of others, and of other times, fills the room, settles on the carpet, marks out the sticky passage from the bed to bathroom.[9]

And as the pale morning light comes through the window we'll helplessly watch the dust falling upon us like a fine snow.

June 2010

---

9   Carolyn Steedman, *Dust* (Manchester: Manchester University Press, 2001), 17.

AFTERWORD

A POSTCARD
FROM BERLIN
BY
DAVID WILLIAMS

1.

The shopping bag, the shuffle, the Old Testament beard, and the pants pulled up around his belly button mark Detlef as gently eccentric, and the couple of thousand people gathered in Berlin's Mauerpark on a sunny Sunday afternoon love him for it. Twenty years ago the Mauerpark was a no man's land between East and West Berlin, and Detlef, singing his almost famous German version of Sinatra's "My Way," would have been shot. The impresario of this celebration of the awkward and the awful (and ironic?) is an Irish bicycle courier who goes under the pseudonym Joe Hatchiban—from the Japanese *Juhachiban*, ("number eighteen" or "lucky karaoke song"). YouTube confirms that like Detlef, Hatchiban is now a local and budding global personality. In his many media interviews he concedes the *strangeness* of hosting karaoke afternoons on a former death strip, but like the journalists who interview him, he struggles to articulate what it all means. *Der Spiegel* suggested that it was "just a good old-fashioned good time."

2.

In "Karaoke Culture," the essay that opens and defines this collection, Dubravka Ugrešić writes that as a cultural critic (a "dubious guild") she is, in karaoke, ready "to see more than just desperate squawking to the backing track of 'I Will Survive'." As she maintains, "karaoke supports less the democratic idea that everyone can have a shot if they want one, and more the democratic practice that everyone wants a shot if there's one on offer." Mauerpark karaoke celebrates *feeling über alles*: the worse the performance, the more enthusiastic the crowd. One struggles to imagine the skinny Canadian tourist squealing Prince's "Kiss" and doing one-armed push-ups in the loneliness of his bedroom, but give him the Mauerpark crowd and he's ready to go. Anonymous and amateur, the Canadian tourist doesn't "display any artistic pretensions, or any particular concern about authorship." His creation is neither plagiarism nor imitation, "because both terms belong to a different time and a different cultural system."

3.

Whether we are polite children of the southern German provinces or *bourgeois-bohemian* migrants from across oceans, Berlin is not so much a projection screen for fantasies of a life more exciting (and certainly more affordable), but a screen on which to play out these fantasies. A little rebellion here, a little self-invention there—karaoke on the death strip is just the start. In the spirit of the mayor of Berlin's declaration that the city is "poor but sexy," we think of ourselves the same way. We don't wonder whether the one-in-five Berliners who are structurally unemployed would perhaps be happier being a little less sexy, if only they were a little less poor. At this moment Berlin is the ultimate karaoke-city, a place to be "somewhere else, someone else, someone else somewhere else." As Ugrešić writes, "karaoke culture in all its manifestations unites narcissism, exhibitionism, and the neurotic need for the individual to inscribe him or herself on the indifferent surface of the world, irrespective of whether the discontent individual uses the bark of a tree, his or her body, the Internet, photography, an act of vandalism, murder, or art. In the roots of this culture, however, lies a more serious motive: fear of death. From the surface of karaoke culture shimmers the mask of death."

4.

Ugrešić's 1997 novel *The Museum of Unconditional Surrender* was elegiacally named for a museum that no longer existed. The museum, housed in the building in Berlin in which Nazi Germany signed its capitulation to the Soviet authorities, had closed three years earlier. It re-opened in 1995 with the somewhat more benign name, the *German-Russian Museum Berlin-Karlshorst*. The barracks surrounding the museum so poignantly described by Ugrešić's narrator have now largely been torn down, and the Soviet officers' quarters next door to the museum are currently being converted into luxury apartments. As Ugrešić writes in this collection, "freedom from knowledge, from the past, from continuity, from cultural memory and cultural hierarchy, and an inconceivable speed—these are the determinants of karaoke culture."

5.

Christoph Koch, a German journalist, has just published a book about his trauma of going forty days and forty nights without the Internet or a mobile phone. Other journalists have been interviewing him about his messianic survival in the wilderness. In recent years hotels, cafés, airports, and all kinds of other places have advertised Internet access as a selling point, but we can't be far from a time when black zones beyond Google's reach will be priced at a premium.

6.

Ugrešić the essayist has always been a switch hitter. Within collections, and even within individual essays, she writes alternately as elegist, diatribalist, satirist, ironist, and on occasion, moralist. Her first essay collection was published in 1993, and in the original Croatian was called *Američki fikcionar* (*American Fictionary*), but the book appeared in English as *Have a Nice Day: From the Balkan War to the American Dream*. In response to Ugrešić's notes on couch potatoes, organizers, shrinks, and jogging, a reviewer for *The New York Times* wrote "judging by this book, Ms. Ugrešić saw little of the United States, made few friendships of any depth and watched television a lot." Much got lost in translation with that change of title.

7.

Almost three hundred years ago Jonathan Swift modestly proposed that the starving Irish sell their children as food for the rich. At the time, and in the intervening years, some readers have taken Swift literally, but no one has ever taken these people seriously. In "Assault on the Minibar," either Ugrešić or her narrator (which?), fed up with the *totalitarian* assumption of guilt that she is going to steal from the minibar and not pay for it, confesses to scratching "Death to the Minibar!" into the little locked fridge, throwing it in the bath, and turning on the faucet. Thinking about the victimized little minibar in Room 513, the aforementioned *New York Times* reviewer will no doubt be first to call the police.

8.

In this summer of 2010 Ugrešić presented a version of the essay "The Elusive Substance of the Archive" as the closing keynote address at an academic conference in the United Kingdom. Backed by small armies of footnotes and appeals to the authority of literary history and literary theory, we scholars (and those of us impersonating scholars) had hammered the theme of "Archive" for almost a week. At the conclusion of Ugrešić's address the applause continued well beyond that required by courtesy. In three-quarters of an hour, the reflections of a novelist seemed to contain more *truth* about the subject than we had collectively managed, with the help of Benjamin, Joyce, Borges, and Sebald, in days. These lines hit hardest: "We walk through the world with our memory sticks around our necks, each of us with our own homepage, each of us with an archive stored on the web. We, are everywhere . . . And the more voluminous the archive that trails us, the less of ourselves there seems to be . . . We don't communicate with each other . . . Oh so modern, we put things on YouTube so anyone can gawk at them. We used to send out ghostly signals of our existence, and now we make fireworks out of our lives. We enjoy the orgy of being, twittering, buying new toys, iPhones and iPads, and all the while our hunger just grows and grows. We wear memory sticks around our necks, having of course first made copies. The memory stick is our celestial sarcophagus, our soul, our capsule, our soul in a capsule."

9.

A visit to the "Foreigner's Office" (*Auslandsamt*) in Berlin is a bowel-voiding experience, more like a *Battle Royale* fixed by the invisible hand of fear than a tranquilized wander through IKEA. My game began on a January morning at 5:30 A.M. The Office is located in a semi-industrial part of Wedding, a Berlin neighborhood that has all the social problems of a Parisian *banlieue*—with all that word implies about migration and poverty—yet none of the architectural violence. Were it not so poor, Wedding would be pretty. A Bulgarian friend—an experienced player—had given me an insider tip on the unwritten rules of the game. The first and most important rule, she declared, is to be in line outside the building no later than 6:15 A.M. The second is to have memorized the building's complex floor plan, so when doors open just before 7:00 A.M. you'll get to the necessary section among the top dozen finishers. If you don't manage to pull a waiting number by 7:10 A.M., you won't be among the day's competitors. The only consolation is that—at least at this stage—disqualification is only temporary. You can get up at 5:30 A.M. and compete again tomorrow.

10.

The floor plan of the Berlin Foreigner's Office offers a fascinating lesson in German (and European) geopolitics. Asylum seekers are quarantined in a separate building; illegal "new entrants" to Germany aren't allowed above the ground floor (i.e. they're non-starters in the game who never even get to level one); Turks have a spacious floor to themselves; alone together, former Yugoslavs (minus the upgraded Slovenians) get to renew old acquaintances on a floor of their own; the Soviet Union, minus the three upgraded Baltic states (replaced by Thailand, Vietnam, and Taiwan!), is reassembled in Berlin exile—Eastern Europe is certainly not lost; while a wild mix of countries, from Indonesia to the United Arab Emirates to Somalia, mingle in an exclusively Muslim brotherhood. Even the grouping together of the entire Americas, Oceania, Israel, much of wealthier Asia, and central and southern Africa has its own "leftover" logic.

11.

With the dulcet inflections of my New Zealand accent, my German is gentle on local ears, and a Danish bloodline on my maternal grandfather's side has granted me a fortunate "northern" complexion. When longer than a couple of inches, my hair resembles sheep's wool from my homeland, and so I keep it closely-shorn. Even the most distinctive piece of clothing I own—calf-height sheepskin-lined winter boots—make me look more like an Austrian high-country farmer than a "real" foreigner. I mean, it's not like I'm a Romanian Gypsy in Sarkozy's France, I think—I'm not even a Romanian Gypsy in Romania. But sitting in the waiting room, I'm convinced that disqualification looms. Maybe they have it on file that twelve years ago I got caught without a ticket on the Munich S-Bahn? And that, like all unreliable foreigners, I gave a false address? And what of my history with minibars?

12.

The setting has changed, but the smell of anxiety in the room is one I know well. I remember it from over a decade ago when traveling the *Gastarbeiter* bus routes between Sarajevo and Munich. I'll never forget the silence at every westwards border crossing, a silence that could hang in the air for over an hour, which is often how long it took for Croatian, Slovenian, Austrian, or German border guards to enter the bus. The delay seemed like a carefully calibrated fear multiplier—and it worked. On a bleak January morning in Berlin, the same delay does its work on me. Like the narrators of "Battle Royale" and "The Fly," I go back over the details that have gotten me to the waiting room, hoping to exonerate myself from blame while simultaneously "stitching" them together. My parents may have taken me away from my first homeland of Fiji at a young age, but the rest I did on my own. I sometimes think of my *willing* departure *for* Bosnia in my early twenties as "an irreparable mistake committed at the age of ignorance" (a Kundera line from my internal repository). But the "thread" continues to this day in Berlin, as I, neither *Ossie* nor *Wessie*, working on the translation of this collection, find myself in so many of its scenarios.

13.

Most often we talk about certain musicians providing the sound-tracks to our lives, or of friends who act as mirrors in which we see our own changing reflections. Whether in the sadness of Bosnia, the museum and karaoke-city of Berlin, or lost in the fibre optic Google galaxy, worried that its speed is wrecking my capacity to watch *Andrei Rublev* from beginning to end, Dubravka Ugrešić's writing has been with me for some time now. From former Yugo-slavs at "home" and in the diasporic cities of Western Europe, North America, and Australasia, to inquisitive New England college students and their well-educated parents, to the global metropolitan literati dreaming of having the guts to write like her, Ugrešić's writing undoubtedly accompanies a mass of unnamed others. The essays in *Karaoke Culture* are new postcards sent from a space both inside and outside the global village. They are written by an author who when making jokes makes sure she has her turn on the receiving end, when mourning or moralizing questions her right to do so, and who when serving up satiric indictments has her own name appear among the accused. In a less anonymous and less liquid epoch, these things might have been called the responsibility of the writer.

Berlin, February 2011

Dubravka Ugresic is a writer of novels (*Baba Yaga Laid An Egg, The Ministry of Pain*), short story collections (*Lend Me Your Character, In the Jaws of Life*) and books of essays (*Nobody's Home, Thank You for Not Reading, The Culture of Lies*). Born in the former Yugoslavia, Ugresic took a firm anti-nationalistic stand when war broke out in 1991, and she was proclaimed a "traitor," a "public enemy," and a "witch," and was exposed to harsh and persistent media harassment. As a result, she left Croatia in 1993 and currently lives in Amsterdam.

David Williams is currently completing his Ph.D. in Comparative Literature at the University of Auckland, his doctoral research centering on the post-Yugoslav writings of Dubravka Ugresic and the idea of a "literature of the Eastern European ruins." *Karaoke Culture* is his first major translation.

Ellen Elias-Bursać has translated works by several writers from the former Yugoslavia, including David Albahari's *Götz and Meyer*, for which she was awarded the ALTA National Translation Award in 2006.

Celia Hawkesworth was senior lecturer in Serbian and Croatian at the School of Slavonic and East European Studies, University College, London, until her retirement. She now works as a freelance writer and translator.

Open Letter—the University of Rochester's nonprofit, literary translation press—is one of only a handful of publishing houses dedicated to increasing access to world literature for English readers. Publishing ten titles in translation each year, Open Letter searches for works that are extraordinary and influential, works that we hope will become the classics of tomorrow.

Making world literature available in English is crucial to opening our cultural borders, and its availability plays a vital role in maintaining a healthy and vibrant book culture. Open Letter strives to cultivate an audience for these works by helping readers discover imaginative, stunning works of fiction and by creating a constellation of international writing that is engaging, stimulating, and enduring.

Current and forthcoming titles from Open Letter include works from Catalonia, China, Czech Republic, Poland, Russia, and numerous other countries.

www.openletterbooks.org